IMAGES
*of America*

# FARMINGTON

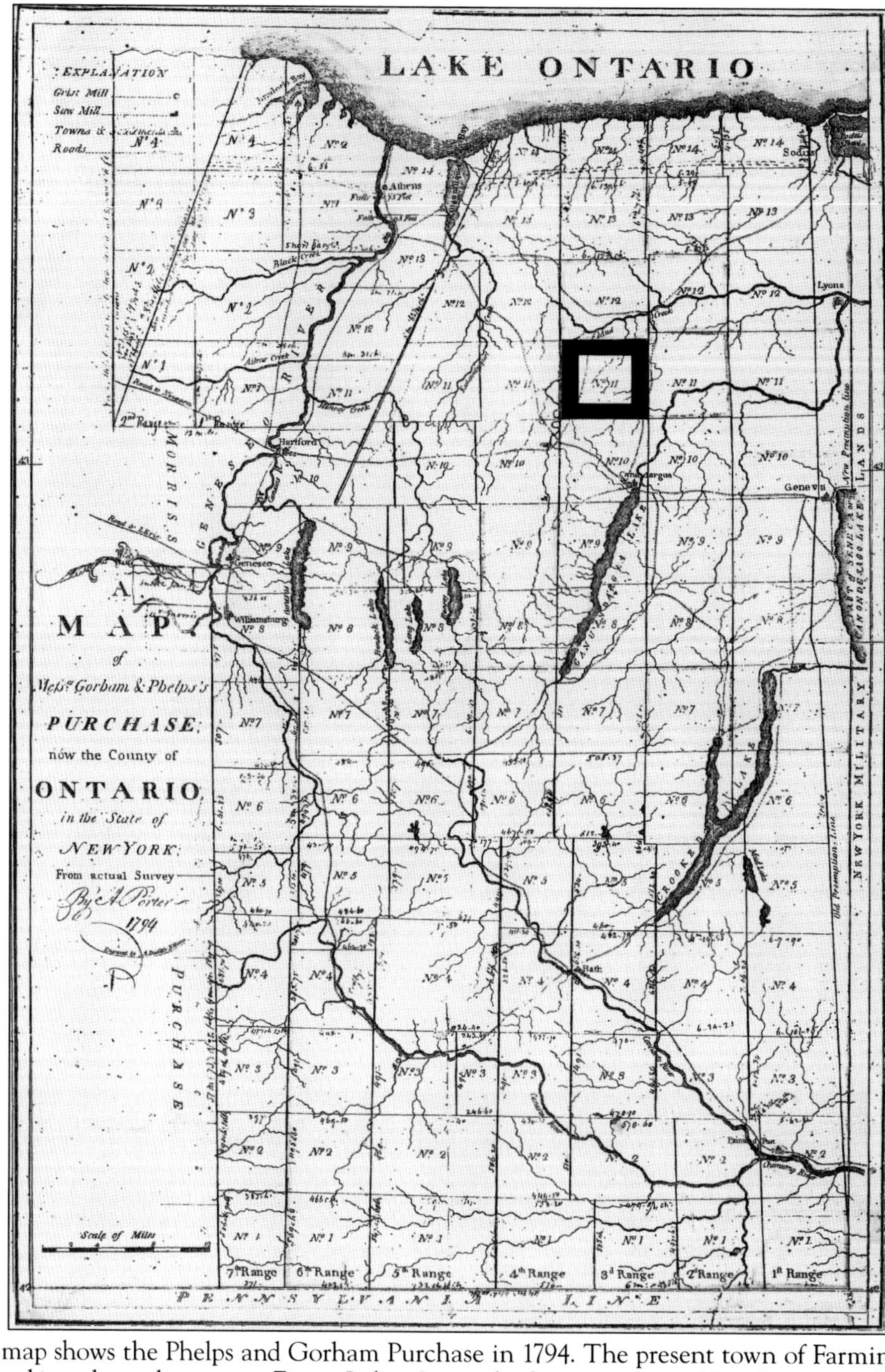


This map shows the Phelps and Gorham Purchase in 1794. The present town of Farmington is outlined just above the western Finger Lakes. It was the first township sold in this vast wilderness. (Courtesy Ontario County Archives and Records Center.)

**On the Cover:** This remarkable image of a Farmington barn raising shows the community working together to build a barn for Edward W. Stevenson in 1910. The Stevenson farm was near the corner of Holtz Road and County Road 8. (Courtesy Farmington Town Historian.)

IMAGES
*of America*

# FARMINGTON

Reginald W. Neale
Foreword by Margaret Hartsough

ARCADIA
PUBLISHING

ISBN 978-0-7385-7356-4

Published by Arcadia Publishing
Charleston, South Carolina

Printed in the United States of America

Library of Congress Control Number: 2010922406

For all general information, please contact Arcadia Publishing:
Telephone 843-853-2070
Fax 843-853-0044
E-mail sales@arcadiapublishing.com
For customer service and orders:
Toll-Free 1-888-313-2665

Visit us on the Internet at www.arcadiapublishing.com

*This book is dedicated to my wife, Mary Lyn Neale.*

# Contents

Foreword 6

Acknowledgments 7

Introduction 8

1. The Importance of Friends 9

2. Early Farmingtonians and Their Homes 25

3. Children and Education 63

4. Community life in Old Farmington 81

5. Agriculture, Commerce and Transportation 99

# FOREWORD

In his book *Farmington*, Reginald Neale has offered many interesting photographs with brief informative captions to tell readers about this rural community.

Ontario County was established in January 1797 by the Court of General Sessions, with Farmington listed as one of the original towns. We believe the judge of that court gave the town its name, undoubtedly taking the name from Farmington, Connecticut.

The first town meeting was held in April 1797. Those records still exist here in Farmington and in the Ontario County Archives.

Members of the Society of Friends purchased, in the name of Nathan Comstock, about 25,000 acres in the vast Phelps and Gorham Purchase. They were disowned by their home church in North Adams, Massachusetts, for this rash action. The first families arrived in Farmington early in 1790. By 1796, they had constructed a log building to be used as a meetinghouse and school and had set aside land for a cemetery. They were welcomed back into the Society of Friends. These early Quakers believed in equality for all, tolerance toward all, peaceful dispute settlement, and education for all. The Friends' influence spread throughout New York and the rest of the United States in the 19th century and contributed to many of the human rights we enjoy today. These things all have roots in Farmington. Today Farmington is a mix of rural and residential area and is known as a great place to call home. We hope you enjoy learning more about this friendly community.

—Margaret Hartsough

# ACKNOWLEDGMENTS

This book would not have been possible without the help and cooperation of Margaret Hartsough, town of Farmington historian, whose dedication to the preservation of Farmington history is exceptional. Many individuals provided invaluable assistance. Among them are Wilma Townsend, Ed Varno and Bruce Stewart of the Ontario County Historical Society; Ray Henry, Canandaigua town historian; Dr. Preston Pierce, Ontario County historian; and Dr. Hans-J. Finke, director of the Ontario County Records and Archives Center. Several people graciously agreed to read drafts of this book and offered valuable comments and suggestions. Among them are Leslie O'Malley, Hans-J. Finke, Ted Fafinski, Jessica Youngman, Babette Huber, Marjory Allen Perez, Judy McLaughlin Snyder, and Judy Wellman. The following individuals either reviewed materials or generously contributed items from their personal collections, or both: Leo and Audrey Everdyke, Pat and Don Ford, Helen Kirker, Christopher Densmore, Charles Lenhart, Rudy and Diana van der Velden, Barbara Wehrlin, Pat and George Ayres, Nathan and Elma Aldrich, Miriam Padgham, Lillian Keefe, Don and Evelyn Batterby, Royal and Nancy Purdy, Jake Repard, and Lewis Martz.

Unless otherwise noted, all images are courtesy of the Town of Farmington historian.

# INTRODUCTION

Ideally these historic photographs of Farmington would represent every family, individual, location, and institution that influenced the town. Realistically, surviving records tend to be somewhat arbitrary. As a result, there are certain to be some families who, through no intention of the author, are missing from this record.

It may be surprising to learn that Farmington residents were at the forefront of radical social and political change in the 19th and 20th centuries. The early settlers had strong views on racial equality, gender equality, and pacifism. Farmington was an important stop on the Underground Railroad, which helped slaves escape to freedom. At least 25 members of the Quaker Church associated with Farmington attended the first women's rights convention in 1848. Others helped negotiate the Treaty of Buffalo Creek, which preserved Seneca Indian land rights. Farmington residents traveled widely, speaking in support of social changes. The ideals of these early settlers helped to shape the community values that still resonate in Farmington.

Because Farmington was an important center of progressive activity, many controversial issues were debated by Farmingtonians in the historic 1816 Farmington Quaker Meetinghouse. The central role of this extraordinary structure is discussed further in the following pages.

Although this collection of photographs draws on the work of many individuals, historians are especially fortunate to be the heirs of a remarkable photographic legacy in the work of farmer and photographer Edwin J. Gardner. Beginning at a time when photography still required cumbersome equipment and toxic chemicals, Gardner applied his considerable talents to documenting the Farmington individuals, institutions, and events that were part of his life. He also solicited commercial portrait and event work. If he had a studio, it was probably located in his home at 238 Hook Road. Most of his photographs are known only from prints; no one knows what happened to the original glass-plate negatives.

Gardner's technical expertise was combined with a keen eye for detail and a wonderful sense of humor. His photographs are a truly unique record of a period from the 1890s to the 1920s in a community that should be more widely appreciated as a leading progressive influence in the 19th and 20th centuries.

# *One*

# The Importance of Friends

Farmington would not exist in its present form without the efforts of the Society of Friends, commonly known as Quakers. In 1788, a group of Quakers agreed to buy the entire 25,000-acre township, sight unseen. Since most of the first settlers were Quakers, this first chapter inevitably features many of the individuals, locations, and buildings associated with that denomination. The town soon became home to residents of many religious traditions.

It is also important to realize that it was not just Quakers, but all Farmingtonians, who debated the radical social changes being proposed in the 19th century. Nationally known figures such as Susan B. Anthony, Lucretia Mott, and Frederick Douglass came to Farmington to speak to huge crowds on the topics of abolition and women's suffrage.

Many of these debates took place in the 1816 Farmington Quaker Meetinghouse, known after 1828 as the Hicksite Meeting House. It was located on the northwest corner of Allen-Padgham Road and County Road 8. The building was said to have accommodated crowds as large as 1,000 persons. It was the largest available venue for public meetings in a wide area. In 1834, the Friends regional meeting brought Quakers from all over western New York, Canada, and Michigan. The building served the congregation for more than a century, but as it reached the age of 111 years, it was no longer needed. It was repurposed as a storage barn, moved several hundred feet north from its original site, and gradually began to deteriorate. A group of concerned citizens who understand its historical significance is spearheading a major effort to restore the structure, move it to the southeast corner of the intersection, and open it to the public as a historic site and museum.

In 2007, the 1876 church on the northeast corner of County Road 8 and Sheldon Road, the cemetery behind it, and the 1816 meetinghouse described above were placed on the National Register of Historic Places as the Farmington Quaker Crossroads Historic District.

Some of the pioneer family names still found in the area today are Aldrich, Allen, Brown, Fish, Hathaway, Herendeen, Lapham, Payne, Power, Sheldon, and Smith.

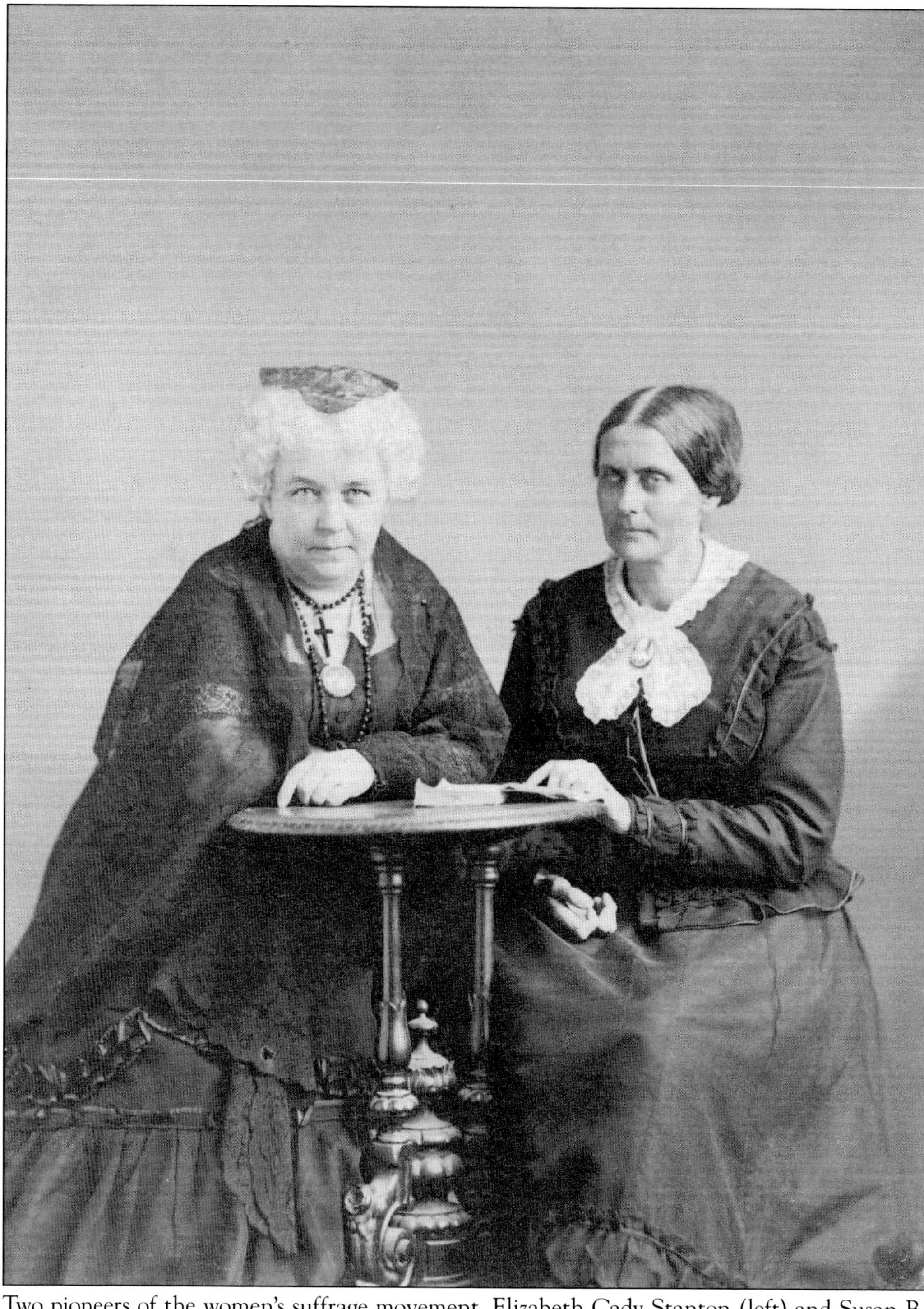

Two pioneers of the women's suffrage movement, Elizabeth Cady Stanton (left) and Susan B. Anthony, are seated at an ornate Victorian table. Both women spoke to large audiences at the 1816 Farmington Meetinghouse. A foundation named for Stanton later became the custodian of the meetinghouse. (Courtesy Ontario County Historical Society.)

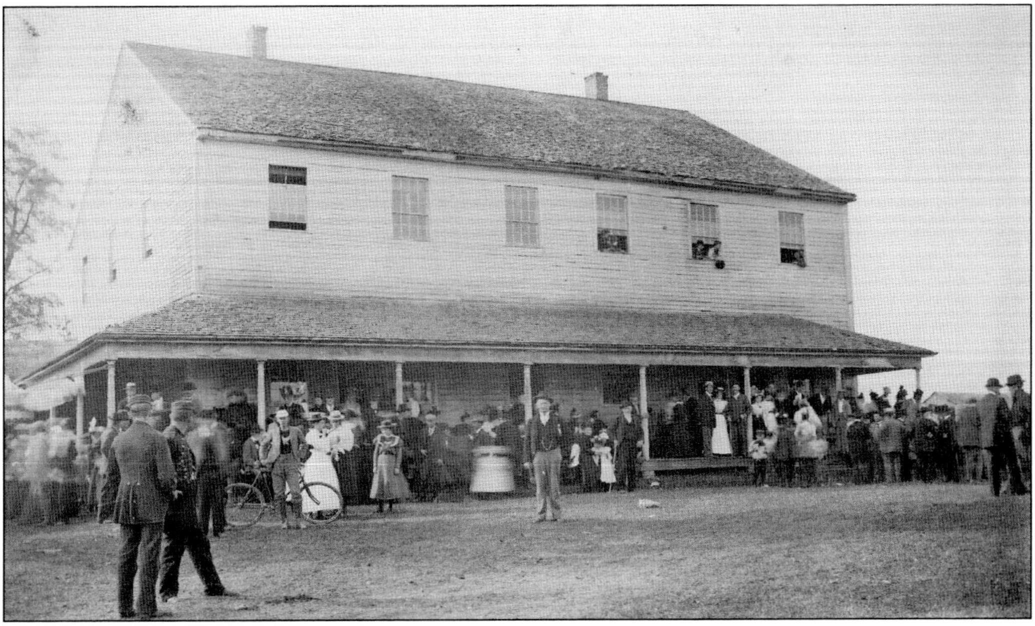

The 1816 Farmington Meetinghouse was originally erected to replace a smaller building, located almost directly opposite, on the east side of County Road 8. Around 1828, there was a nationwide doctrinal split between Orthodox Quakers and the followers of Elias Hicks. The Orthodox group left the new building and returned to the structure on the other side of the road. The new building was used mainly by the Hicksites. Frederick Douglass and many other noted figures spoke to large audiences there. Many years later, the Orthodox church was destroyed by fire. It was replaced by the present Farmington Friends Church in 1876.

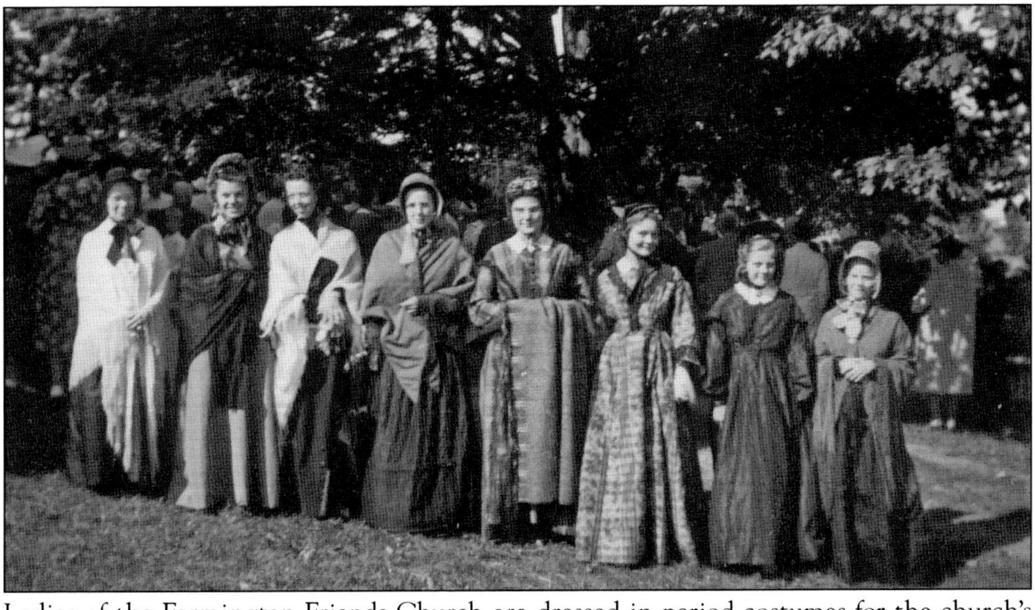

Ladies of the Farmington Friends Church are dressed in period costumes for the church's sesquicentennial celebration on August 27, 1939. From left to right are Edna Lapham, Elma Baker, Myrle Baker, Margaret Allen, Mary Lee Herendeen, Gertrude Pritchard, Doris Wyman, and Dorothy Wyman. (Courtesy Farmington Friends Meeting.)

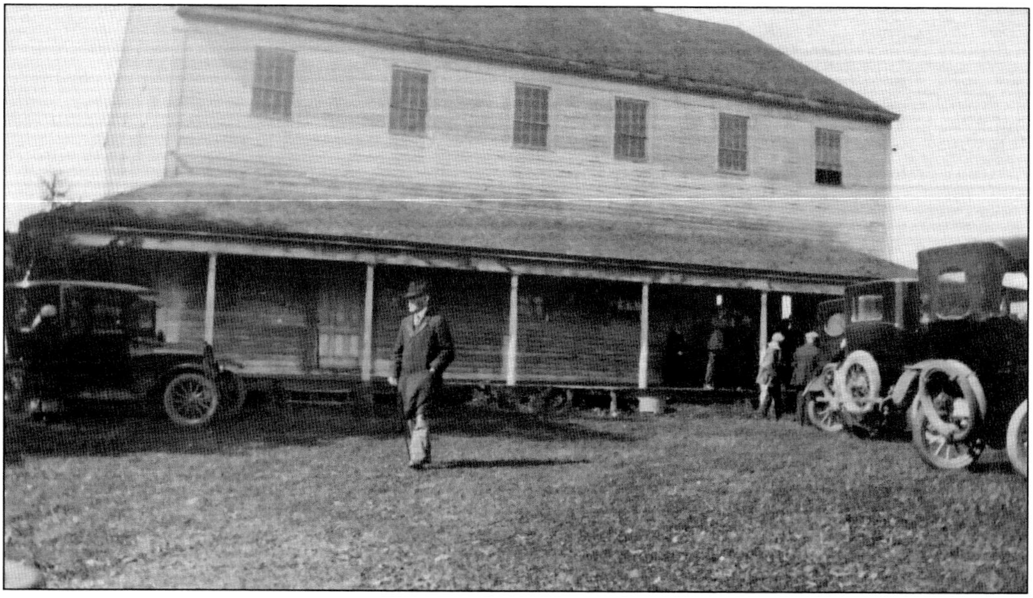

Here are two photographs of the 1816 meetinghouse, taken while it was still in use for its original purpose. The gentleman in the above photograph is Ed Mott in 1924. The photograph below was taken in 1926 on the occasion of the last religious service in the building. By this time, horses and buggies had been replaced by automobiles. (Courtesy Farmington Friends Meeting.)

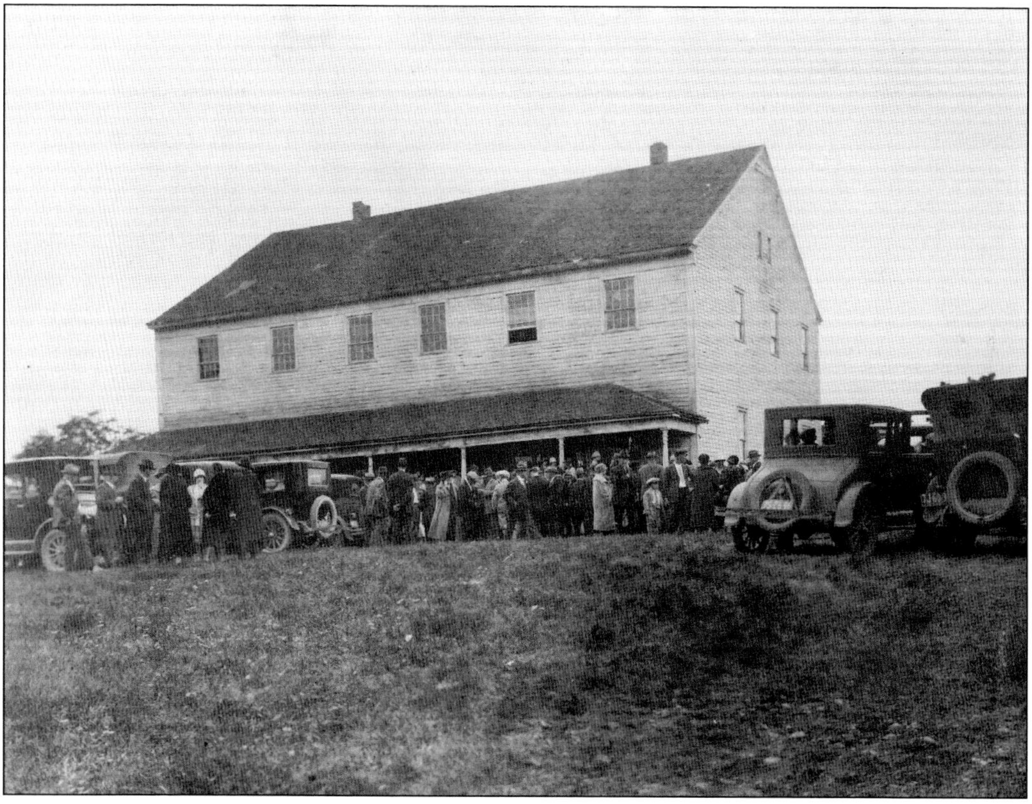

The inscription on the back of this photograph identifies it as a portrait of Mary S. Knowles. She was a pastor in Farmington in the late 1800s. The November 6, 1897, edition of the *New York Times* noted that she was one of the members of the New York Orthodox Meeting charged with considering "the compilation of a uniform book of discipline and the organization of a National Friend conference." (Courtesy Farmington Friends Meeting.)

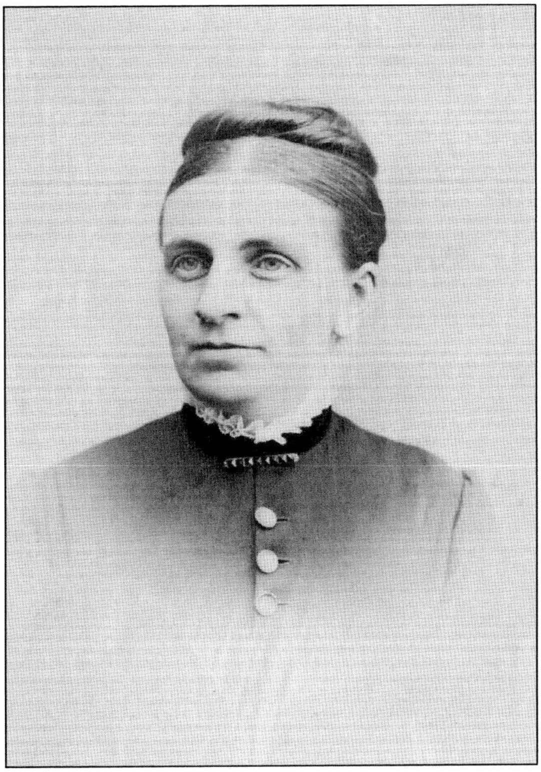

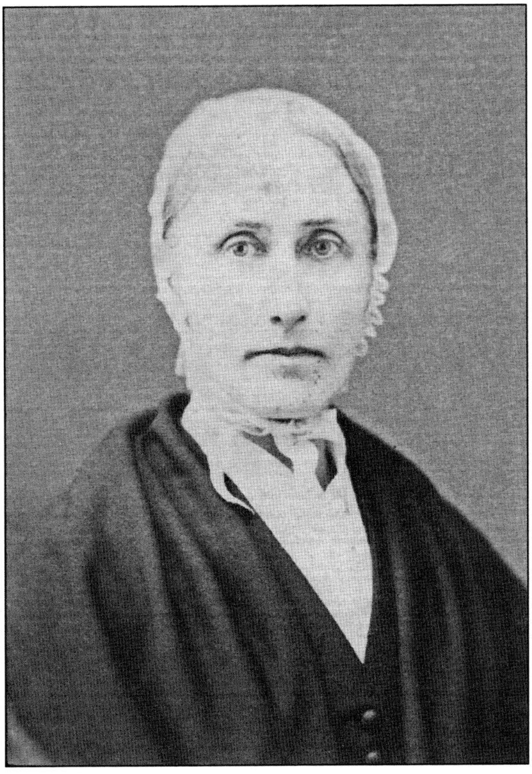

This is a portrait of Margaret Macomber Hathaway, a Quaker minister of the Friends Church in Farmington. Margaret was active in the Farmington Female Anti-slavery Society. Members of her family supported women's suffrage and the Underground Railroad. (Courtesy Farmington Friends Meeting.)

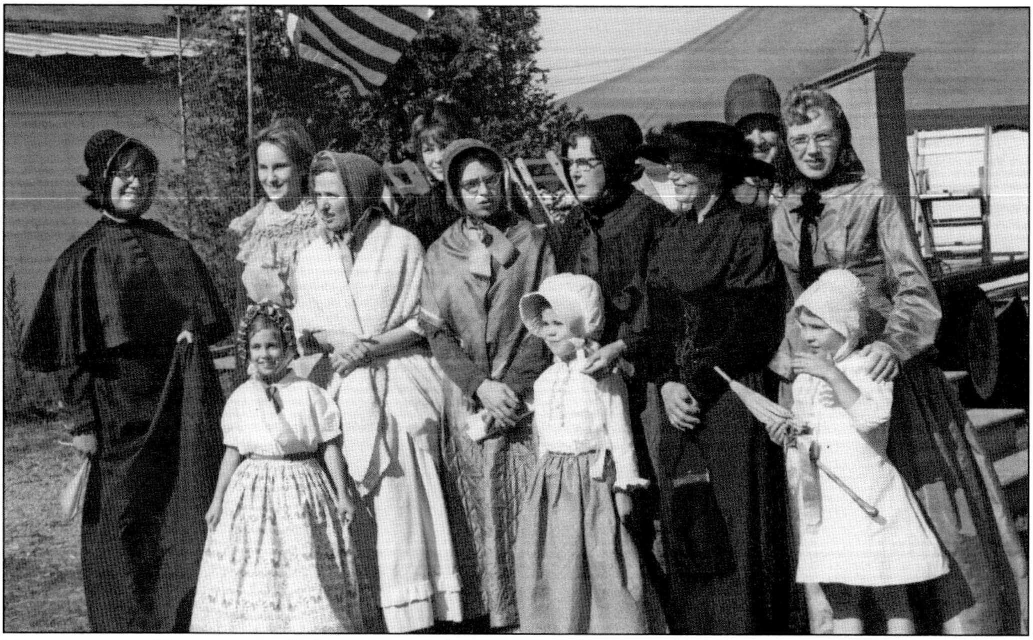

Here are more Farmington ladies in period costumes, this time to celebrate the 175th anniversary of the Farmington Friends Meeting (1788–1963). On the right, in the light-colored dress with her arm on her daughter's shoulder, is Farmington town historian Margaret Hartsough. This photograph was taken after a parade in front of the firehouse in Pumpkin Hook. (Courtesy Farmington Friends Meeting.)

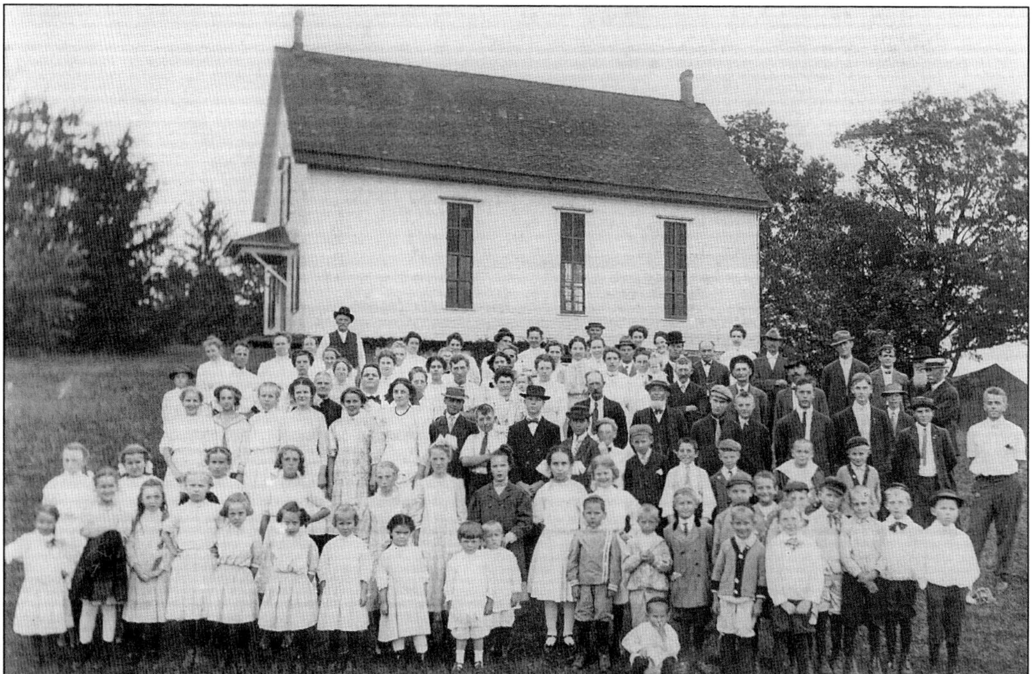

With the 1876 church in the background, members of the Farmington Friends Meeting pose for a group portrait taken around 1915. (Courtesy Farmington Friends Meeting.)

Thomas E. Williams led the Farmington Friends Meeting as clerk and pastor from 1900 to 1903. This is a 1905 portrait of his mother, Rachel Atkinson Williams, with her Bible. (Courtesy Farmington Friends Meeting.)

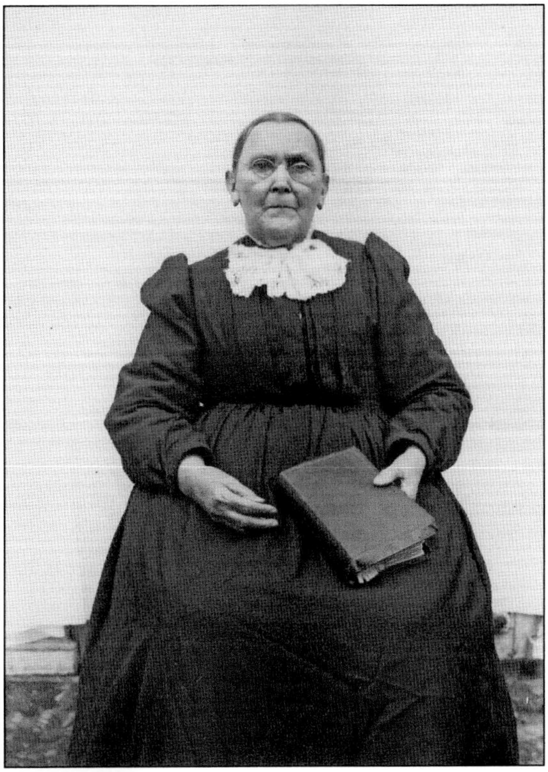

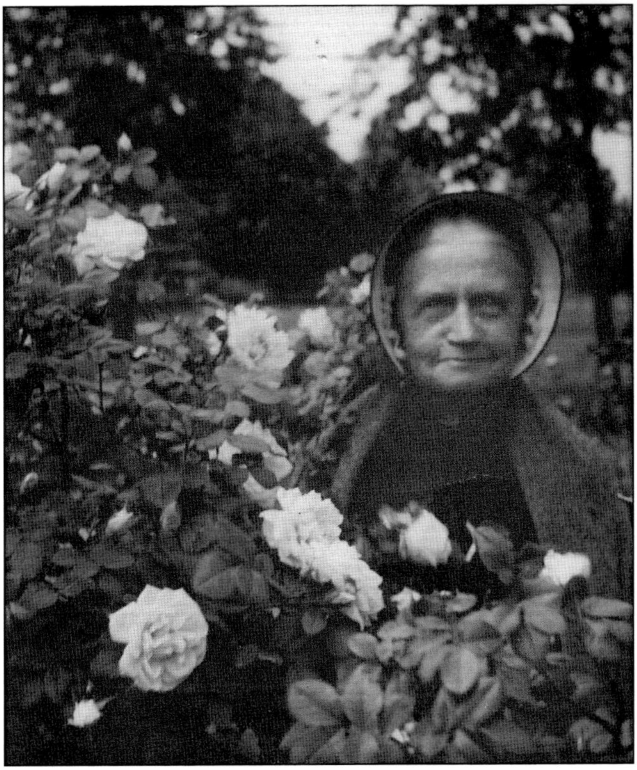

Sara Peckham, born in 1828, is surrounded by flowers. She was an ancestor to many Farmingtonians and was noted as being "the last person to wear a Quaker bonnet in Farmington Friends Meeting." Peckham died in 1917.

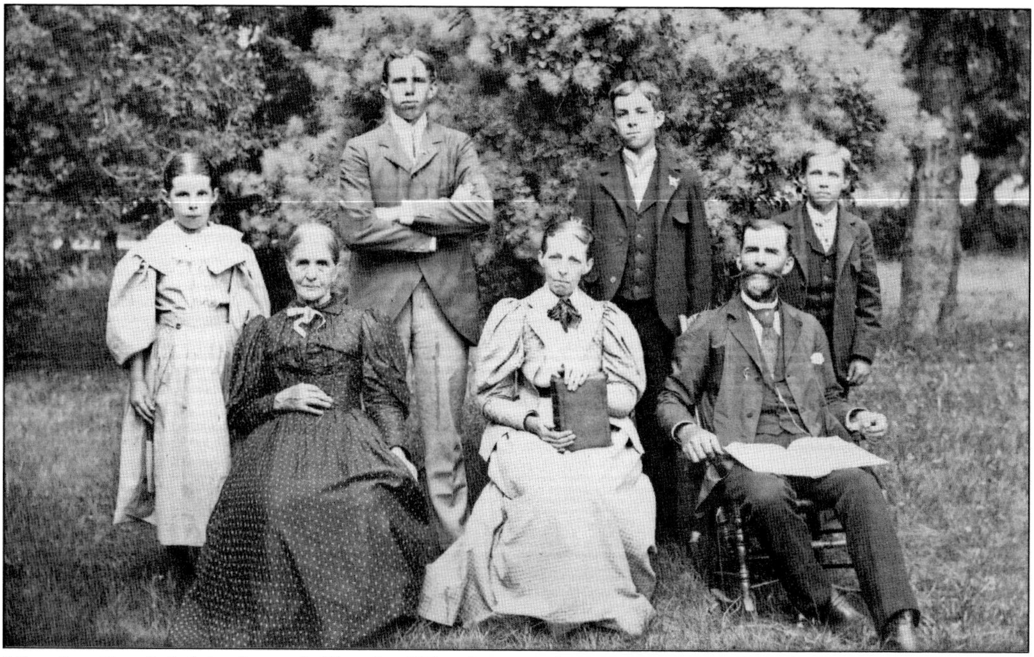

The family of Adelaide and Charles Wood poses for a portrait. Adelaide (holding the Bible) was clerk of the Meeting from 1893 to 1899 and also a Friends minister. (Courtesy Farmington Friends Meeting.)

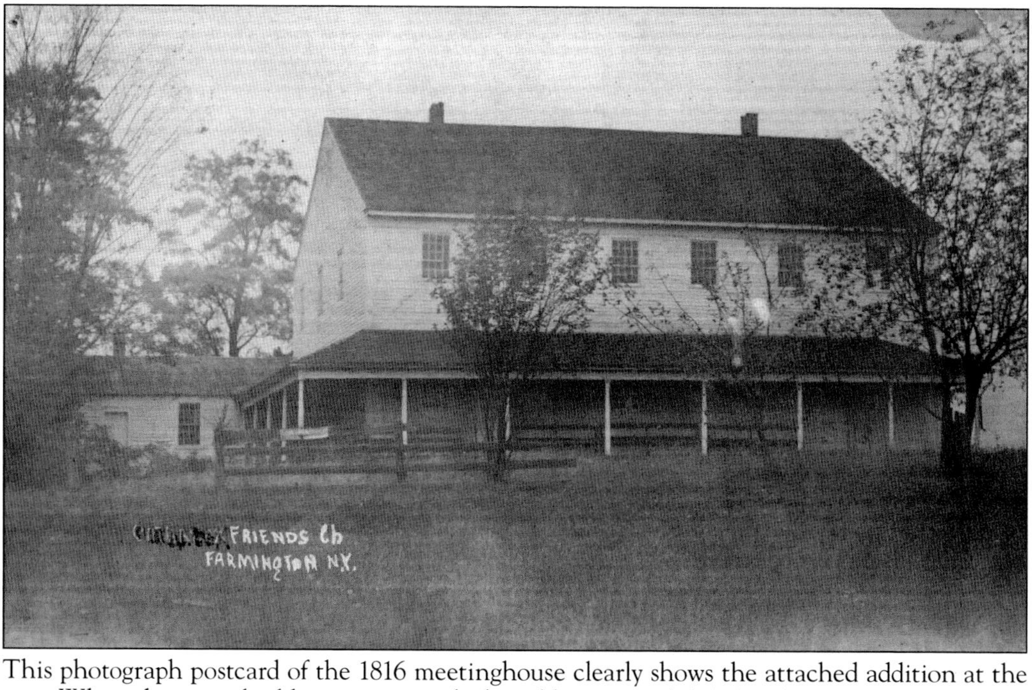


This photograph postcard of the 1816 meetinghouse clearly shows the attached addition at the rear. When the main building was moved, the addition was left behind and converted into a private dwelling, which was later destroyed by fire. (Courtesy Farmington Friends Meeting.)

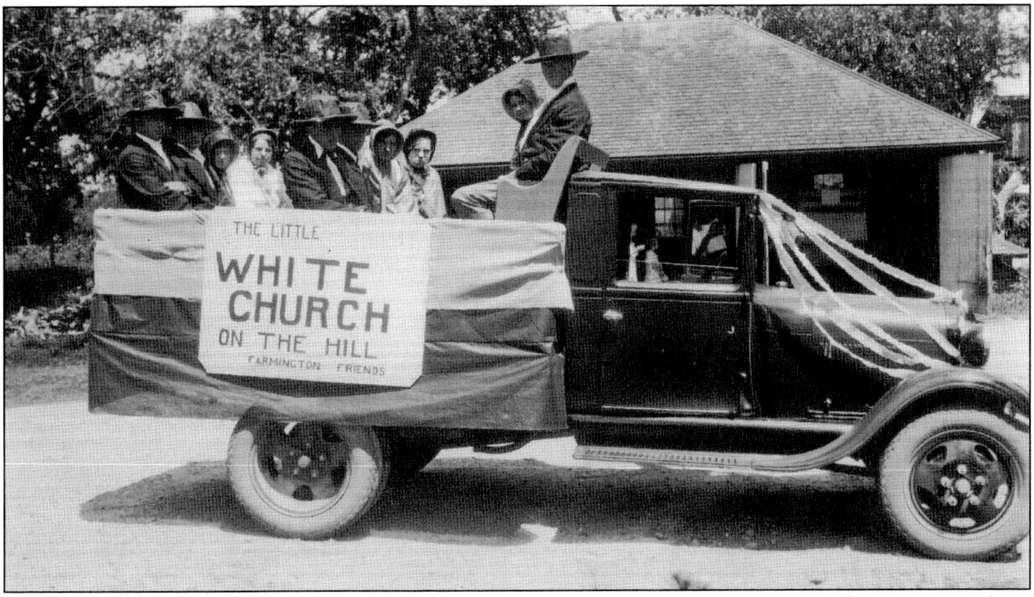


This 1938 photograph was taken during the Friends Church sesquicentennial celebration. The "White Church" designation was probably to contrast it with the 1816 meetinghouse across the road, which was unpainted. (Courtesy Farmington Friends Meeting.)

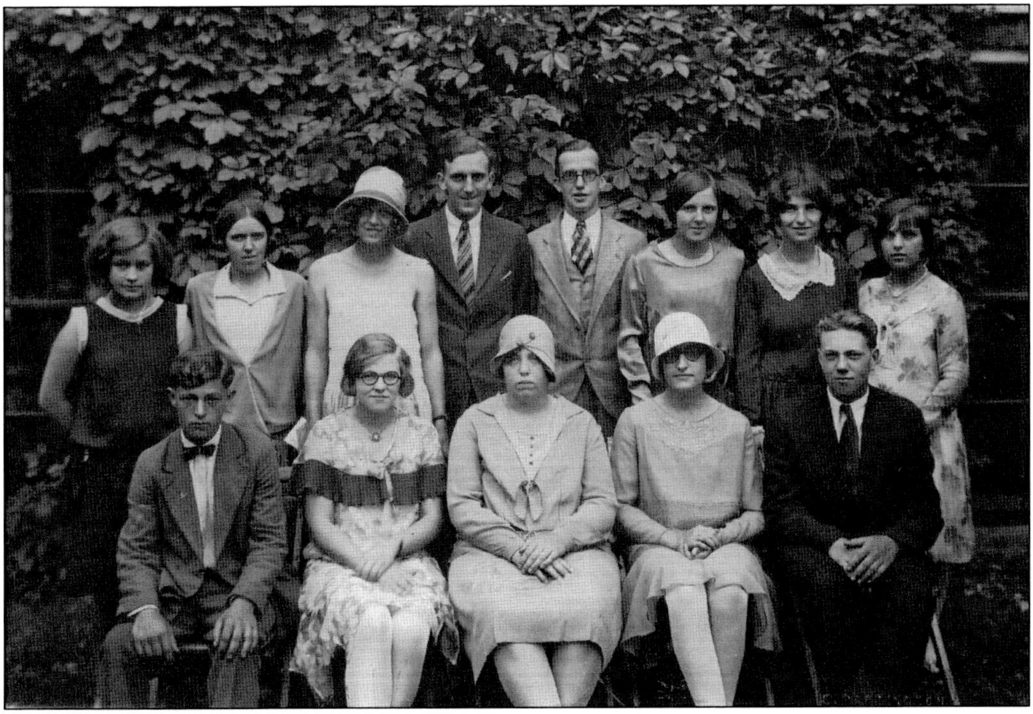

These men and women are members of the 1929 Farmington Friends Sunday school class. The women's hats are characteristic styles of the 1920s. Some of the individuals in this photograph are Harold Young, Jennie Cockle, Gertrude Van Lare, Olga Keith, Walter and Esther Partington, and Edith DeMay. (Courtesy Farmington Friends Meeting.)

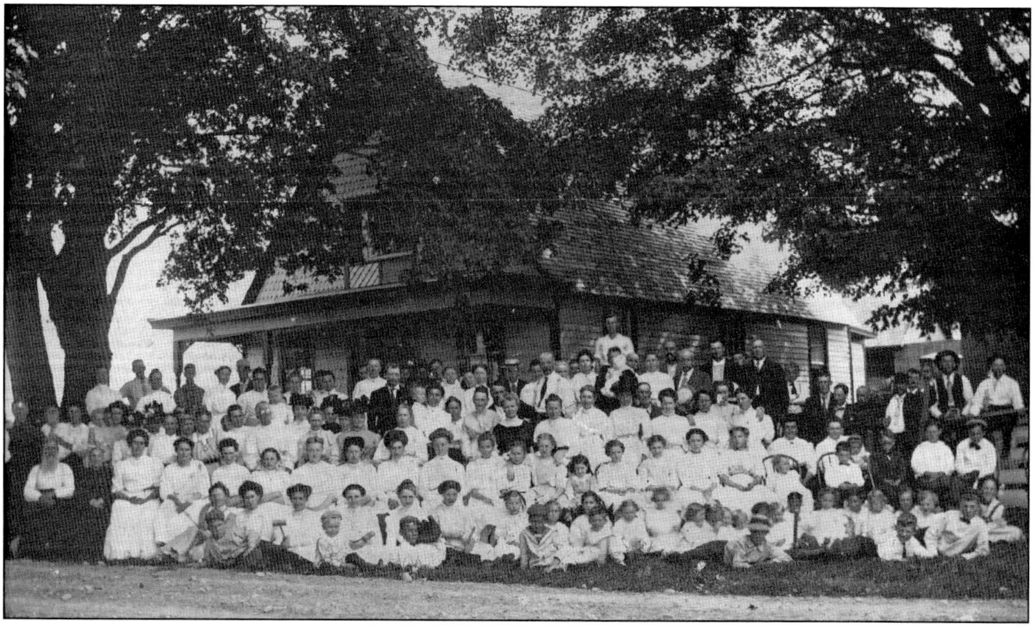

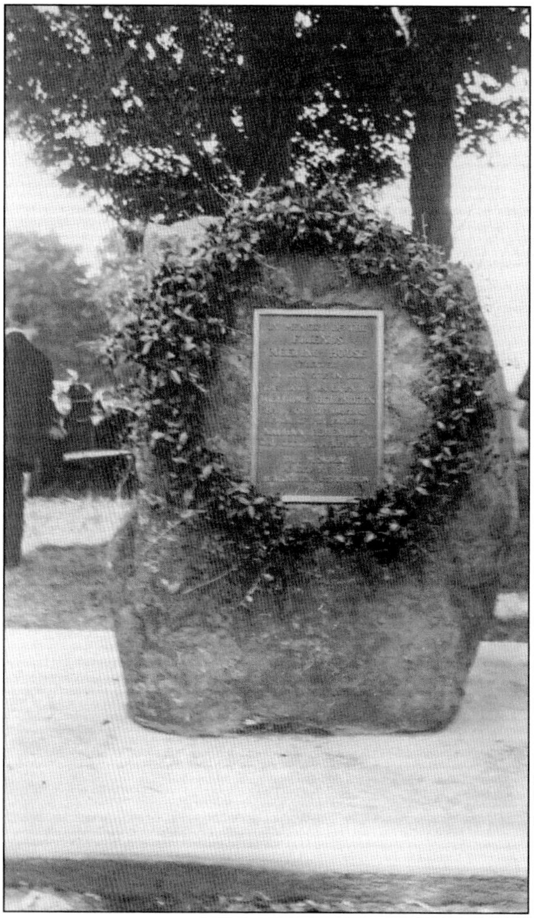

This is a photograph of a Hathaway/Herendeen family reunion in 1915. The group is posing in front of the South Farmington Chapel. This building is no longer used, but it still stands on the southwest corner of Shortsville Road and County Road 28. Off to the right of the chapel, not visible in this photograph, is the South Farmington Cemetery. Charles H. Herendeen, who lived on County Road 28 just south of this intersection, served several terms as town supervisor in the late 1800s.

Across the road from the above building is a combined plaque and stone monument in what is now known as Meeting House Park. The inscription reads, "In memory of the Friends Meeting House erected on this site in 1823. The land was given by Welcome Herendeen, being on the original farm of his father, Nathan Herendeen, who settled here in 1790. This memorial placed by the Herendeen Association, 1928."

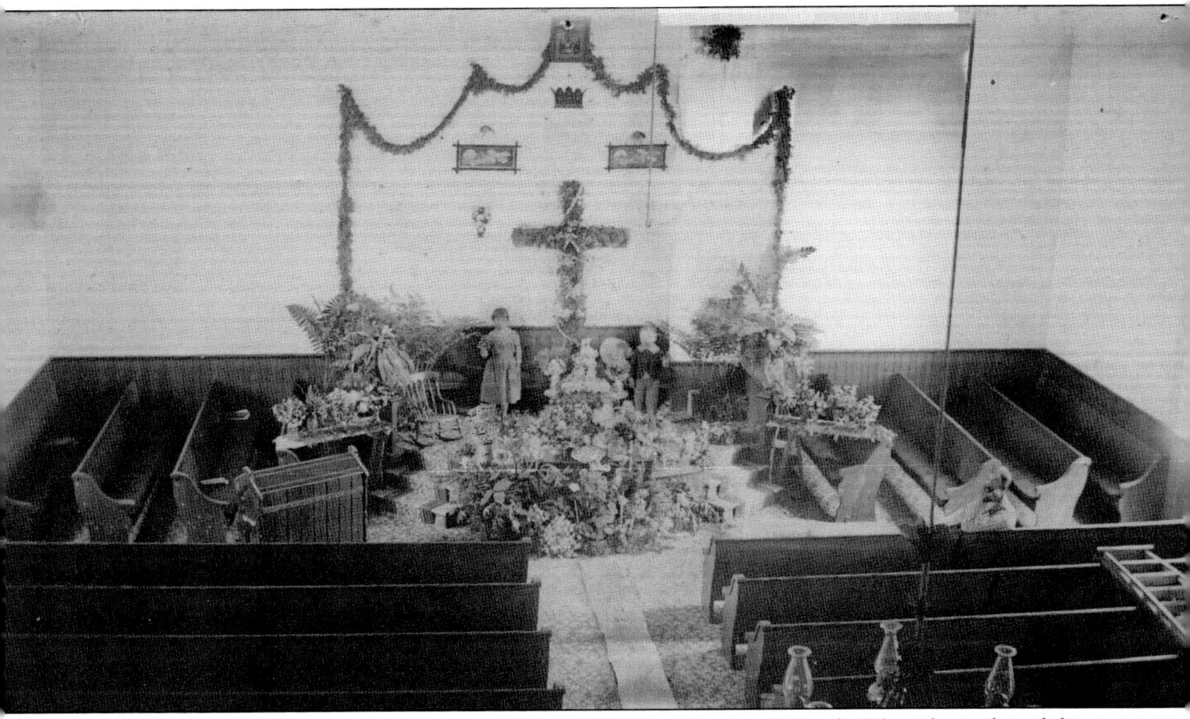

In this unusual shot from the balcony of the 1876 Farmington Friends Church, a chandelier of kerosene lamps is visible at lower right. The man seated in the front pew is probably the photographer. The two children and the masses of flowers suggest that this was taken on Easter Sunday or Children's Day. (Courtesy Farmington Friends Meeting.)

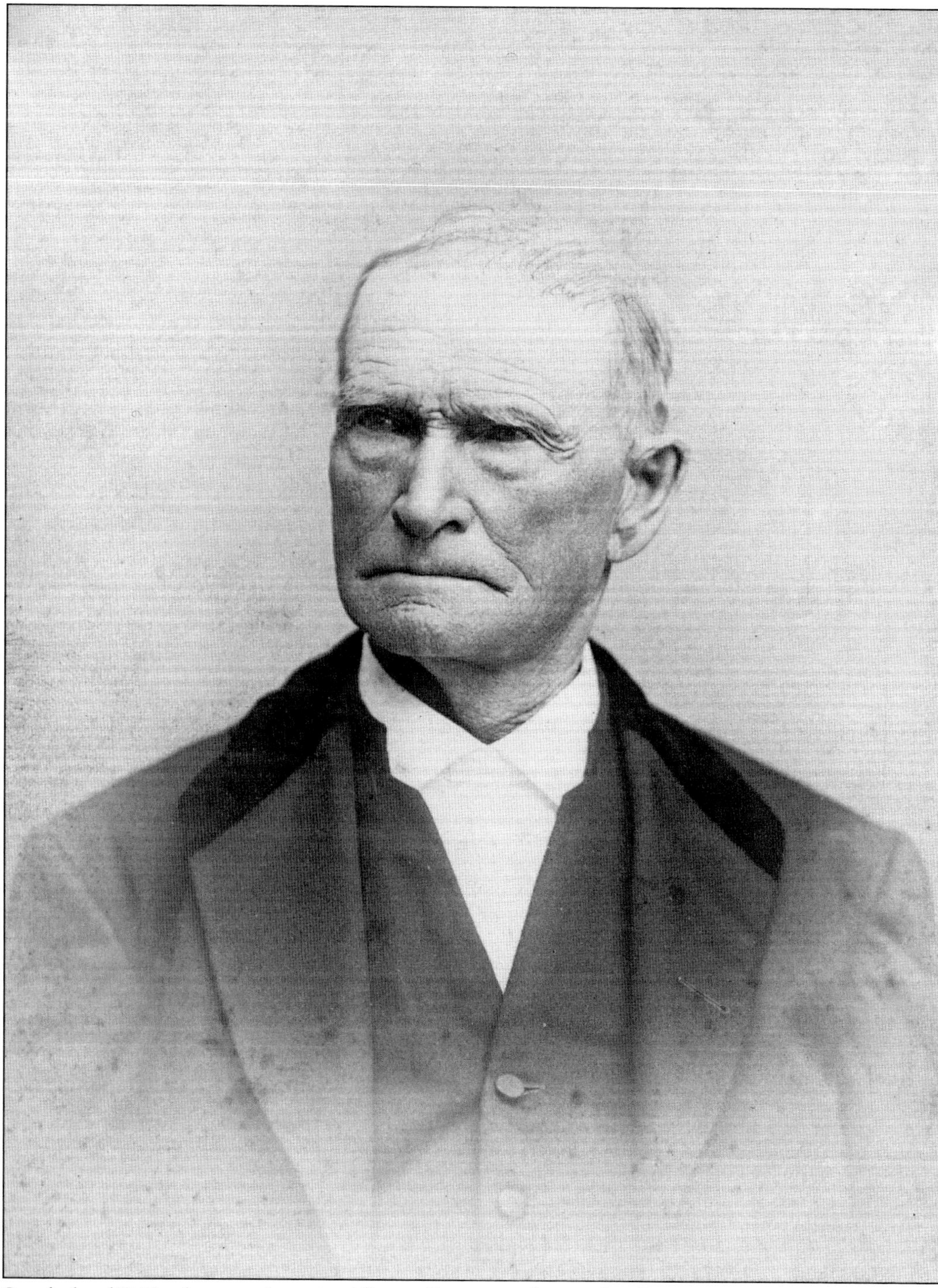

Sunderland P. Gardner was born in Albany County and moved to Farmington at the age of 14. At the age of 30 he became a Quaker minister. During the 1800s, he was one of Farmington's most well-known residents. He estimated that during his preaching career he traveled 9,000 miles in the United States and Canada. At a meeting in 1889, when he was 87 years old, nearly 1,000 people gathered to hear him preach. (Courtesy Friends Historical Library of Swarthmore College.)

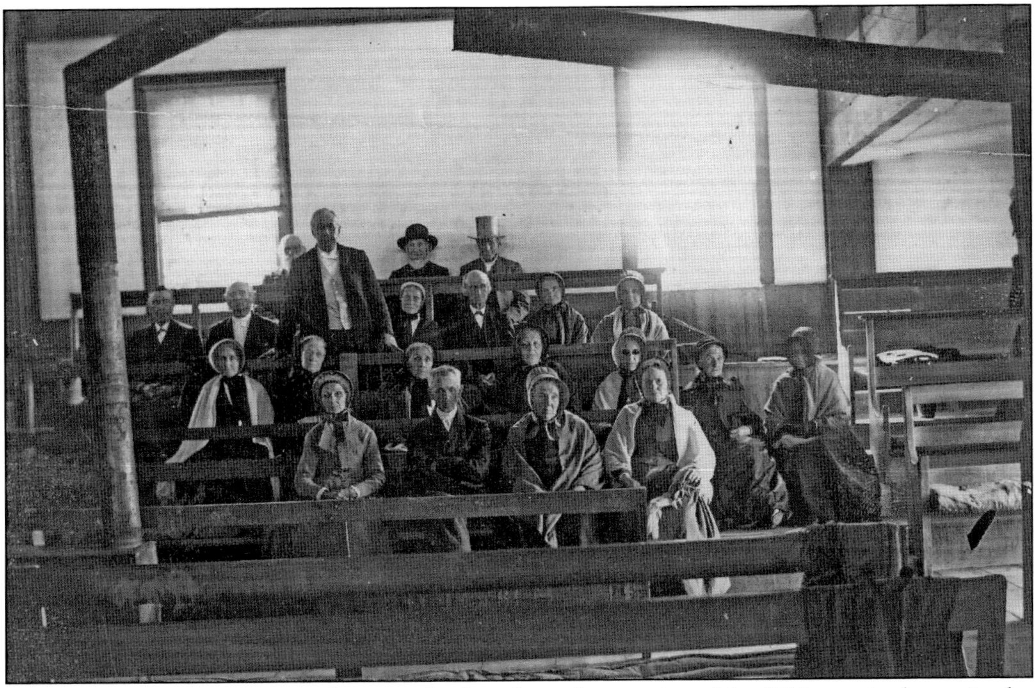

This is one of the few known photographs that show the interior of the 1816 meetinghouse in the late 1800s. The standing man without a hat is John Cornell, a Quaker minister from Mendon. Mr. Cornell was a popular and renowned speaker who traveled to meetings all over the country. (Courtesy Farmington Friends Meeting.)

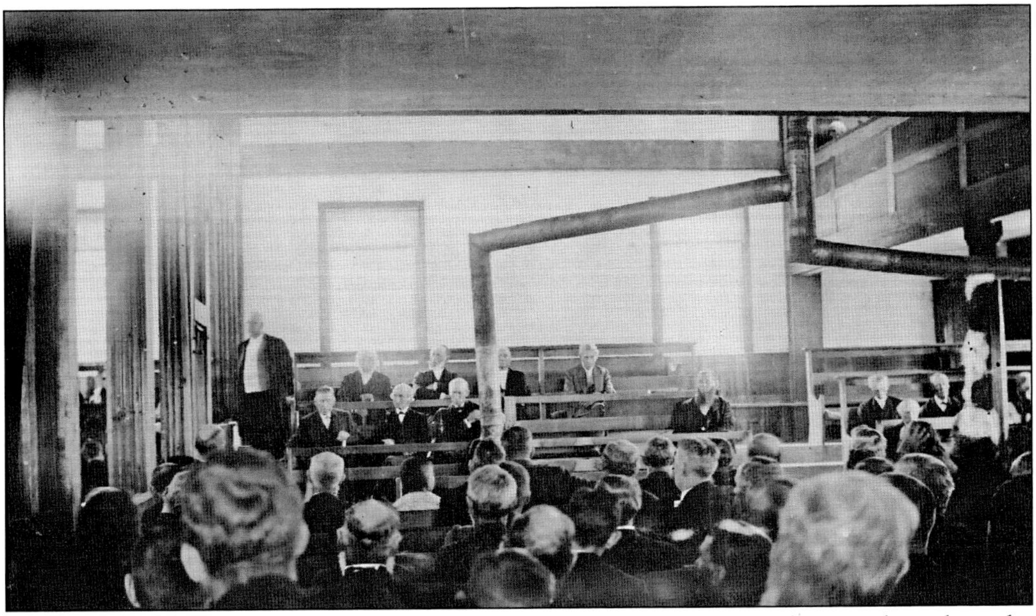

Here is another photograph of the interior of the 1816 meetinghouse. This one shows how the benches for seating were arranged. Meeting leaders, elders, and guest ministers sat on the benches facing the congregation. (Courtesy Farmington Friends Meeting.)

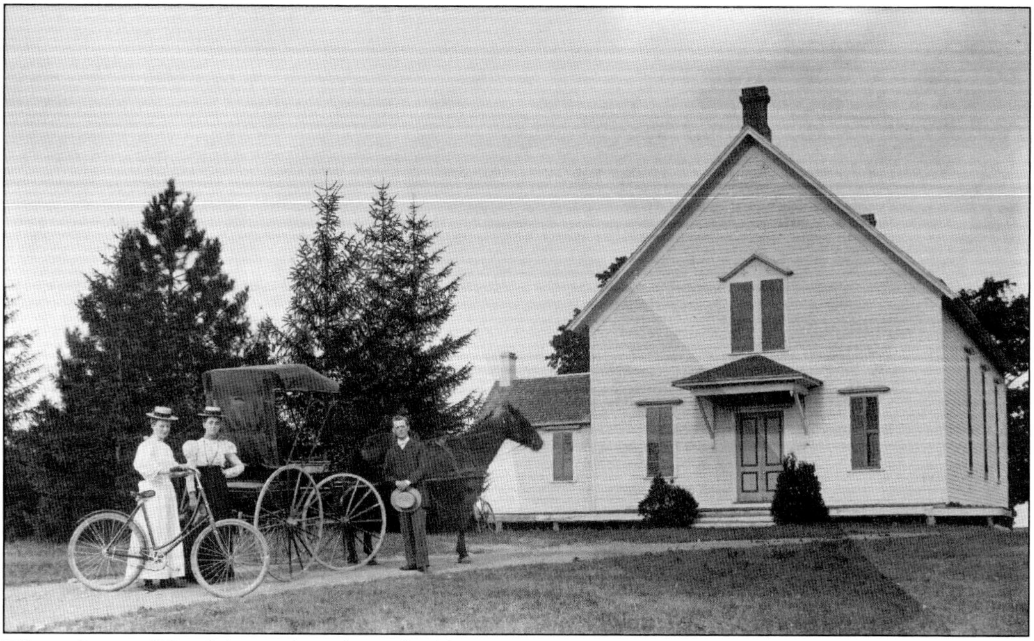

Edwin Parrot Wood, his wife Helena (holding onto the bike), and his sister Grace are pictured in front of the Farmington Friends Church about 1900. The front view of this building looks much the same in 2010. The church was constructed in 1876, but this same site had been used as early as 1803 for a combination meetinghouse and school. (Courtesy Farmington Friends Meeting.)

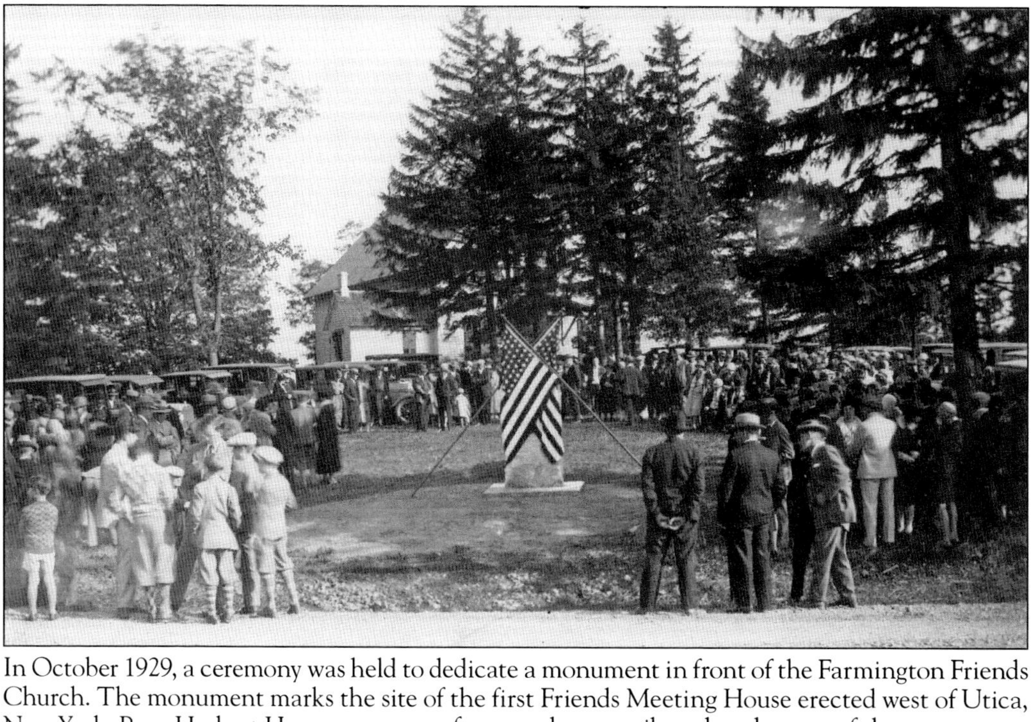

In October 1929, a ceremony was held to dedicate a monument in front of the Farmington Friends Church. The monument marks the site of the first Friends Meeting House erected west of Utica, New York. Pres. Herbert Hoover was one of many who contributed to the cost of the monument, as he and his family were Quakers. (Courtesy Farmington Friends Meeting.)

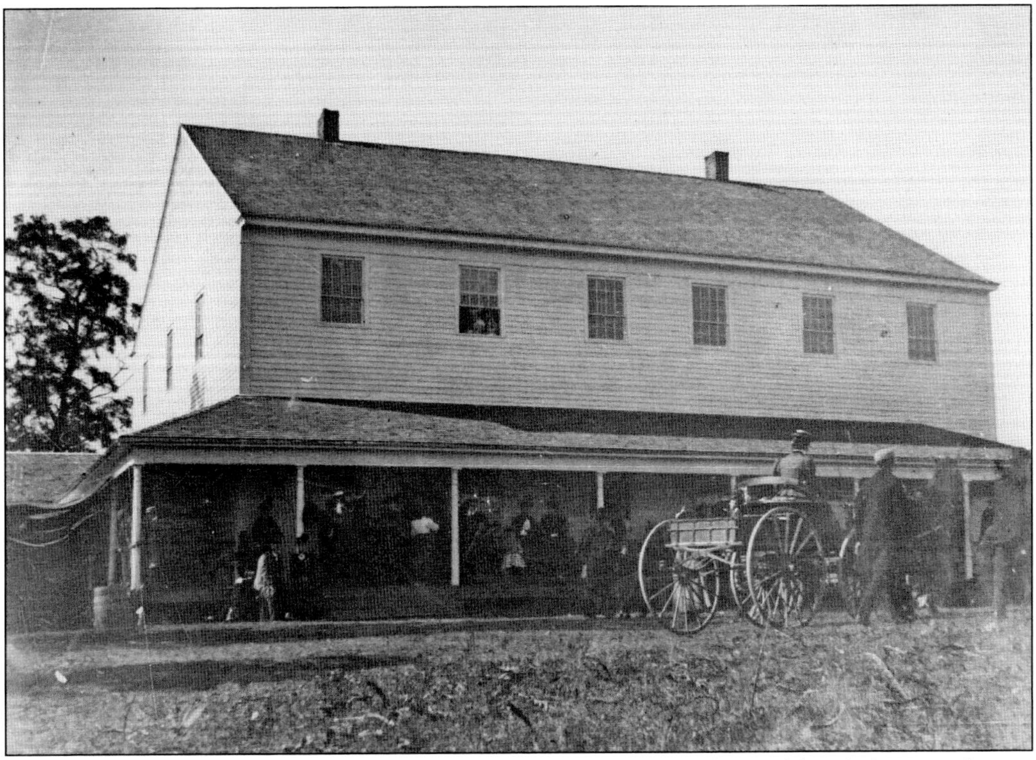

Taken at the turn of the century, this photograph shows carriages in front of the 1816 meetinghouse. (Courtesy Farmington Friends Meeting.)

### Farmington Friends Ministers

In the early history of the meeting many names of ministers are noted. They were unpaid and ofter traveled from meeting to meeting. The first minister to receive a salary was Edwin Wood. He was also the first minister to live in the parsonage. This list of ministers is taken from Margaret A. Baker's records.

Caleb McCumber
Thomas Ellison
Beersheba Herendeen
Ira Lapham
William Clark
Edward Dorland
Margaret Hathaway
Jarvis Rider
Alexander M. Purdy
Robert Knight
Mary Knowles
Adelaid H. Wood Clerk 1893-1899
Edwin P. Wood 1899-1903
Thomas Williams-Clerk and Pastor 1900-1903
George Evans 1903-1906
Leverite Rugg 1906
James Renfrew 1908-1913
Reuben J. Payne 1913-1922
LeRoy DeMarsh 1923
Arthur Santmier 1924-1925
Lizzie M. Leggett 1925
Eliezer Partington 1925-1929
Arthur Hammond 1929-1937
Parker Boroughs 1937-1938
Charles Lampman 1938-1941
Leonard Hall 1941-1945
Robert Rumsey 1946-1949
Wilbur Kamp 1949-1950
Kent Larabee 1951-1952
Herbert Kimball 1952-1954
Donald Deer summer 1954
Richard Faux 1954-1962
Adolph Baker
Graham Wilkins 1962-1966
Paul Walaska Feb. 1966-Oct 1966
Adolph Baker Oct. 1966-Jan. 1967
Richard Hartman 1967-1973
Herbert Kimball 1973-1981
John Fitzgerald 1981-1986
Dale Dorrell 1986-1990
Ruth Kinsey 1990 to present

This list of Farmington Friends ministers shows that women were well represented as ministers in the church, even in its earliest times. (Courtesy Farmington Friends Meeting.)

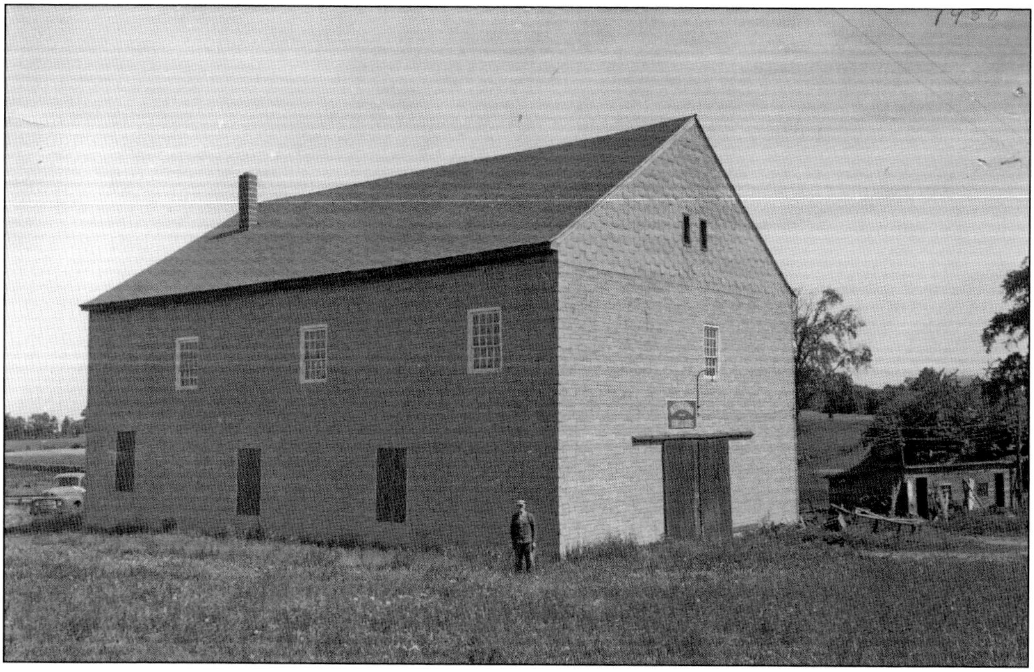

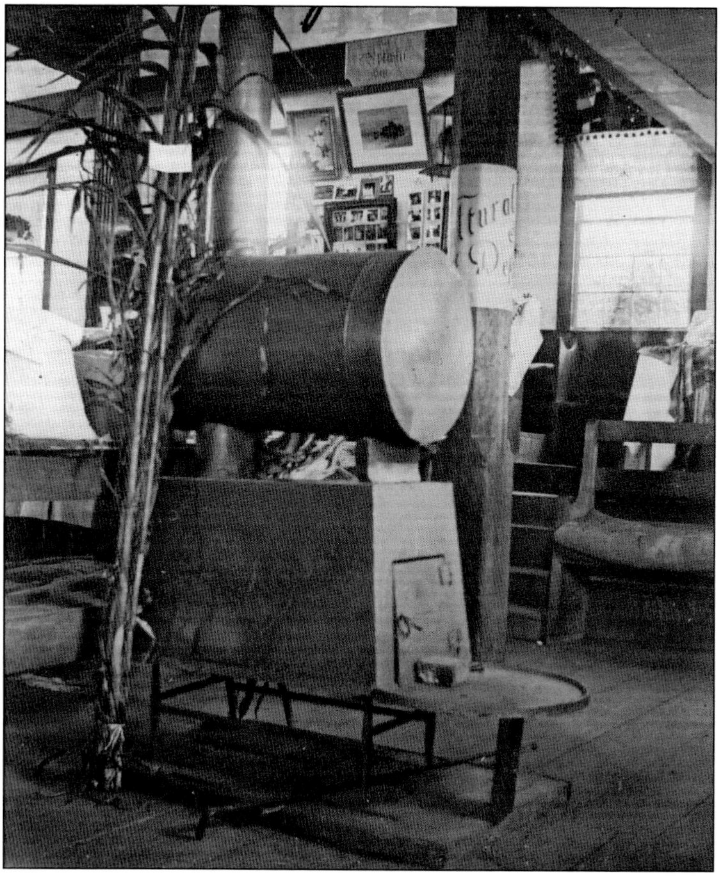

Here is a c. 1958 photograph of the 1816 meetinghouse after it had been moved and converted into a storage barn for celery. Over the next few decades, it deteriorated significantly. After a windstorm blew off one of its walls in 2006, a group of concerned citizens began the project that is currently underway to move it to a more appropriate location and open it to the public as a historical site and museum.

This is one of two stoves that heated the interior of the 1816 meetinghouse. They were both probably fueled by wood. The photograph was taken in 1899, when the meetinghouse hosted the Farmington Grange Fair.

# *Two*

# Early Farmingtonians and Their Homes

The first settlers strongly believed in individual equality. To make sure no one received favored treatment, they drew lots—sight unseen—for land in their new town. Thus, some settlers owned parcels in widely separated parts of the town. This helped to distribute the population over a wider area.

The pioneer homes of the first Farmingtonians were temporary primitive log shelters with dirt floors. But the pioneers were blessed with abundant natural resources, and they were willing to work hard. In only a few years, they constructed the mills, forges, and tool works they needed to be self-sufficient. The more prosperous settlers began to build spacious homes, with large barns and other buildings. Farmington still has one of the largest concentrations of homes built early in the 19th century—and before—of any township in central or western New York, including many beautiful examples of the historic cobblestone houses characteristic of this region.

Farmington has always welcomed immigrants. During the 19th century, waves of immigrant families came here from Germany, Ireland, Holland, and other places.

For a large part of Farmington's existence, the hamlet of Pumpkin Hook, originally known as New Salem, was a major center of commerce. At one time, when an outsider spoke of "Farmington," that meant the hamlet at the intersection of Hook and Allen-Padgham Roads. The location was never incorporated, and once automobiles became dominant, activity began to concentrate in other areas, closer to main routes of travel.

Several explanations have been offered for the origin of the name "Pumpkin Hook." Most are variations of this story: settlers grew lots of pumpkins to feed themselves and their livestock, but many of the fruits disappeared. Some individuals were suspected of surreptitiously "hooking" the pumpkins.

Photographs required a lot of effort to achieve an acceptable result, and in many old images the subjects are not smiling. Some adults believed they should look serious, while some individuals avoided smiling to hide primitive dental work. And, because of the awkwardly long exposure times required with glass-plate negatives, photographers sometimes told their subjects not to smile.

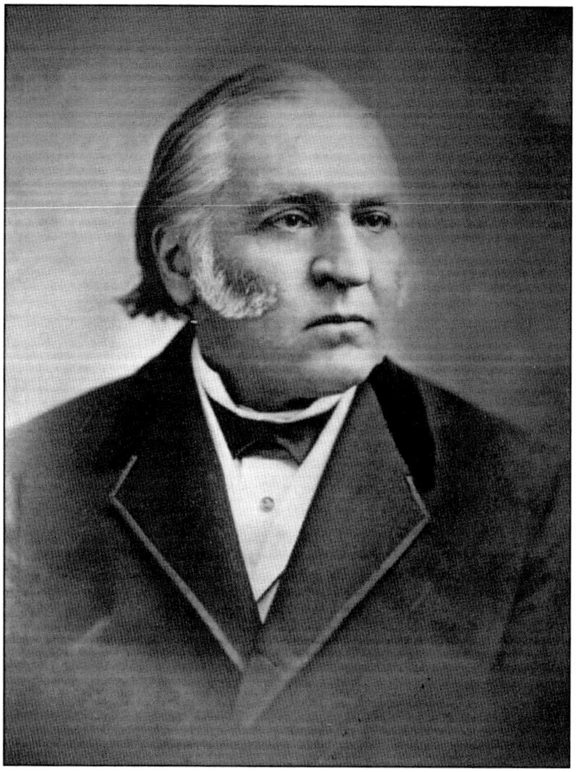

Elbridge Gerry Lapham was born in Farmington in 1814. He was named after Elbridge Gerry, a U.S. vice president and signer of the Declaration of Independence. Lapham was a distinguished lawyer who served as U.S. representative and senator from New York. His home was at 6227 County Road 41 (Boughton Hill Road) in the Farmington hamlet of Mertensia. (Courtesy Ontario County Historical Society.)

According to their diaries, much of the courtship of Lewis F. Allen and Marion Hoag Allen took place in this buggy. This photograph was taken around the time of their wedding in 1899.

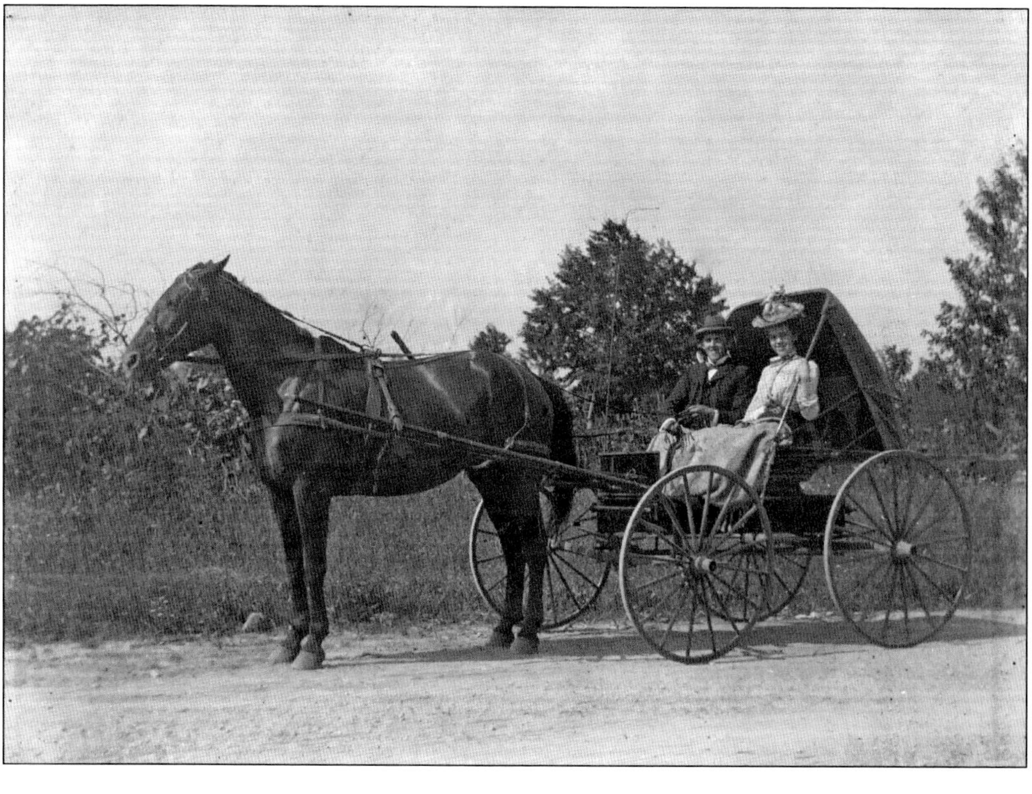

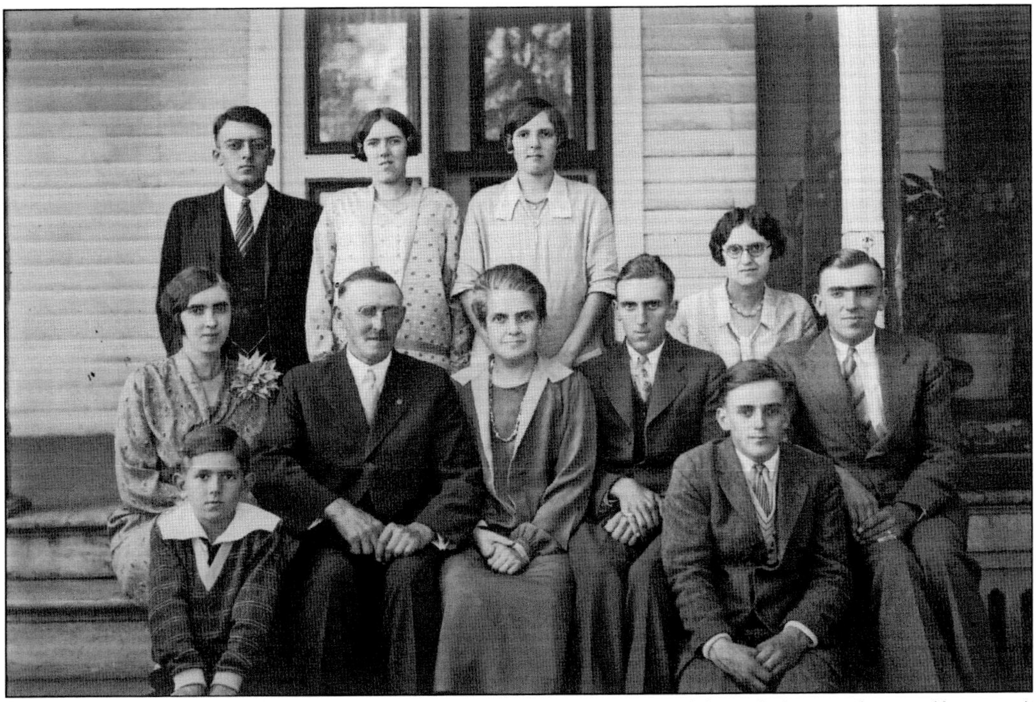

Lewis and Marion's family pose on their porch in 1927. Pictured from left to right are (first row) Seward and Nelson; (second row) Leora, Lewis, Marion, Herbert and George; (third row) Willard, Mildred, Margaret, and Florence.

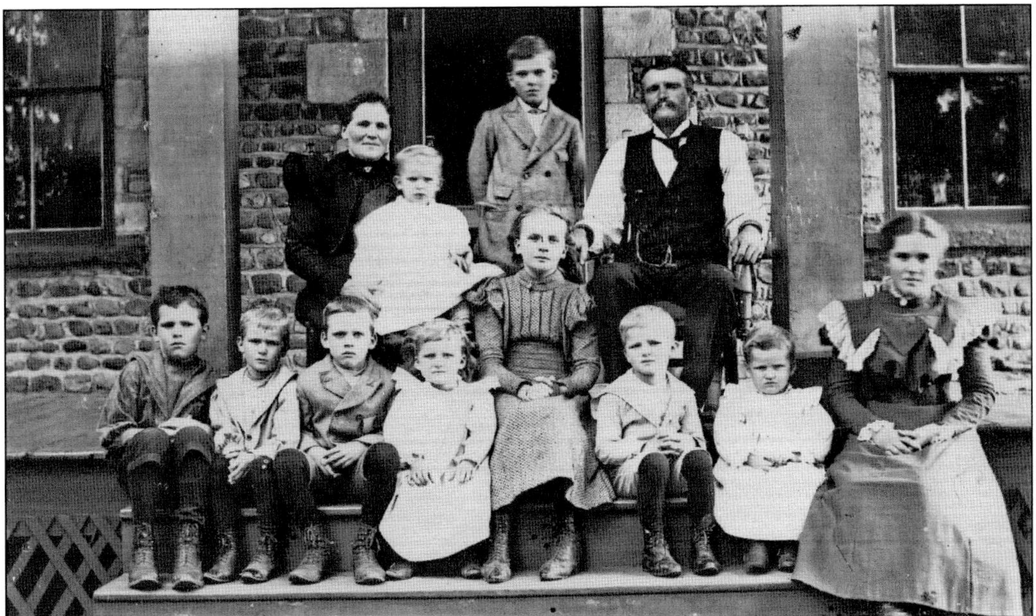

This family photograph of Michael and Margaret Crowley on the steps of their home on Crowley Road was taken about 1898. This historic cobblestone building is still a private home in 2010.

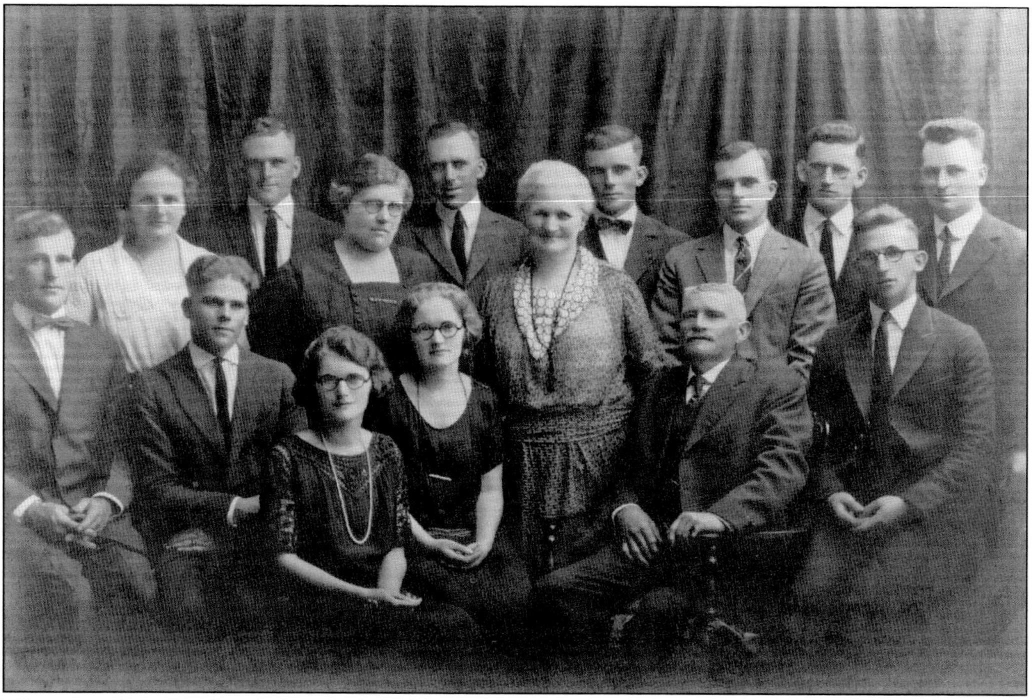

The same Crowley family has gathered here for a studio portrait around 1920.

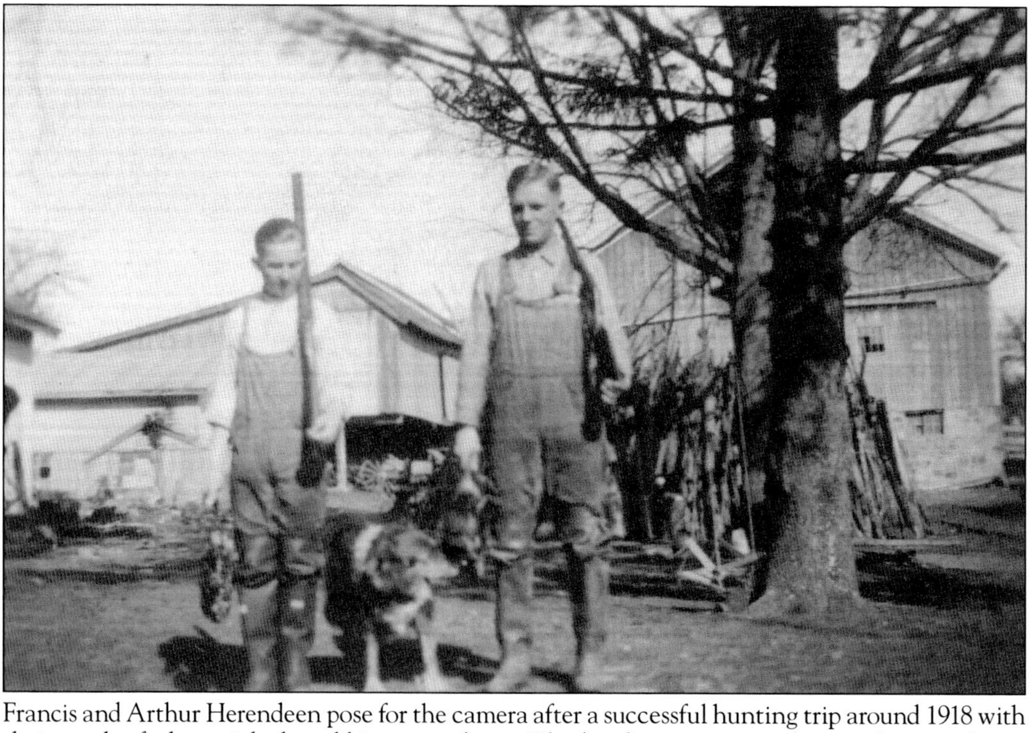

Francis and Arthur Herendeen pose for the camera after a successful hunting trip around 1918 with their catch of what might be rabbits or muskrats. The brothers ran a trap line at the time. Later they operated a fur, wool, and livestock business from the family farm on Allen-Padgham Road.

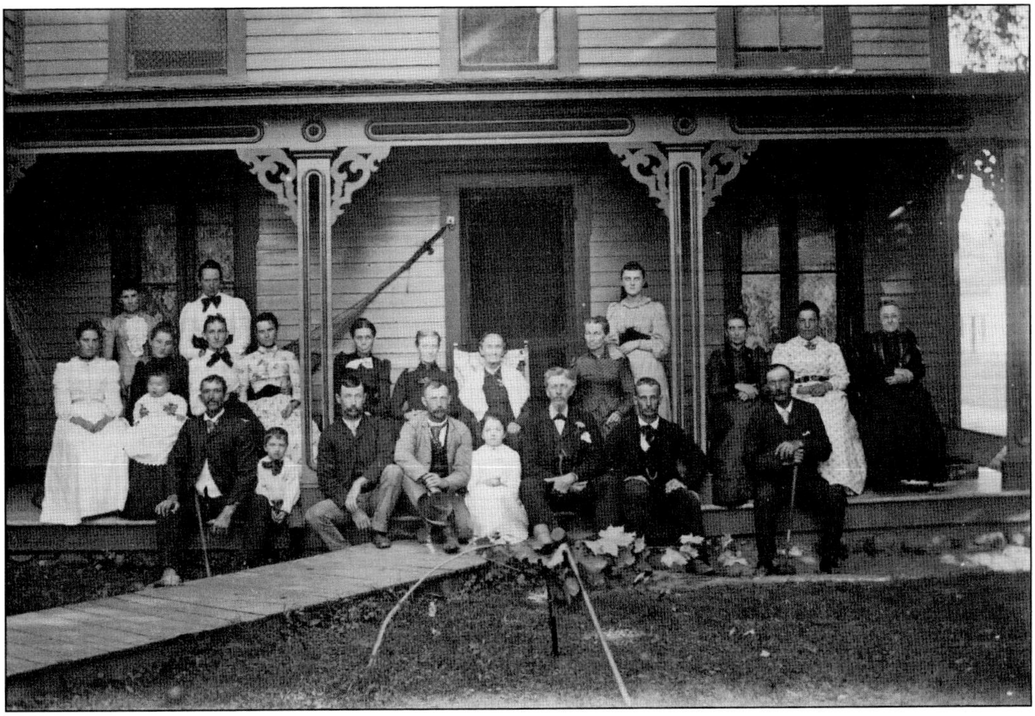

The Stevenson and Webb families interrupted their game of croquet for the photographer to snap this group shot sometime around 1910. Note the board sidewalk in front of the porch.

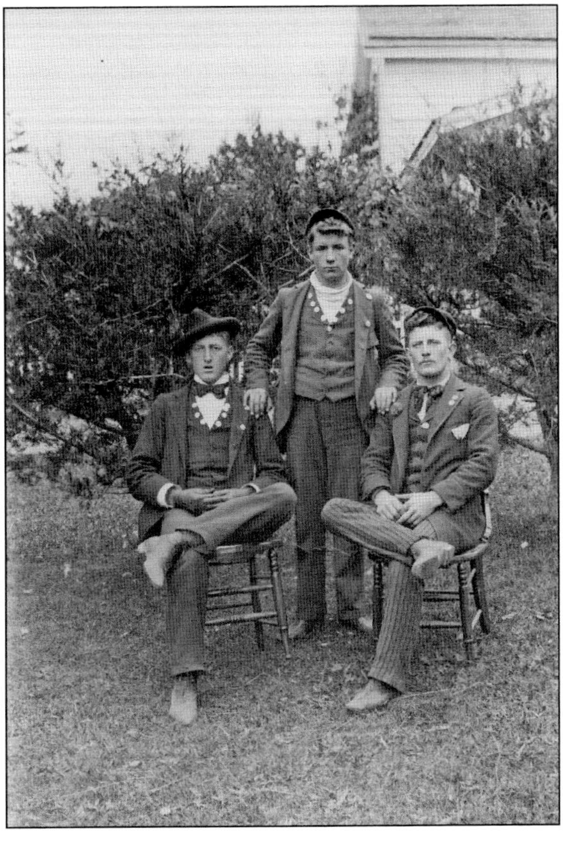

Pictured around 1900, these young Farmington men are, from left to right, Harvey Cheesbrough, Ernest Crocker, and Francis Nussbaumer. The buttons decorating their vests may be political campaign buttons, which were popular at that time. Hats and caps were also fashionable for casual wear.

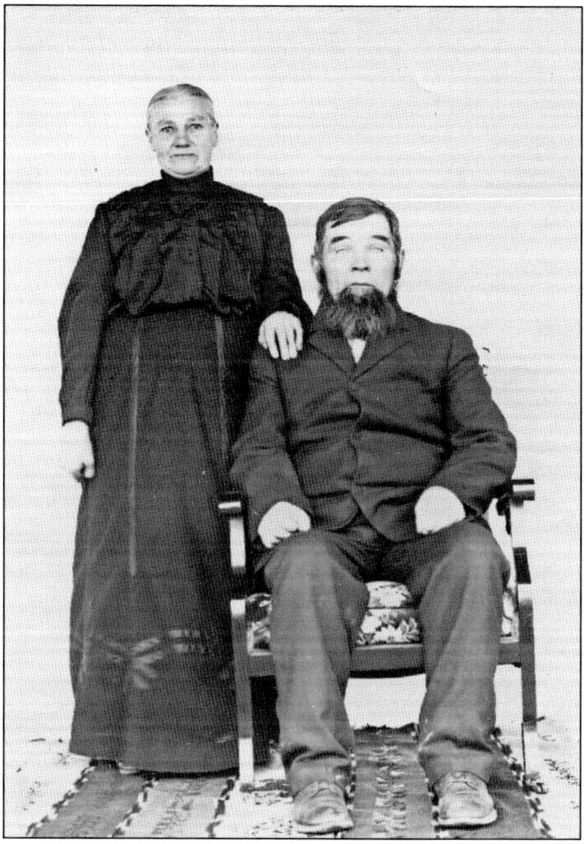

William and Lottie Mamero pose for the photographer about 1900. The Mameros were among several families who came to the Farmington area from Mecklenburg, Germany. Their farm was on Hook Road, near the present crossing of the New York State Thruway.

The photographer captured a portrait of these serious-looking ladies sometime around 1902. Third from left is Nancy Cotton; sitting with her are her daughters, from left to right, Sara Cotton Betz, Carrie Cotton, and Eva Cotton Coon.

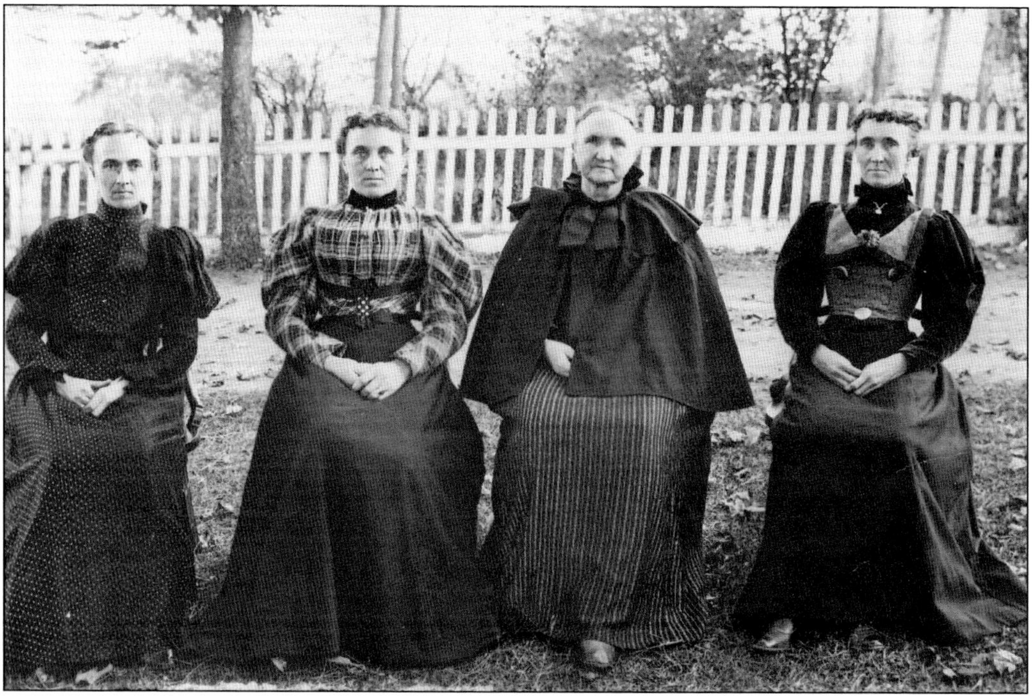

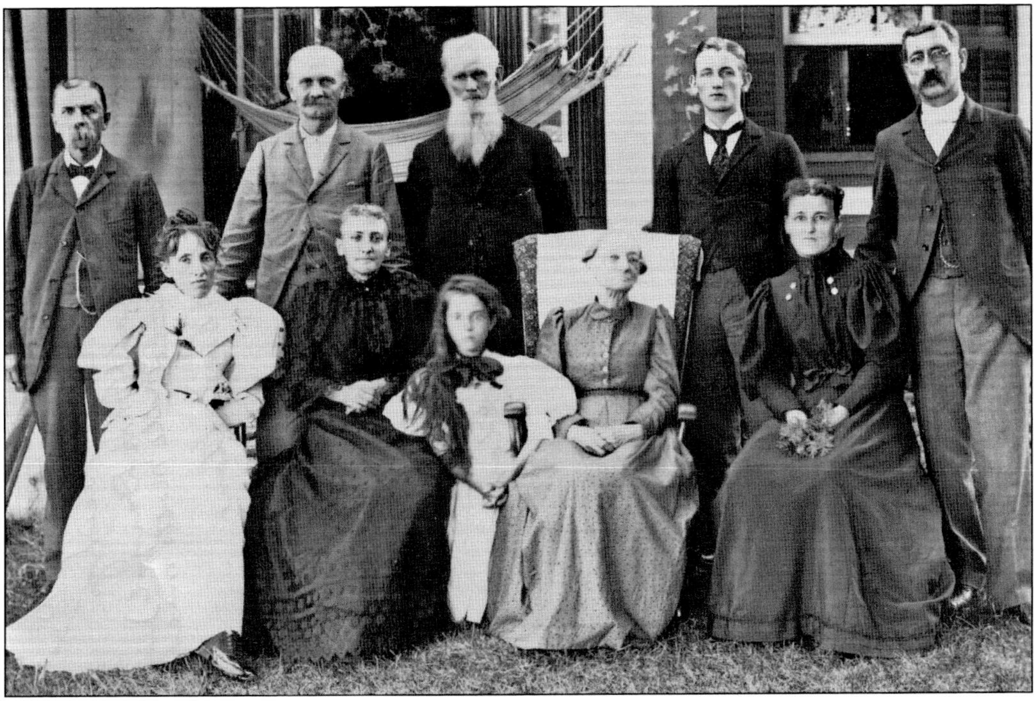

The second couple from the left is Farmington resident Edwin Mott and his wife, Mary, posing with their relatives, the Youngs and Boughtons, about 1898. Leisure-time activities at the turn of the century included lounging in a hammock like the one in the background. The long exposure times required with glass-plate negatives required people to hold very still. The faces of the little girl in the front row and the lady in the chair are blurry because they moved during the exposure.

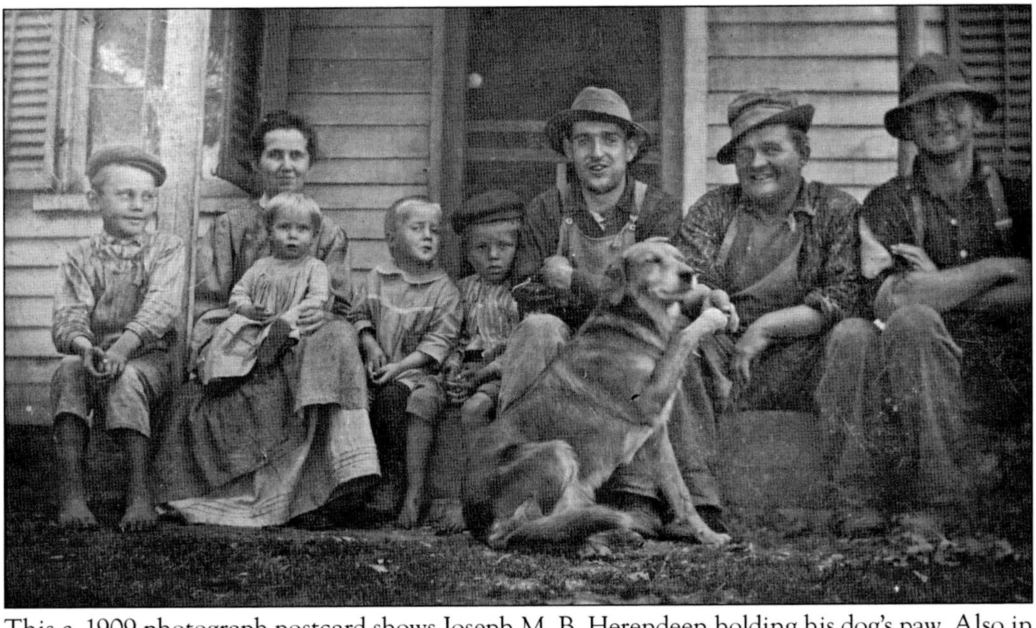

This *c.* 1909 photograph postcard shows Joseph M. B. Herendeen holding his dog's paw. Also in the photograph are Joseph's wife Gertrude, three of their children, and some friends from the Cotton family.

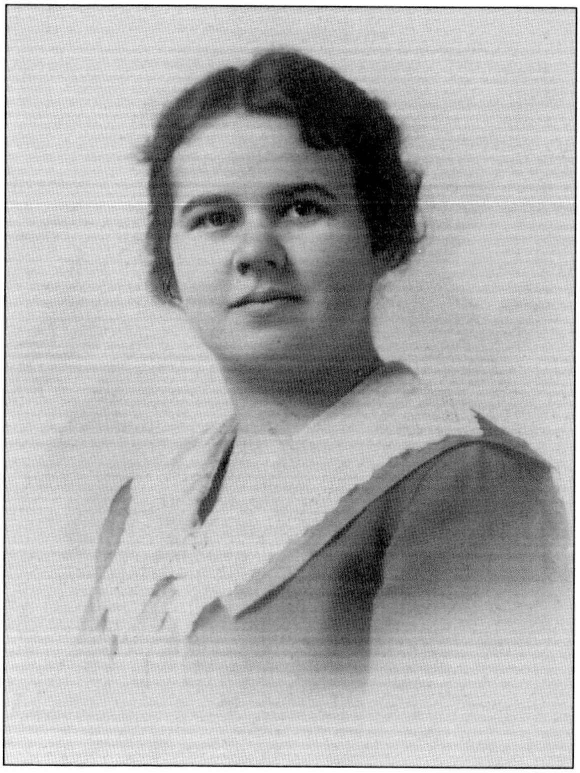

Jane Effie Herendeen was born in Farmington in 1898. She was named for her aunt and became a professional dietician. She served at Clifton Springs Hospital in the 1930s. This portrait is from about 1920.

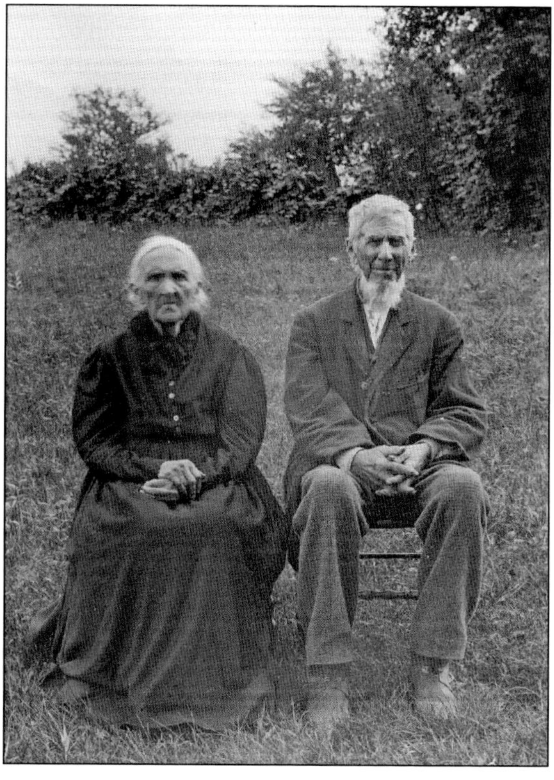

The caption identifies the couple as Fred and Mary Erhardt in this *c.* 1905 photograph. Fred emigrated from Germany in 1864. According to the records, Mary didn't join him until 1894, thirty years later. The Erhardt farm was on Hook Road. It was common for groups of families from one area in their native country to join their relatives and friends in America.

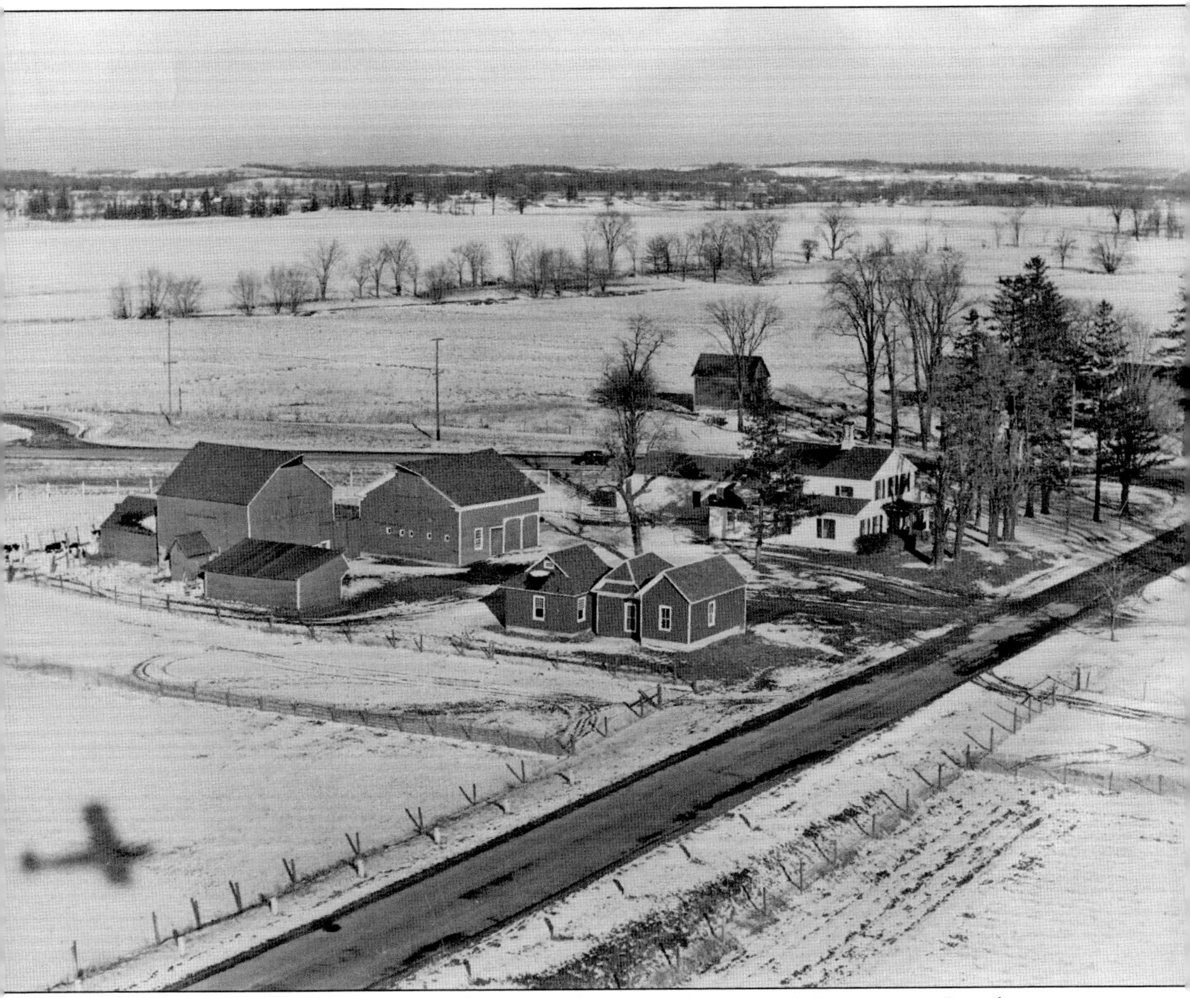

The property in this photograph is the Isaac Hathaway homestead. Isaac was a Revolutionary War veteran, a pioneer settler, and the first town clerk. The view is toward the northeast. The barn near the center is believed to be the oldest framed building in Farmington, constructed for Hathaway by Ananias McMillan in 1793. The future State Route 332 runs horizontally across the middle of the photograph. In 2009, this home was extensively remodeled and opened as the Lyric Arts Academy. (Courtesy Ontario County Historical Society.)

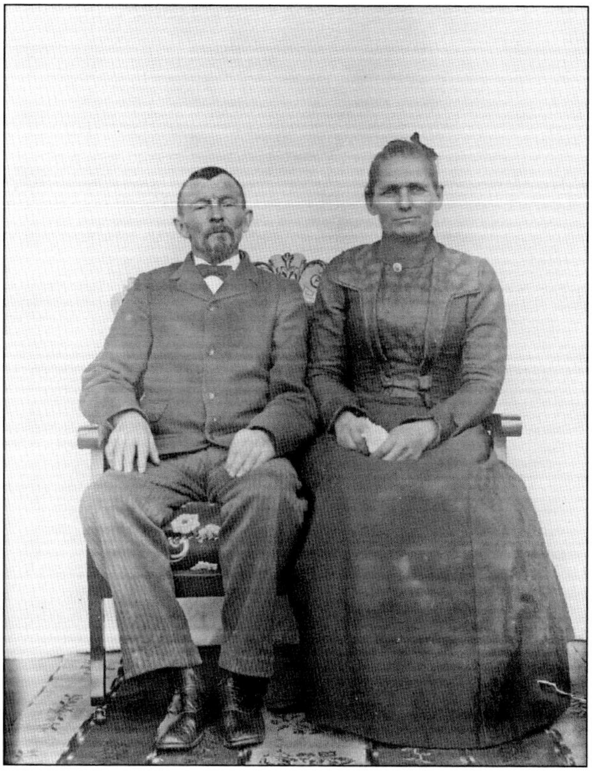

Leonard and Catherine Long pose for this portrait about 1890. The Longs came to Farmington from Wurttemburg, Germany, in 1860. Their farm was known as Meadow Brook Farm and was located on Sheldon Road.

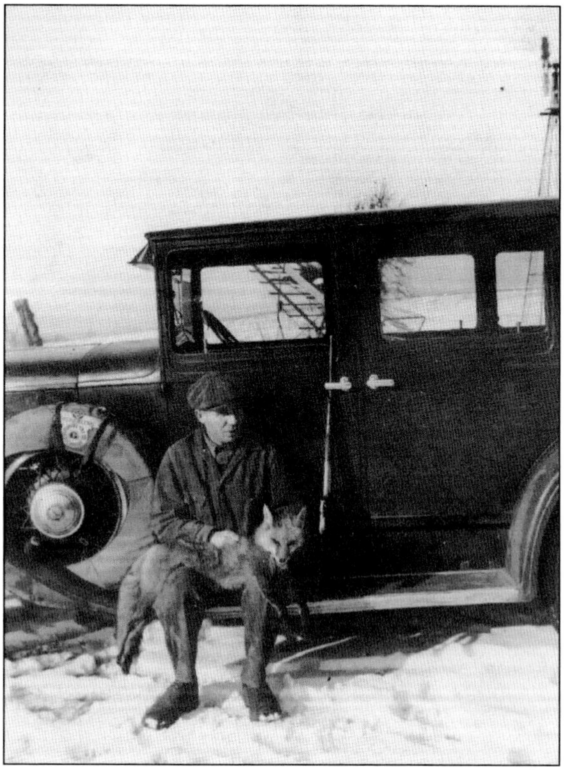

Arthur Herendeen sits on the running board of his automobile with his pet fox at the family farm on Allen-Padgham Road sometime around 1925. Windmills like the one in the background were once a common sight on local farms.

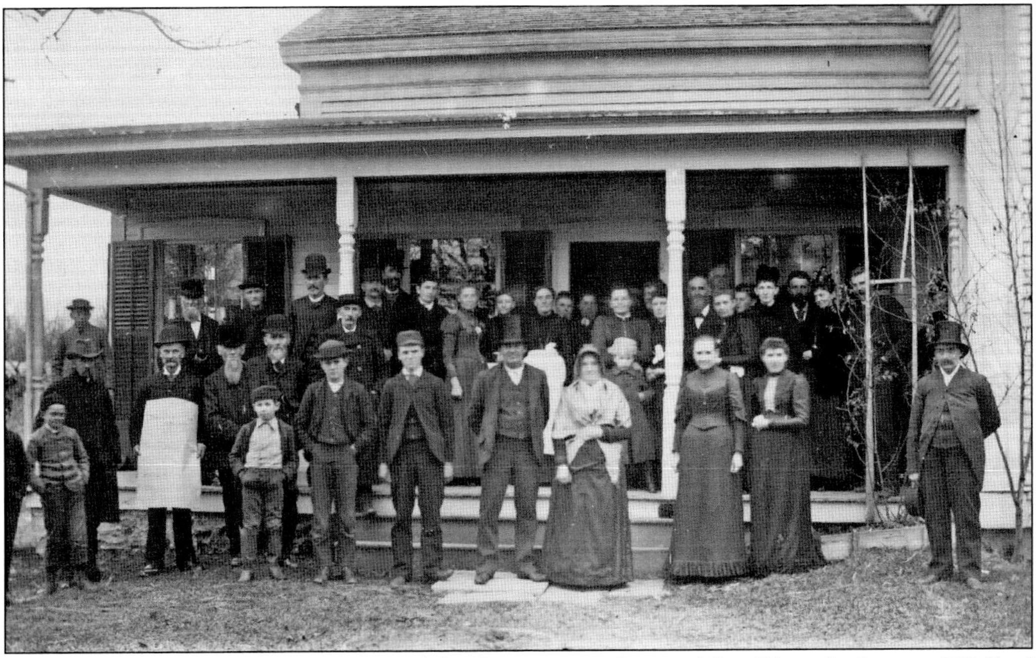

This group is gathered for a meeting of the Farmington Grange No. 431 at the home of Gifford Bowerman around 1890. The man on the left is holding some sort of handwritten proclamation; Bowerman is the man in the center with the tall hat.

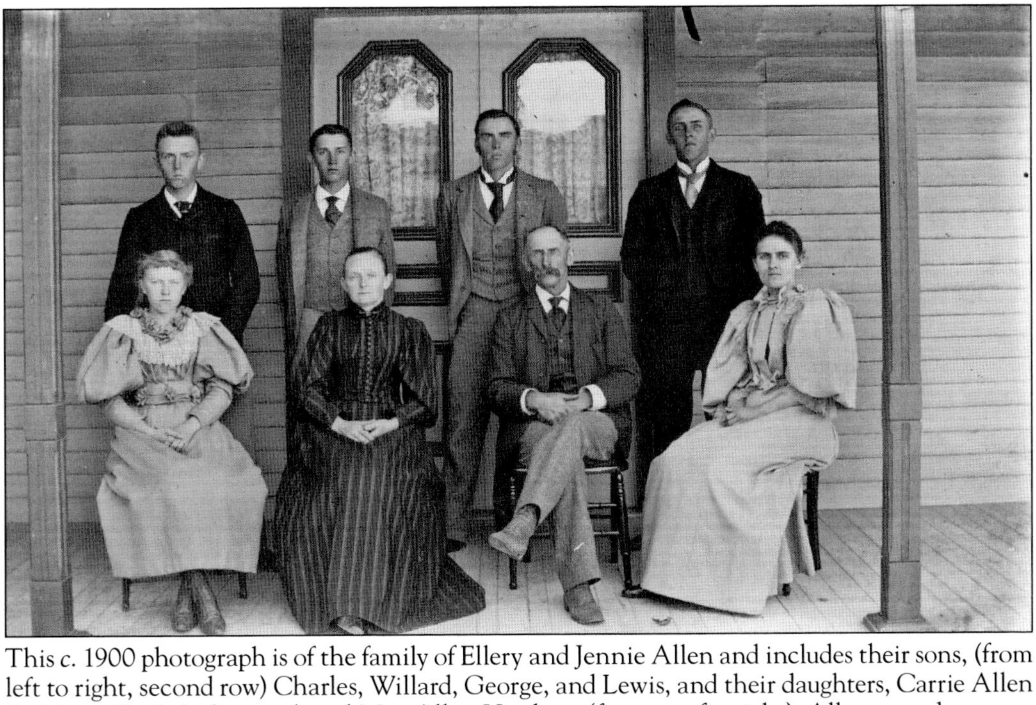

This *c.* 1900 photograph is of the family of Ellery and Jennie Allen and includes their sons, (from left to right, second row) Charles, Willard, George, and Lewis, and their daughters, Carrie Allen Padgham (far left, first row) and May Allen Hawkins (first row, far right). Allen served as town supervisor from 1880 to 1886.

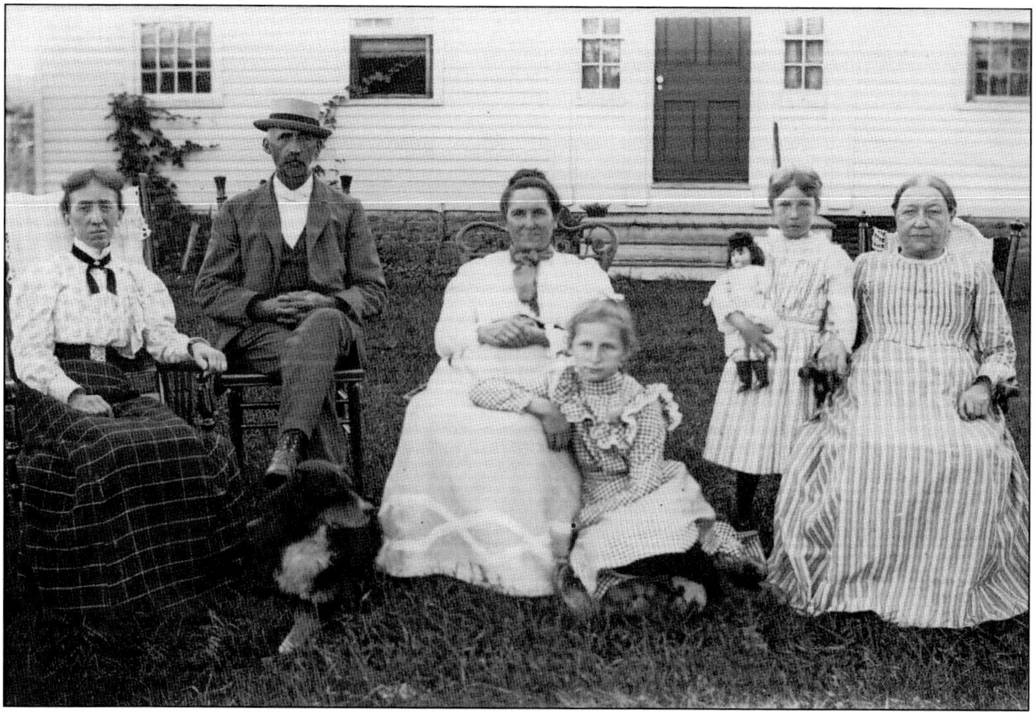

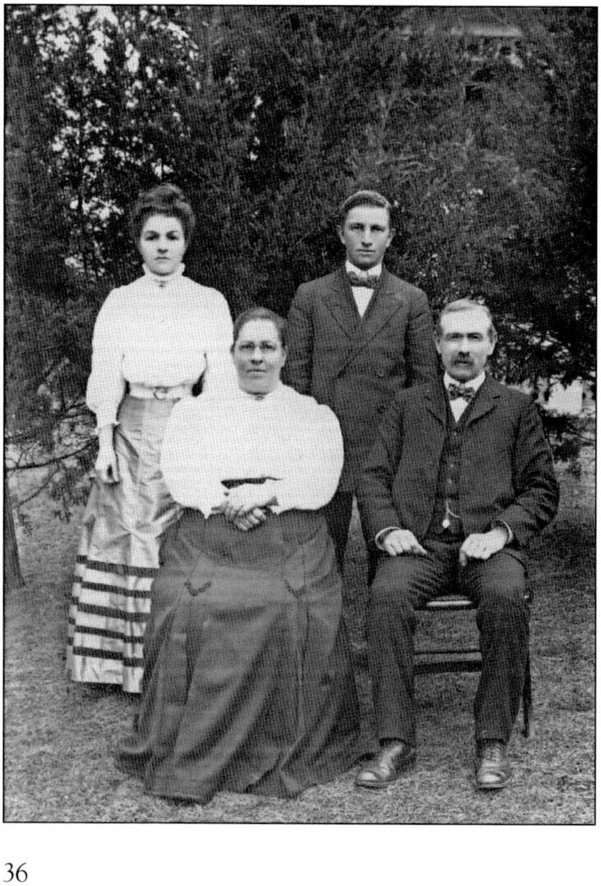

The John and Kate Scribner family pose for a portrait with daughters Helen and Ruth (standing) about 1900. The woman on the left is identified as Aunt Jennie, and the woman on the right as Mrs. Thompson, mother. The Scribners lived on County Road 8 south of Holtz and Martz Roads.

Farmer and photographer Edwin J. Gardner took this portrait of himself, his wife Rosalie, daughter May, and son Lindley about 1905. He served Farmington as a justice of the peace in 1897, as town supervisor in 1902, and later as a member of the board of assessors.

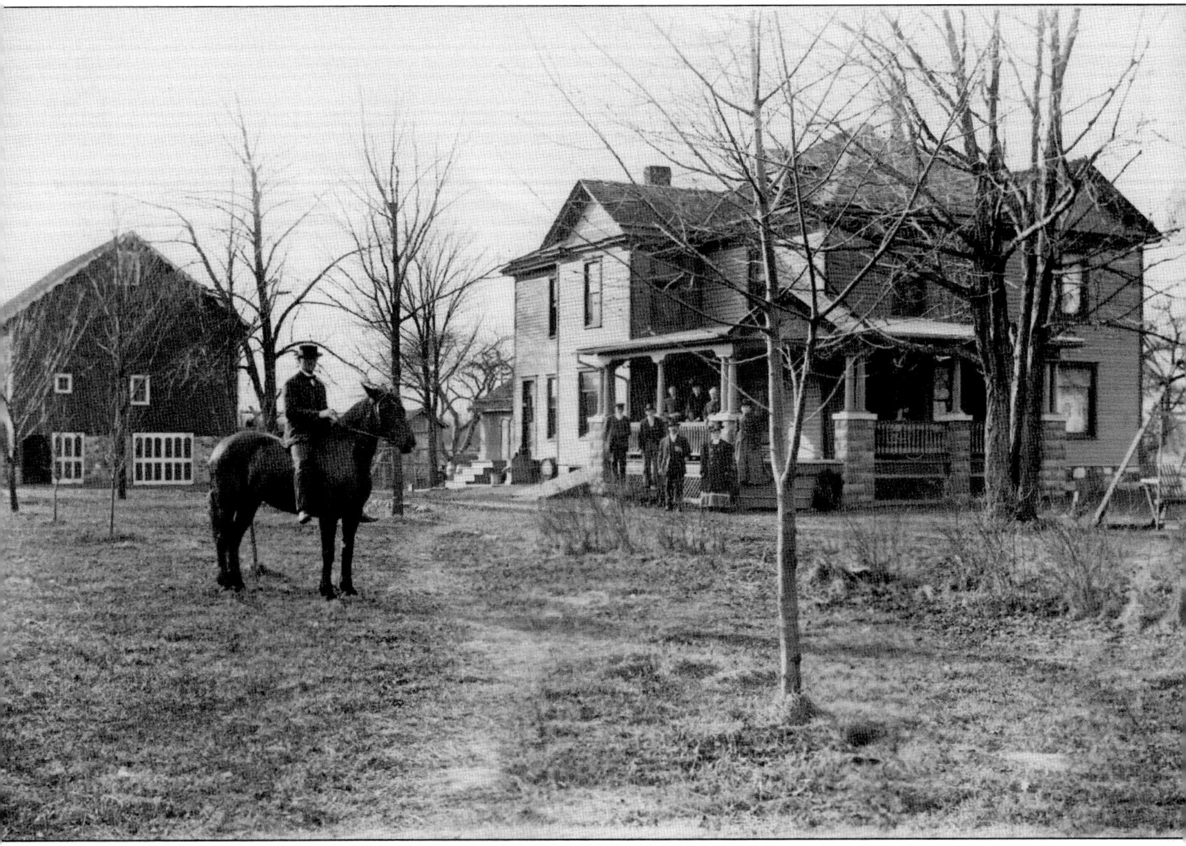

Charles R. Gardner poses on a horse at his home on Hook Road with his family watching from the porch. The barn is known to have built about 1905, so this photograph must have been taken sometime after that.

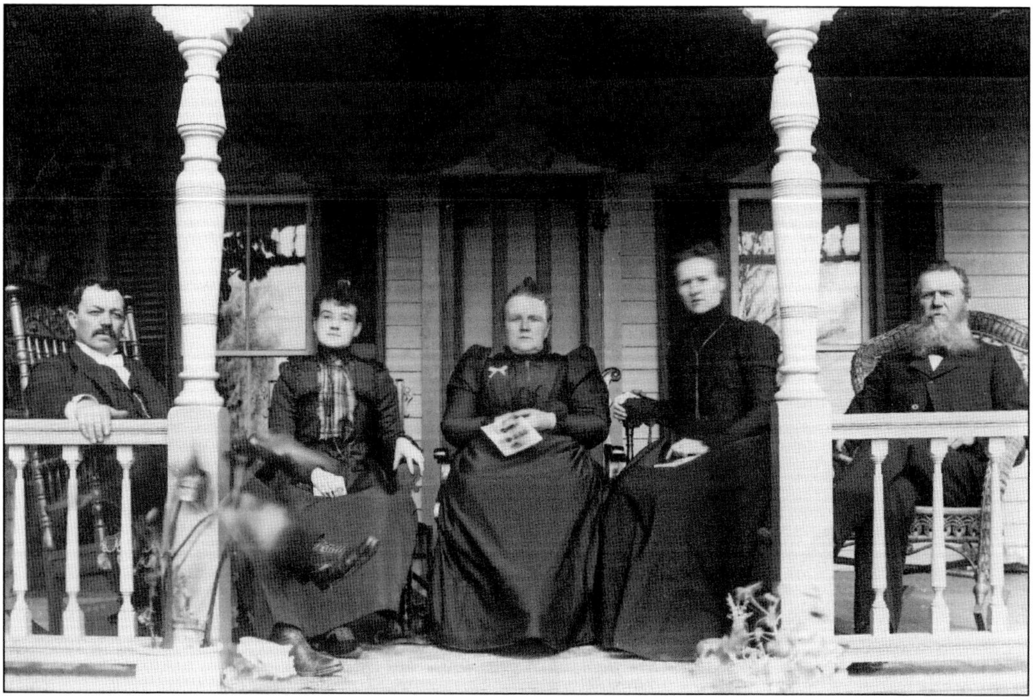

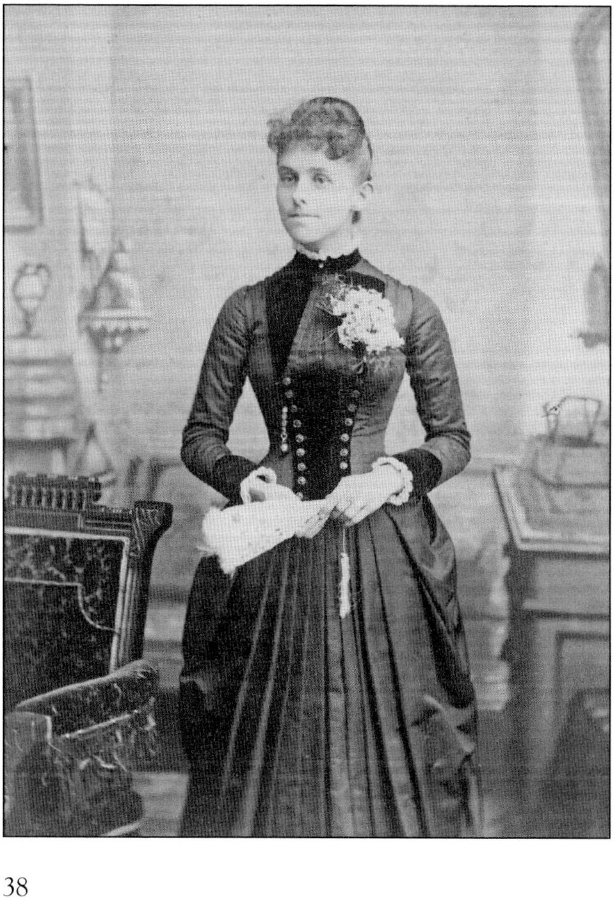

The bearded gentleman on the right and the lady in the center are Henry and Charlotte Selleck Katkamier; their daughter Elizabeth sits between them. Also in the photograph are Charlotte's sister and brother-in-law, Mr. and Mrs. William Schley.

The inscription on this portrait identifies the subject as Luella McLouth of Farmington and notes that she is posing in her wedding dress. She married Clifford Wilber of Farmington and Orleans. The portrait was taken about 1880. (Courtesy Ontario County Historical Society.)

Margaret Allen Baker had a lifelong interest in Farmington history. She was a World War II veteran and is shown here in her WAVES (Women Appointed for Voluntary Emergency Service) uniform. Baker was the honorary chairperson of the Farmington bicentennial celebration.

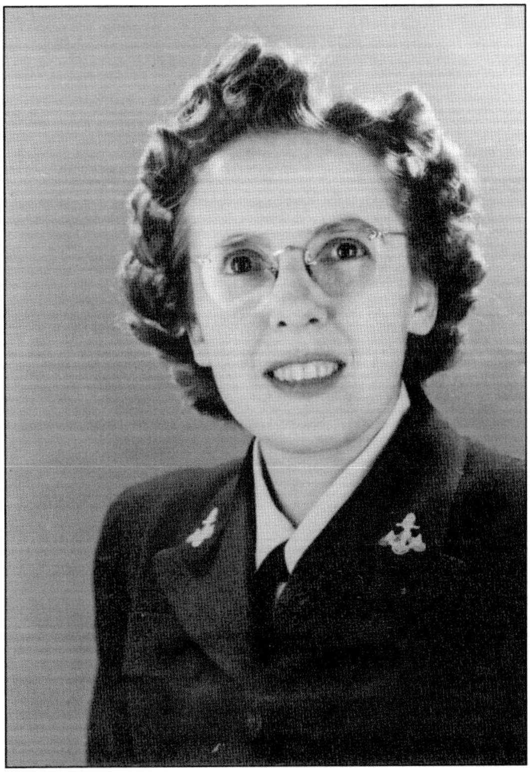

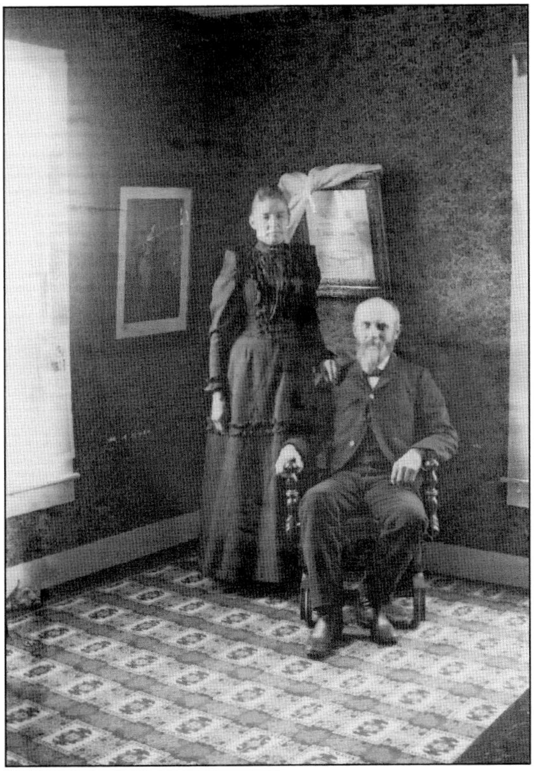

This couple is Darwin and Rebecca Katkamier, parents of Allen B. Katkamier, who became proprietor of Farmington's iris farm, a world-renowned source of irises and other fancy flowers. The framed document behind them appears to be their marriage certificate.

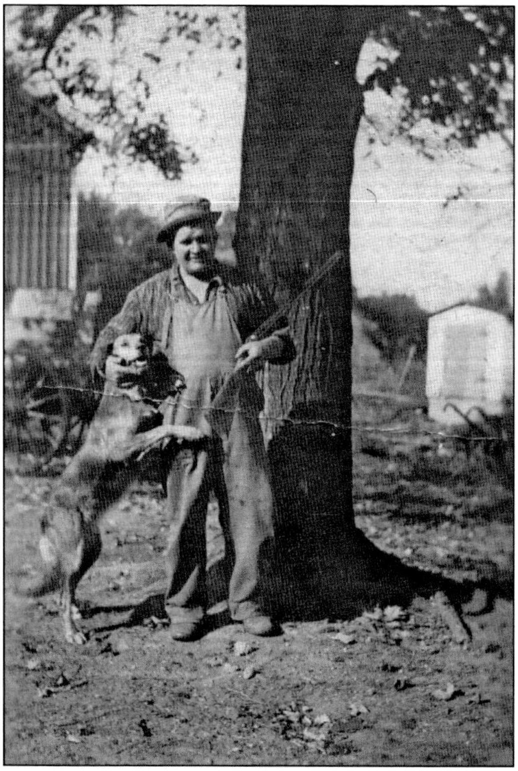

This photograph postcard is postmarked 1909 and is addressed to Edson McLouth. The message reads, "Wishing you all a very Happy New Year. Joseph M. B. Herendeen." Herendeen is pictured with his gun and dog.

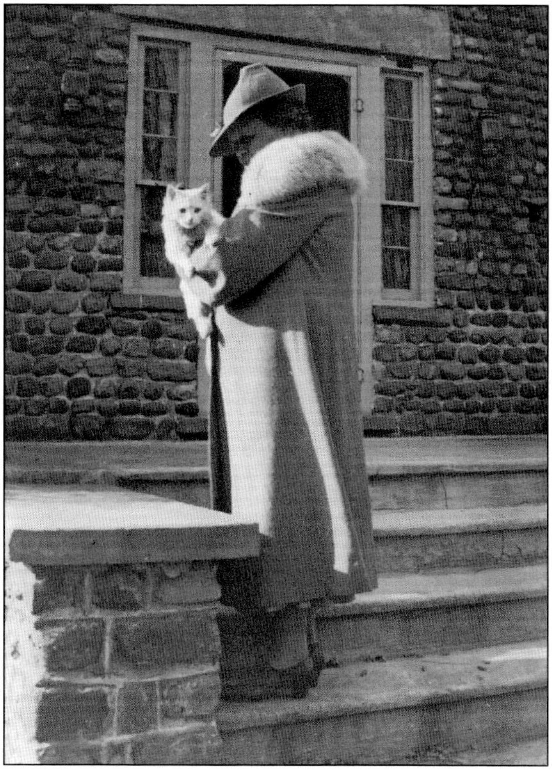

Jane E. Herendeen poses with a furry friend. Jane became a professional elocutionist, which is a person who trains others in the art of public speaking. She taught in New York City at Columbia University. She is shown here on the steps of the Herendeen homestead on County Road 8 about 1930. This historic cobblestone building north of the New York State Thruway is still a family dwelling and has a state historic marker in the front yard.

This 1915 family photograph shows Oscar B. Gardner holding his son Oscar Jr. Also in the photograph are his wife, Julia, and daughters Julia Belle and Florence. Oscar Sr. served twice as town supervisor.

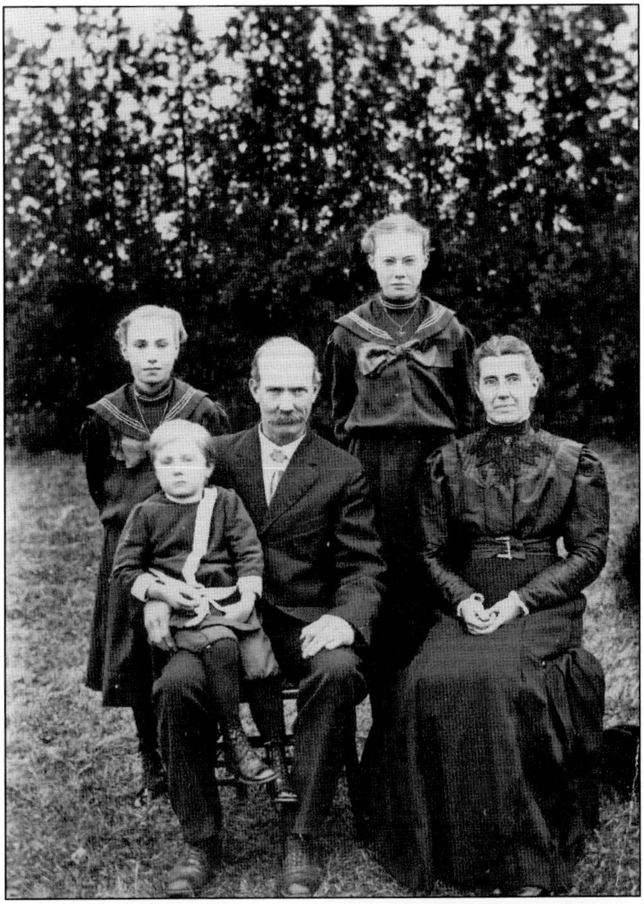

This photograph is part of the E. J. Gardner collection and is almost certainly a Farmington family, but the photograph has no inscription. The Farmington town historian would welcome input from anyone with clues or suggestions about their identity.

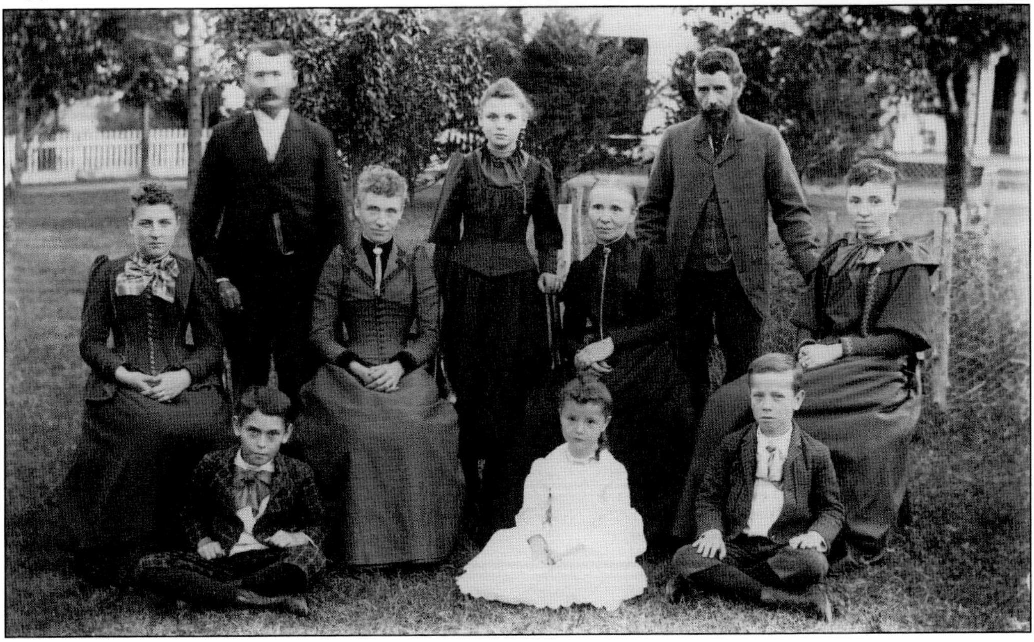

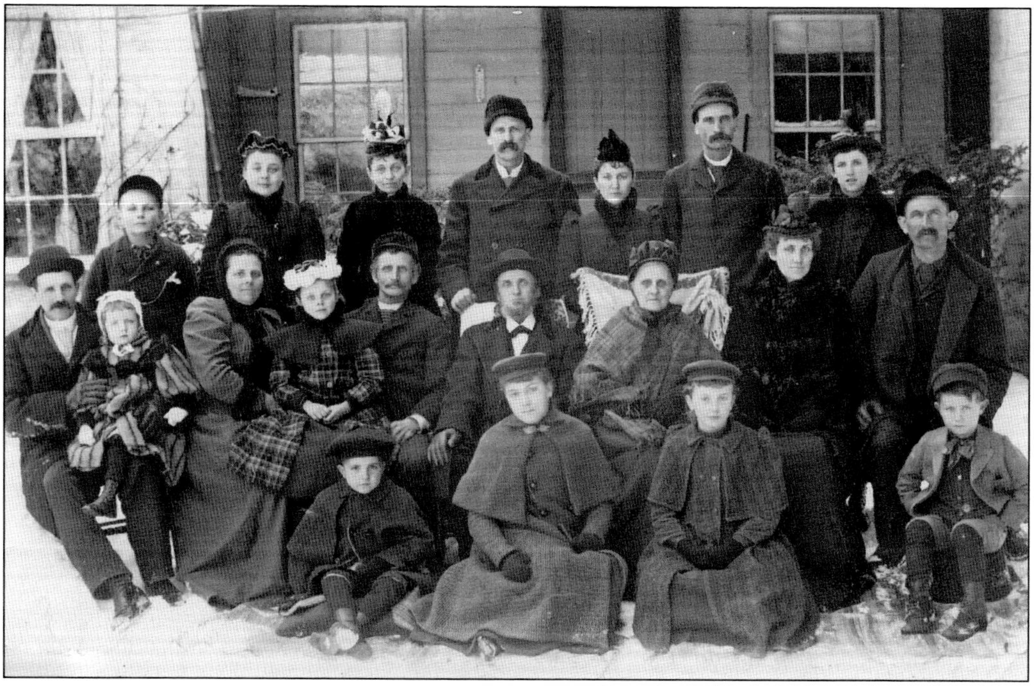

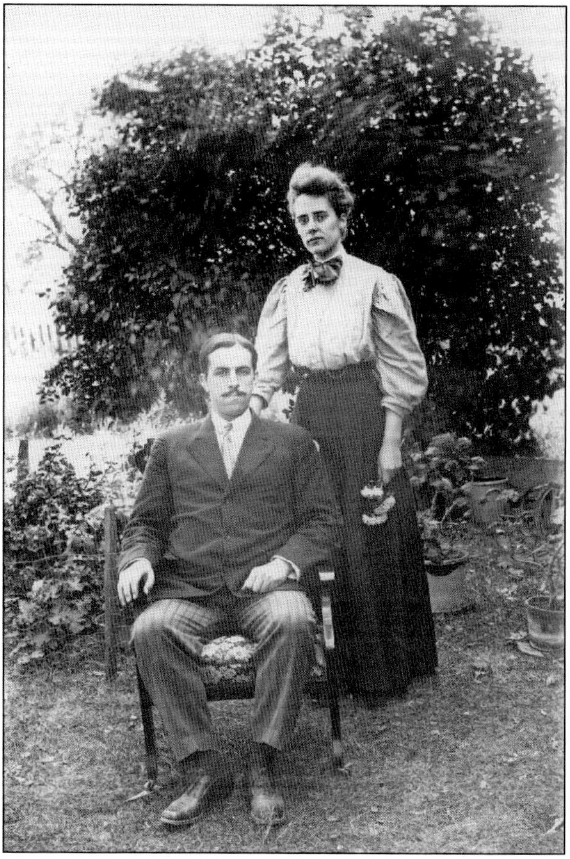

Joseph and Mary Padgham are pictured (center) surrounded by their family sometime around 1895. The photograph was taken at the home of James and Miriam Sheldon Padgham, which was built in the 1860s.

This photograph is of William Carleton Wood and his wife, Alice, taken around 1910. Wood is seated in what appears to be an office chair with casters on the legs.

This is a studio portrait of Nathaniel Herendeen, who was born in Farmington about 1827. He moved his family to the frontier of Kansas for five years before returning to New York. This portrait was made about 1880.

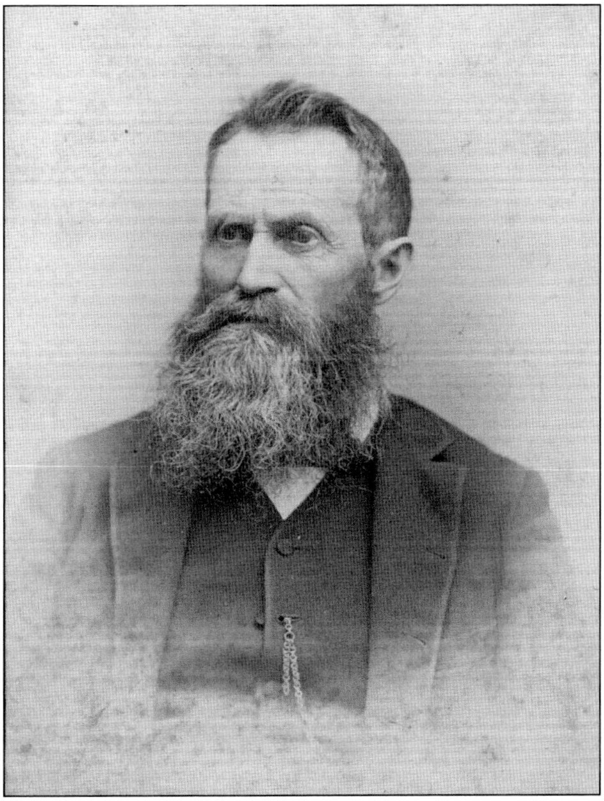

This sketch of the house of pioneer Daniel Arnold, located on Collett Road in Farmington, is from an 1876 Ontario County atlas. Arnold was born in Farmington in 1800. He served terms as town supervisor, commissioner of schools, and county superintendent of the poor.

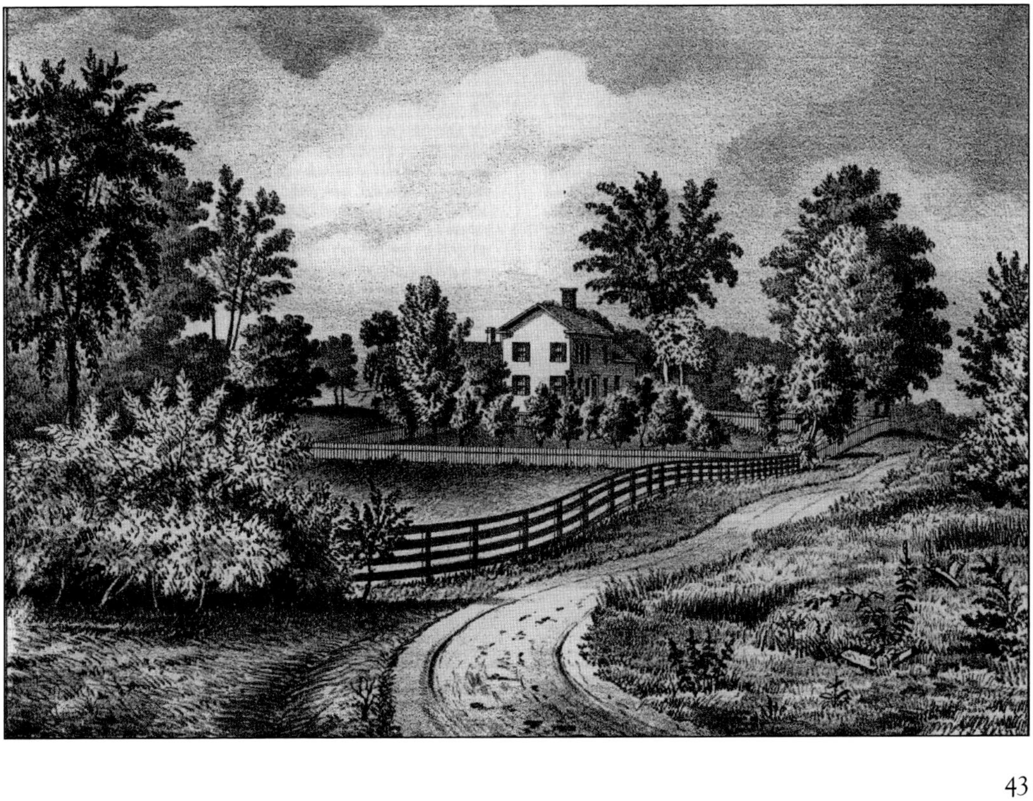

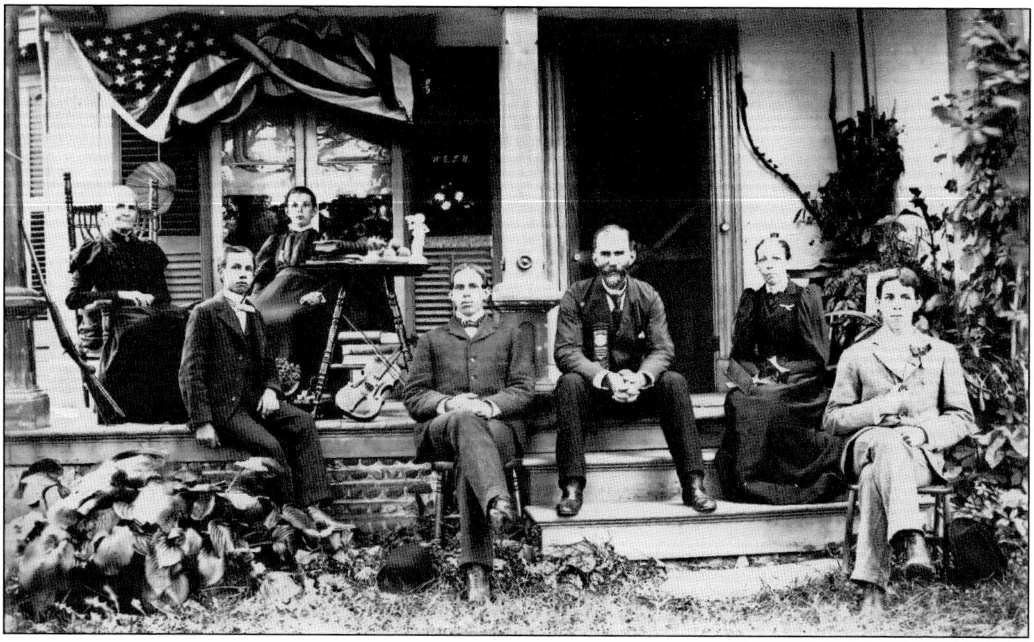

Charles Wood and some members of his family celebrate the Fourth of July. Charles seems to be wearing a prize ribbon on his jacket. Note the prominently displayed flag and the violin under the table. The woman on the steps has a stereoscope on her lap. This photograph was taken about 1905 at the Wood home on Sheldon Road, subsequently occupied by the Popenhusen family and still standing in 2010.

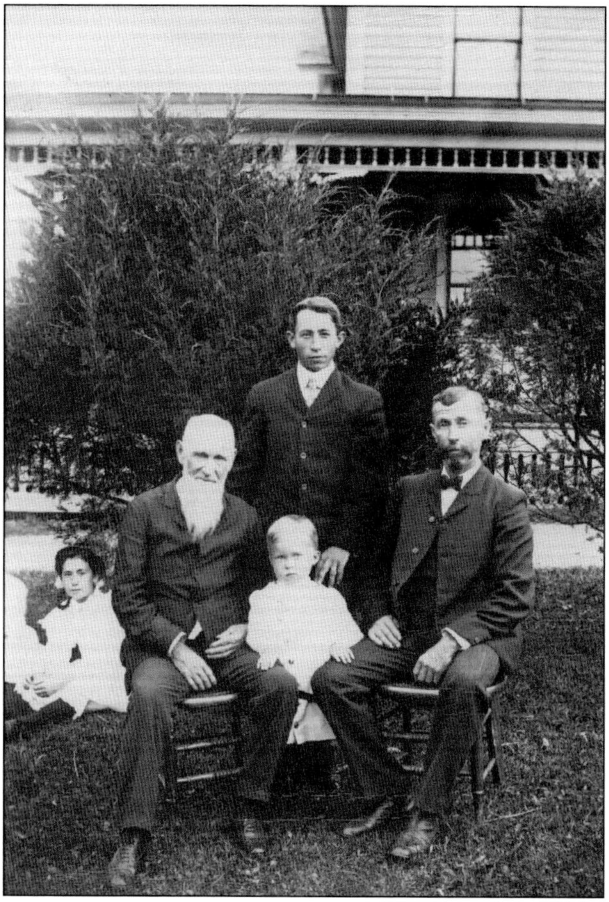

Four generations of Stevenson men pose for this *c.* 1905 photograph: William, Will (standing), Ed, and baby Carl. Members of the Stevenson family were farmers in the northeast part of Farmington. Will's wife, Harriet, was a teacher; she may be the woman in the background.

Farmington residents John Dailor and John Burns are pictured taking a break from their farming chores.

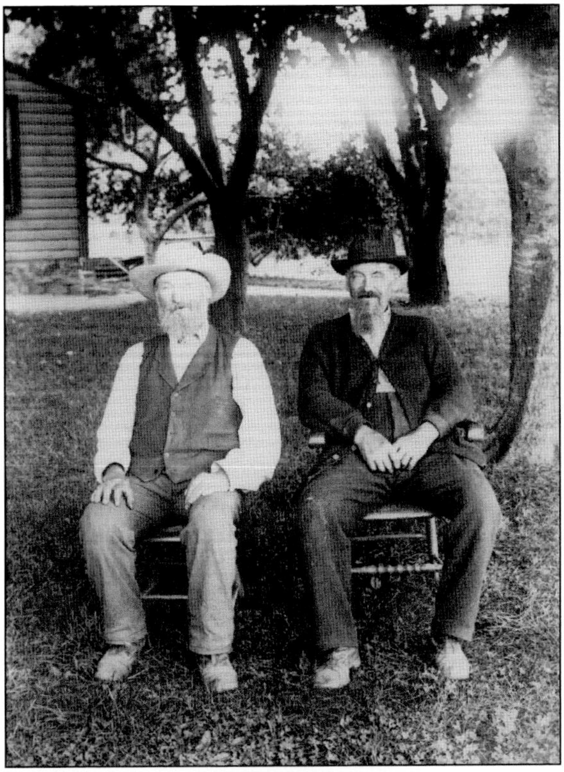

This *c.* 1950 aerial view of Hathaway's Corners looks northeast. This was once known as West Farmington, a busy hamlet with a trolley stop. County Road 41 (also known as Boughton Hill Road) runs from the middle left to the upper right. It was once a Native American trail and later a stagecoach route. (Courtesy Bruce Stewart.)

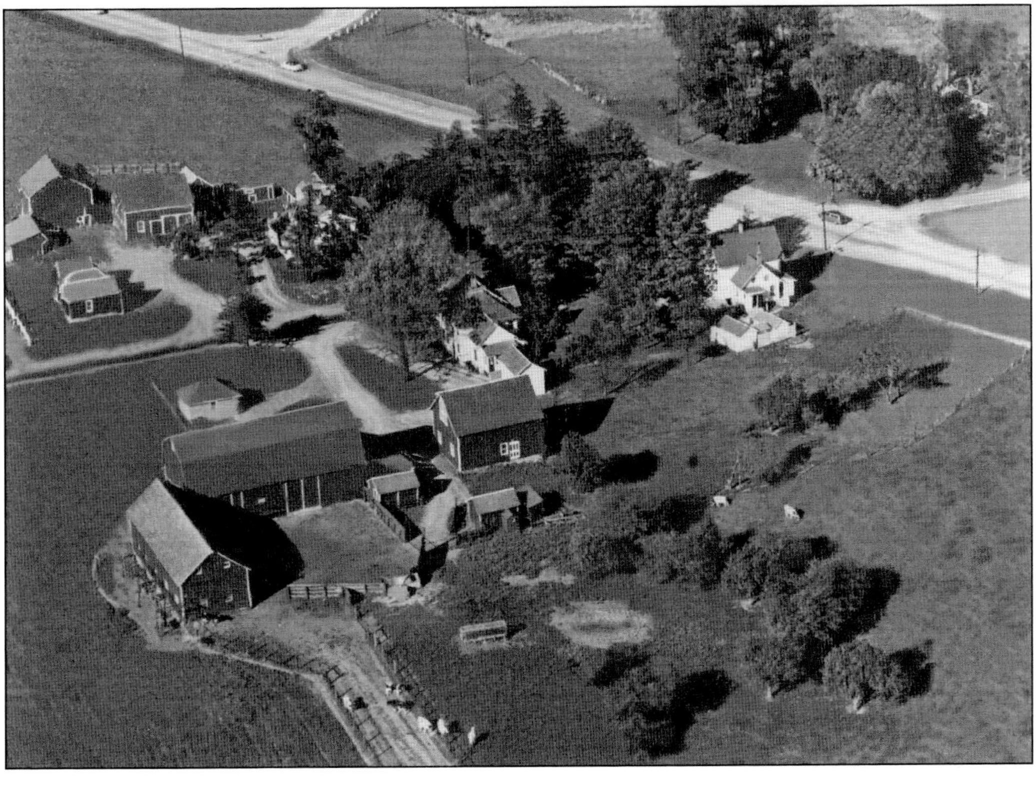

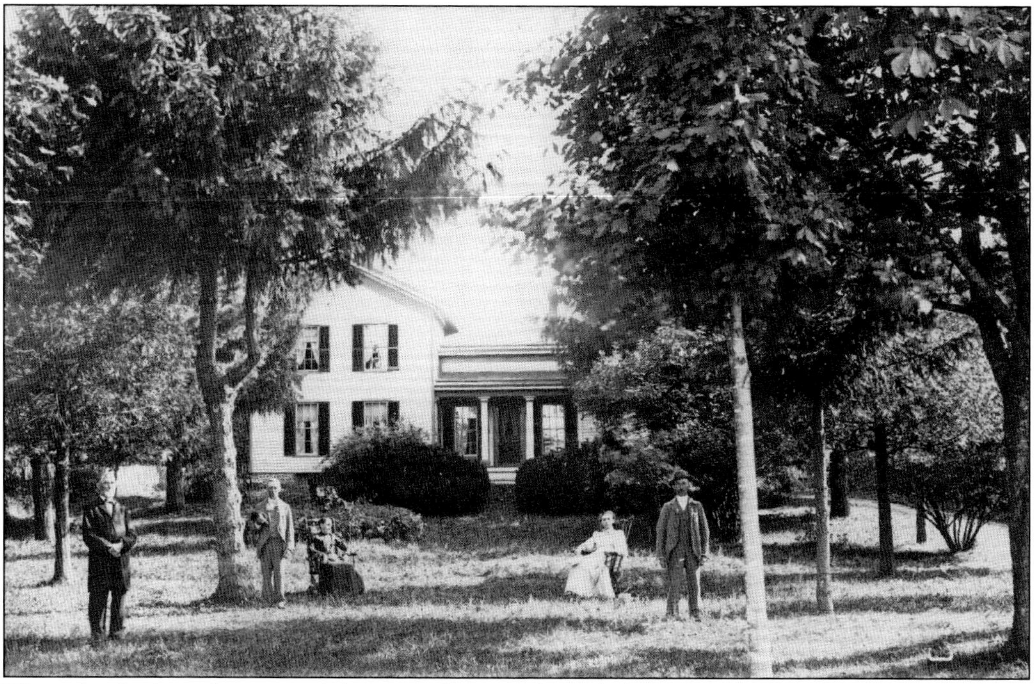

The individuals in this unusual distance photograph are believed to be Henry and Lucinda Moore with their children, Charles, George, and Alice. This photograph was taken around 1900 in the yard of their Farmington home.

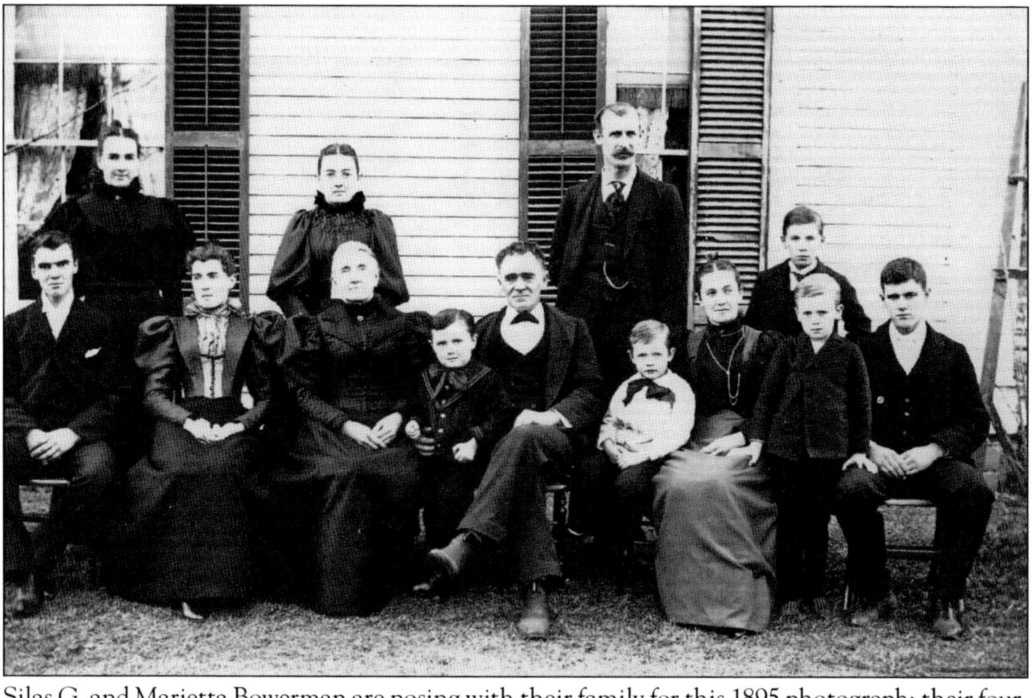

Silas G. and Marietta Bowerman are posing with their family for this 1895 photograph; their four-year-old son Manley is between them. Also in this photograph are Watson and Matie Hulbert and their sons, Robert and Jerome.

These are the Turner sisters, Myrtle Turner Clover and Clara Turner Brewster, pictured sometime around 1900. The seated sister has her hat on her lap that is decorated with a bow and what are probably fresh flowers.

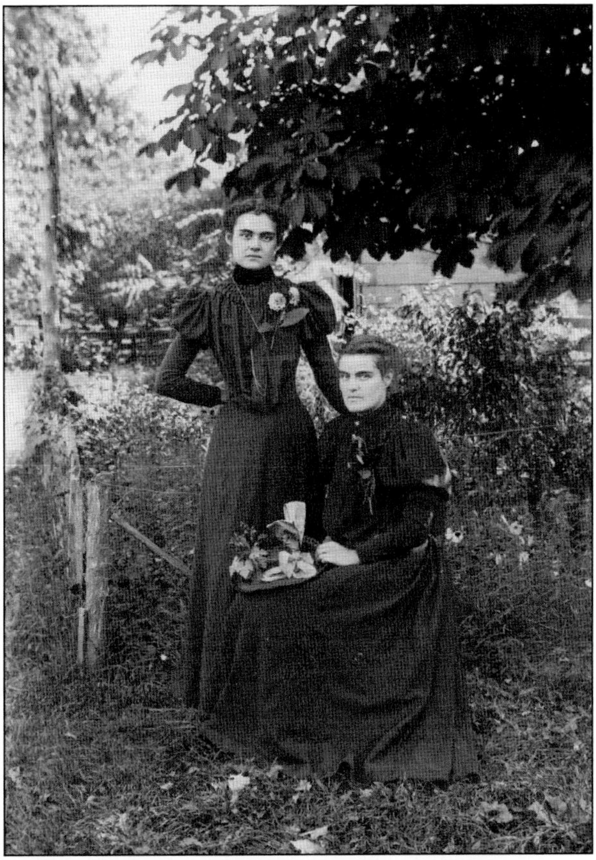

Patriarch William Stevenson and his wife are pictured with their son Edward and his wife, Anna; Edward's son Bert and Bert's wife, Lottie; and Edward's grandson Will Stevenson. This photograph was taken about 1895. Bert and Ed owned adjacent farms near the intersection of Holtz Road and County Road 8.

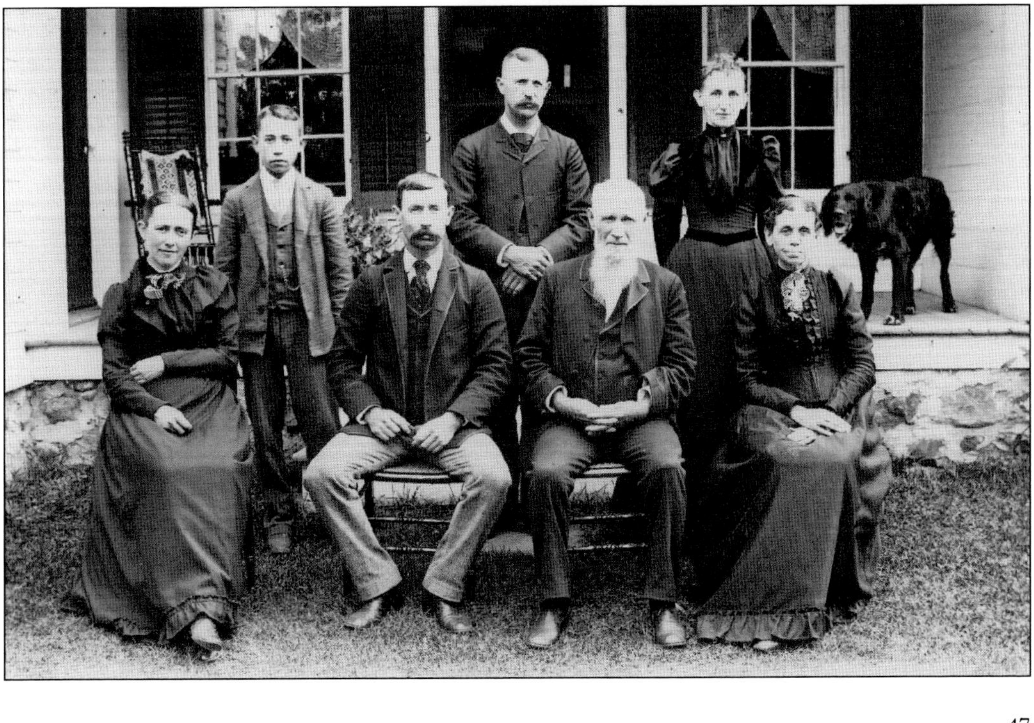

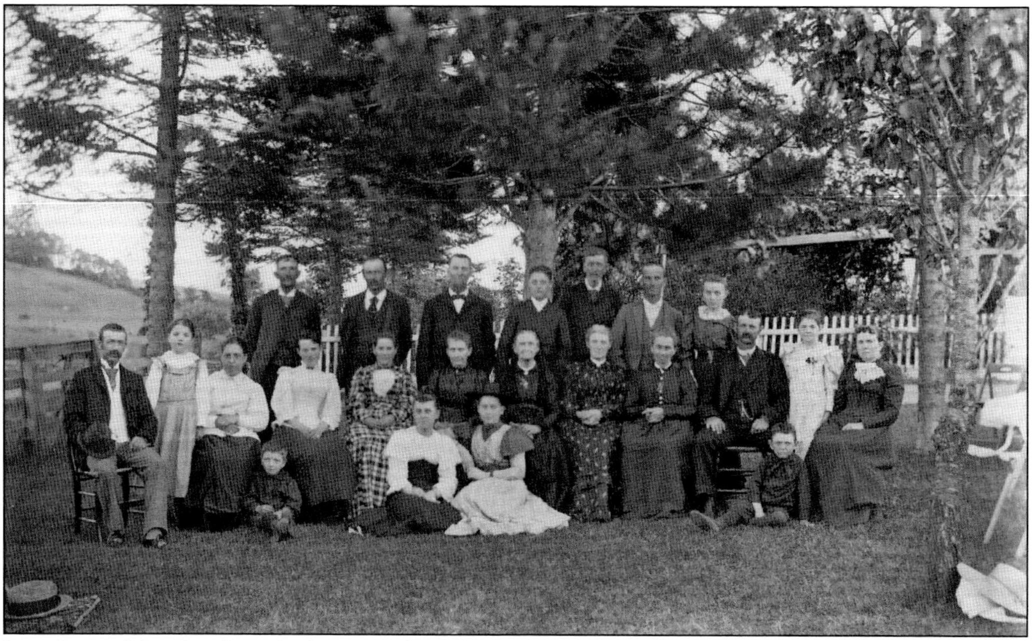

Members of the Gardner, Jackson, and Markham families are pictured enjoying a family reunion about 1892. Photographer E. J. Gardner is seated to the far left.

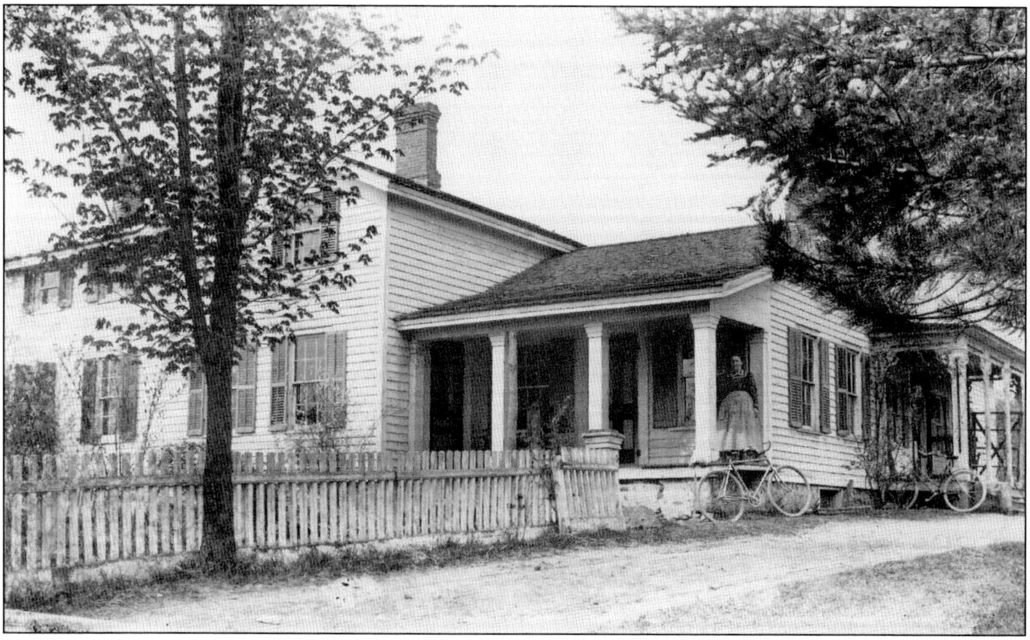

Rosalie Gardner is posing behind the family bicycles on the porch of the E. J. Gardner home at 238 Hook Road sometime before 1900.

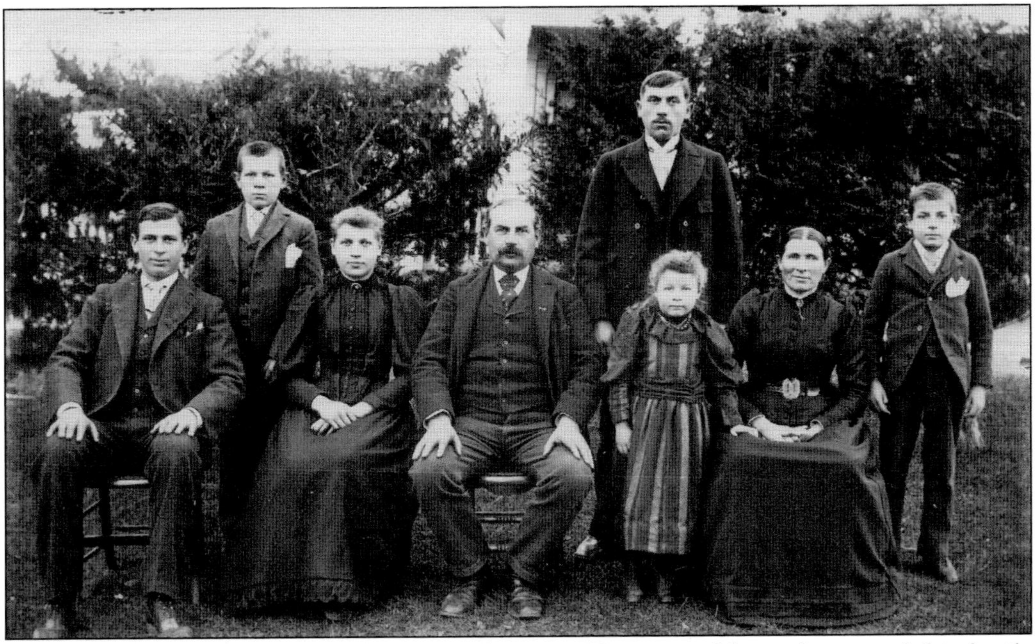

The caption identifies the seated man as Christian Weigert, and he is shown with his family sometime around 1890. In contrast to the grim looks often seen in such photographs, this family at least has a few tentative smiles. Others in the photograph are Mrs. Charles Weigert, Chris Weigert's mother; Edward Weigert, who later lived on Weigert Road; and Ed's brother and sister.

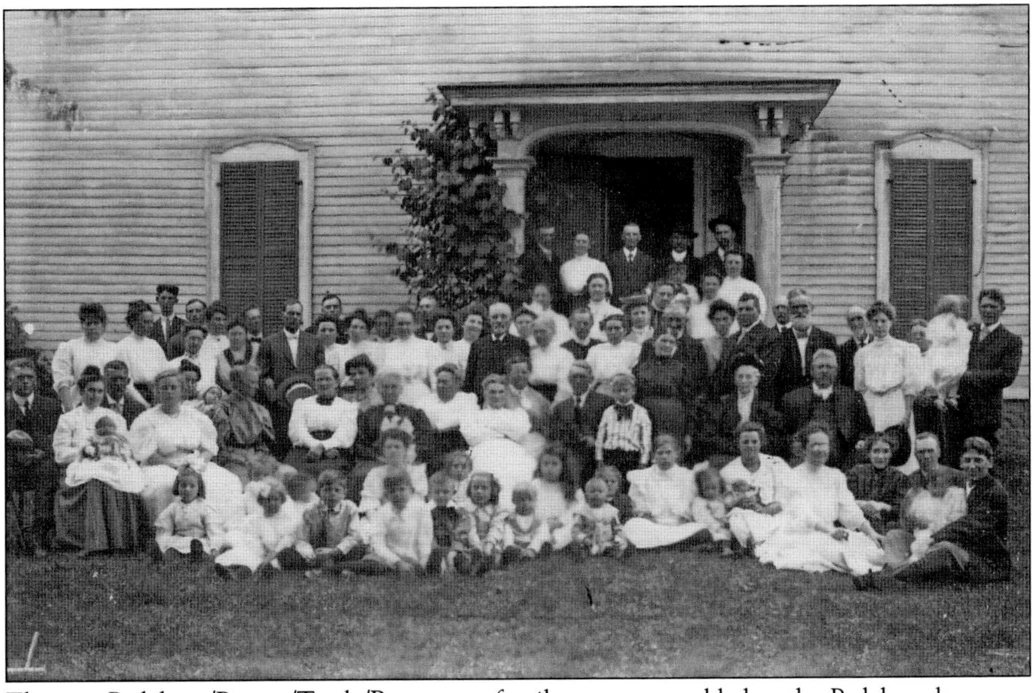

This is a Padgham/Powers/Tuttle/Bowerman family group assembled at the Padgham home on Hook Road about 1904. This home was later sold to the Katkamier family, who operated the iris farm across the road.

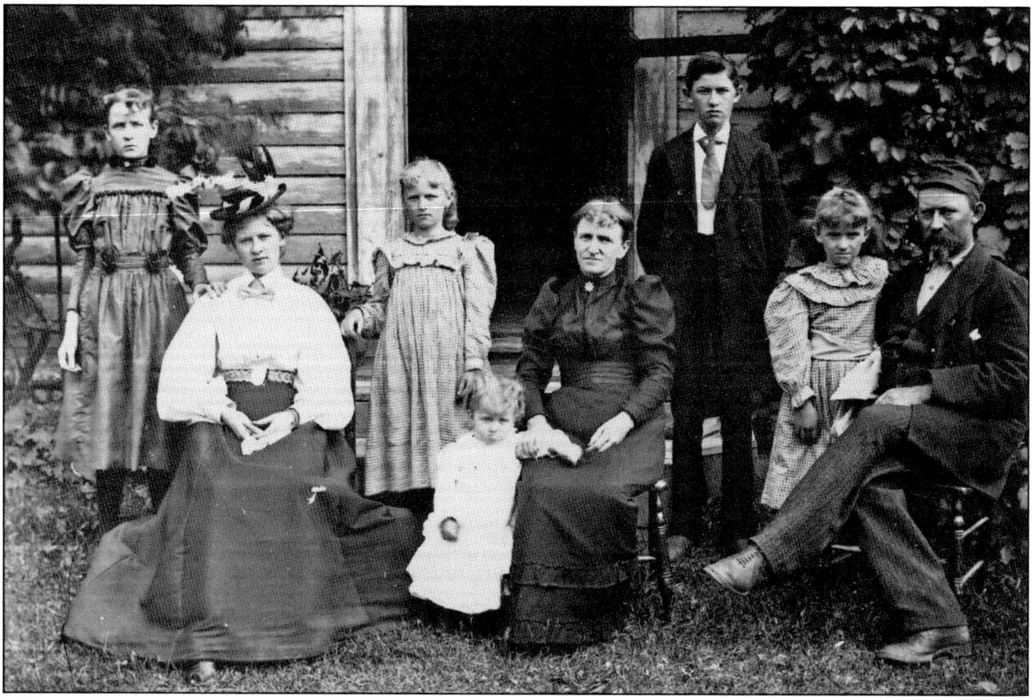

The inscription identifies this as the Thomas Carpenter family, who lived on Church Street in Pumpkin Hook around 1900.

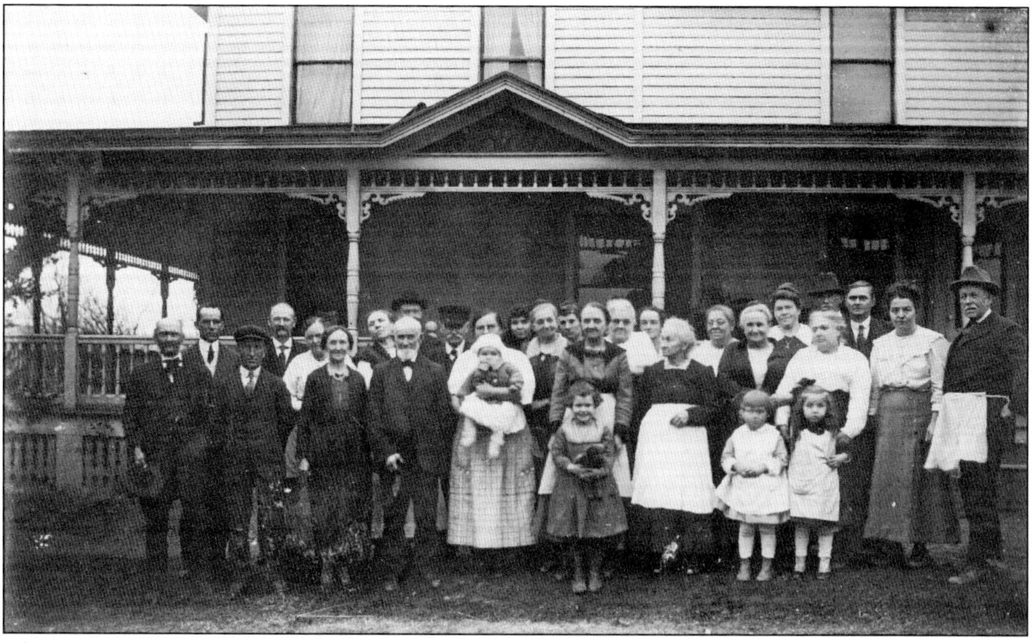

This family group is celebrating a Gardner reunion at E. J. Gardner home on January 22, 1921. On the right is Dr. Orville Mason, a Farmington physician. He was a member of the Masonic Fraternity and is pictured wearing a Masonic apron. In the front row, Ethel Gardner is holding baby Edwin; Charles R. Gardner is fourth from the left.

This 1923 catalog page advertises one of the many models of Bennett Homes, a business that operated out of North Tonawanda, New York. After one of these kit homes was purchased, the materials would arrive at the nearest railroad freight station. The kits included all the lumber, bricks, mortar, nails, glass, and shingles needed to construct the house. Similar kits were available from Sears, Roebuck, and Company. (Courtesy the collections of the North Tonawanda History Museum, used with permission.)

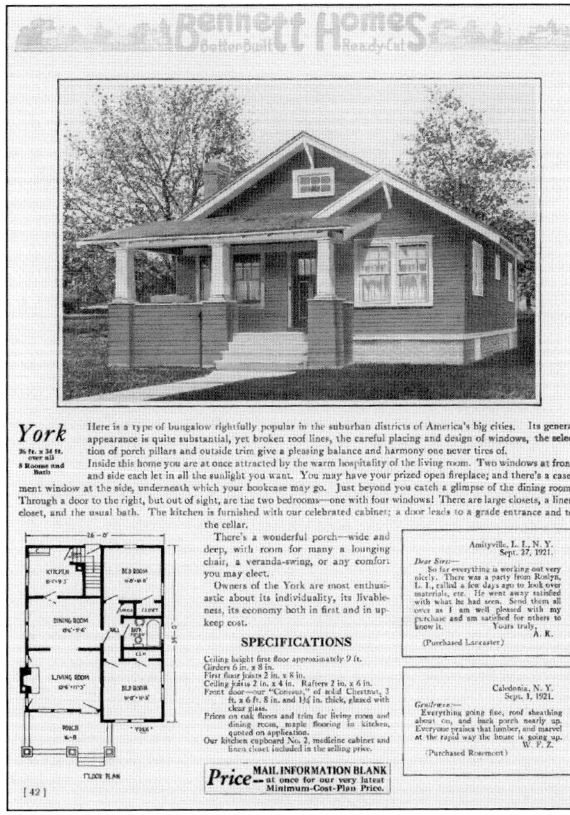

Bennett Homes
Better Built Ready-Cut

**York**
26 ft. x 34 ft. over all
5 Rooms and Bath

Here is a type of bungalow rightfully popular in the suburban districts of America's big cities. Its general appearance is quite substantial, yet broken roof lines, the careful placing and design of windows, the selection of porch pillars and outside trim give a pleasing balance and harmony one never tires of.

Inside this home you are at once attracted by the warm hospitality of the living room. Two windows at front and side each let in all the sunlight you want. You may have your prized open fireplace; and there's a casement window at the side, underneath which your bookcase may go. Just beyond you catch a glimpse of the dining room. Through a door to the right, but out of sight, are the two bedrooms—one with four windows! There are large closets, a linen closet, and the usual bath. The kitchen is furnished with our celebrated cabinet; a door leads to a grade entrance and to the cellar.

There's a wonderful porch—wide and deep, with room for many a lounging chair, a veranda-swing, or any comfort you may elect.

Owners of the York are most enthusiastic about its individuality, its livableness, its economy both in first and in upkeep cost.

**SPECIFICATIONS**

Ceiling height first floor approximately 9 ft.
Girders 6 in. x 8 in.
First floor joists 2 in. x 8 in.
Ceiling joists 2 in. x 4 in. Rafters 2 in. x 6 in.
Front door—our "Conceus," of solid Chestnut, 3 ft. x 6 ft. 8 in. and 1¾ in. thick, glazed with clear glass.
Prices on oak floors and trim for living room and dining room, maple flooring in kitchen, quoted on application.
Our kitchen cupboard No. 2, medicine cabinet and linen closet included in the selling price.

FLOOR PLAN

**Price**—MAIL INFORMATION BLANK at once for our very latest Minimum-Cost-Plan Price.

Amityville, L. I., N. Y.
Sept. 27, 1921.
*Dear Sirs:—*
So far everything is working out very nicely. There was a party from Roslyn, L. I., called a few days ago to look over materials, etc. He went away satisfied with what he had seen. Send them all over as I am well pleased with my purchase and am satisfied for others to know it.
Yours truly,
A. K.
(Purchased Lancaster)

Caledonia, N. Y.
Sept. 1, 1921.
*Gentlemen:—*
Everything going fine, roof sheathing about on, and back porch nearly up. Everyone praises that lumber, and marvel at the rapid way the house is going up.
W. F. Z.
(Purchased Rosemont)

[42]

This is a photograph of a Bennett kit home built by Anson H. Tuttle in the 1920s. He customized it in some ways, but it is still recognizable as the York model in the advertisement to the right. This home on County Road 8 is currently occupied by Royal Purdy and his family; Purdy is Tuttle's grandson. It is one of two kit homes known to exist in Farmington, with the other across from the Finger Lakes Race Track. (Courtesy Royal Purdy.)

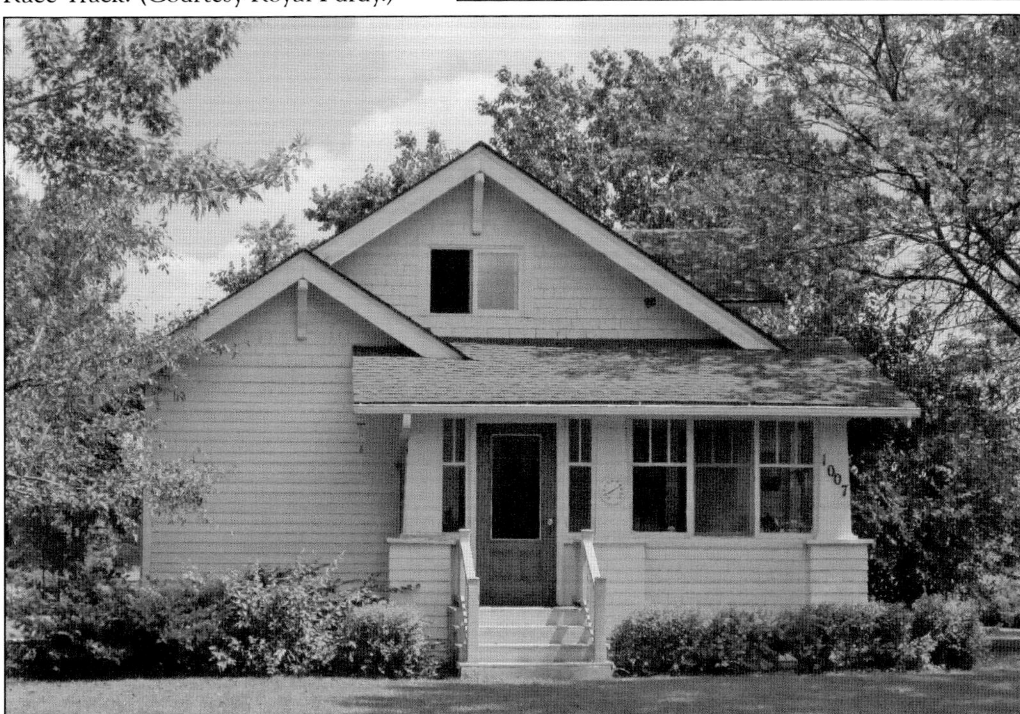

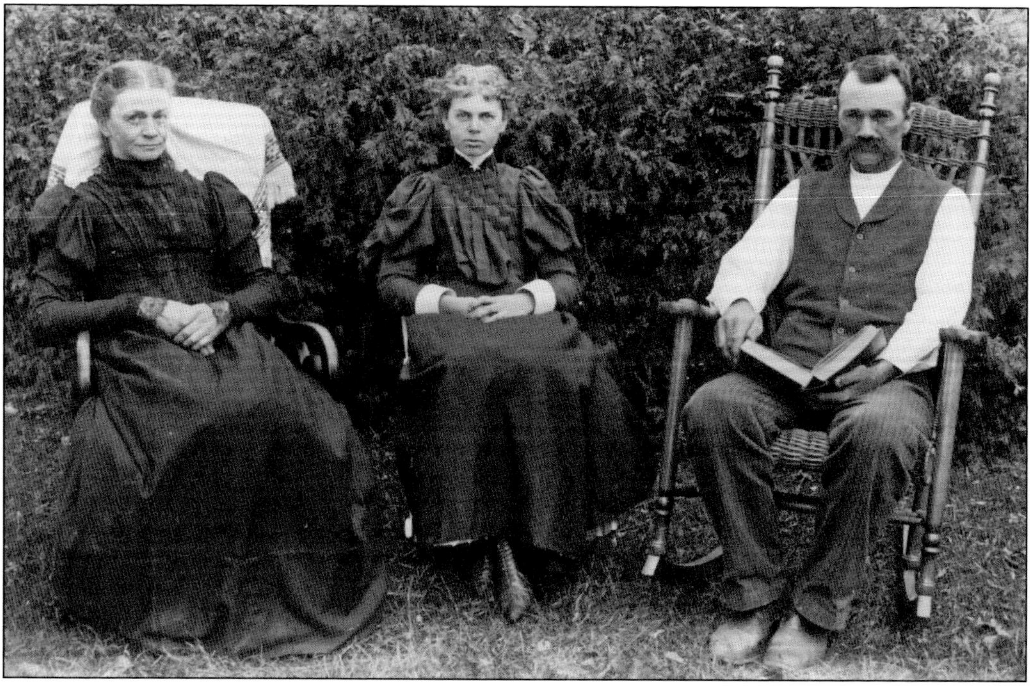

This 1900 family photograph shows, from left to right, Sara, Verna, and Loren Cotton. Loren was Farmington's veterinary surgeon, and he could be reading a book about veterinary surgery, but it is more likely a Bible—the book customarily featured in these traditional photographs.

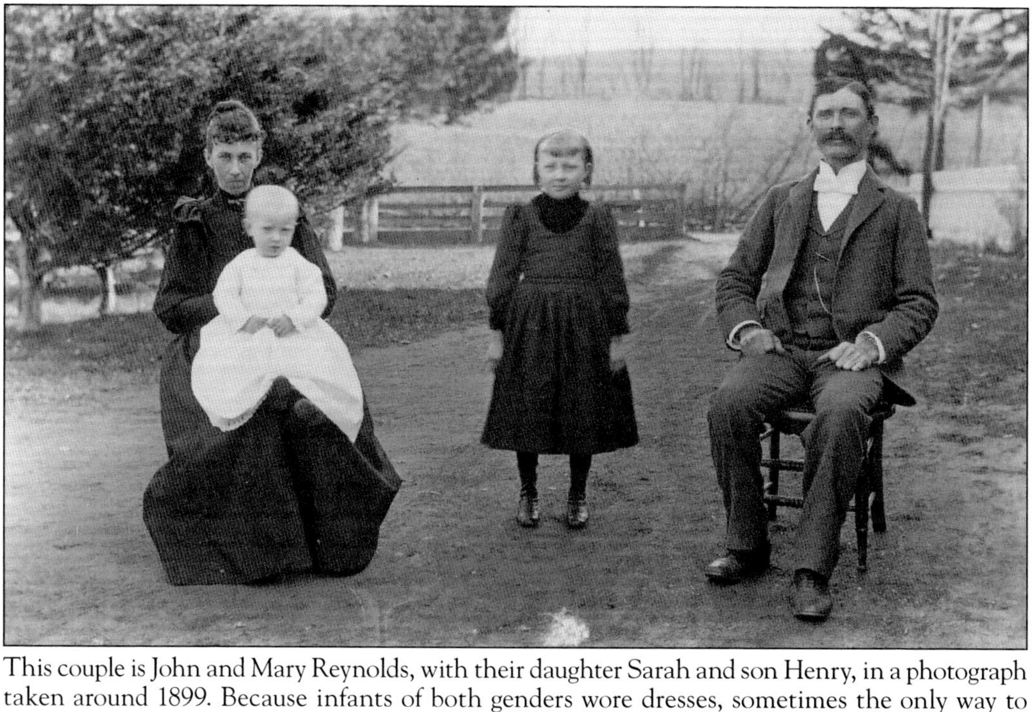

This couple is John and Mary Reynolds, with their daughter Sarah and son Henry, in a photograph taken around 1899. Because infants of both genders wore dresses, sometimes the only way to discern whether the child was male or female was paying attention to their hairstyle; boys' hair was usually parted on the side, while girls' were in the middle.

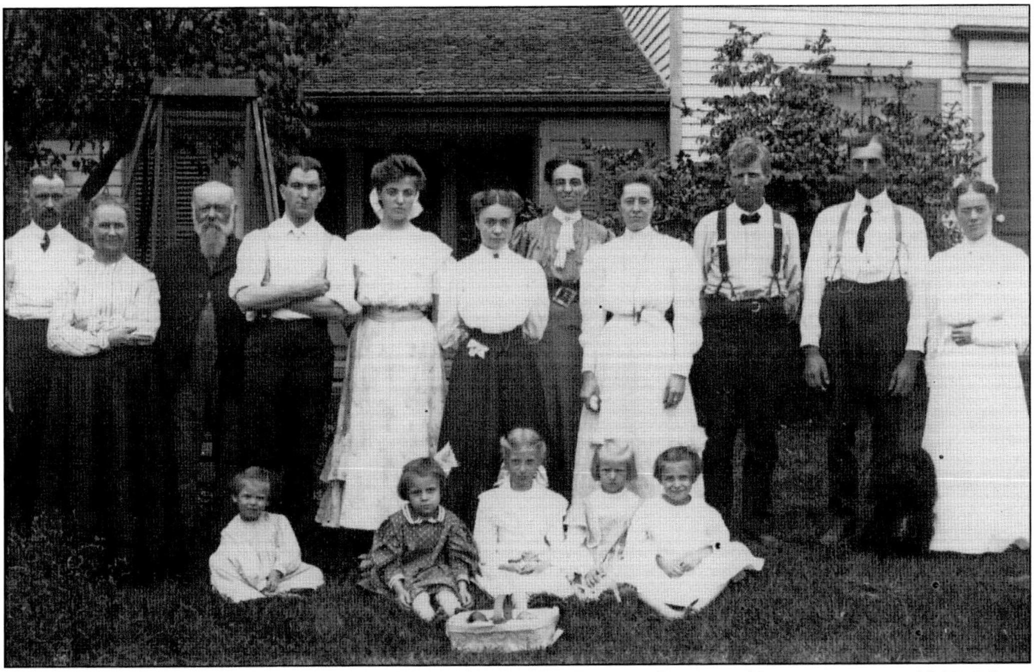

The third person from the left is John Seely Reed, who was born in Farmington in 1842. He is shown with his extended family about 1912, when he was 72 years old. The basket in the foreground looks like a bed for the little girl's doll.

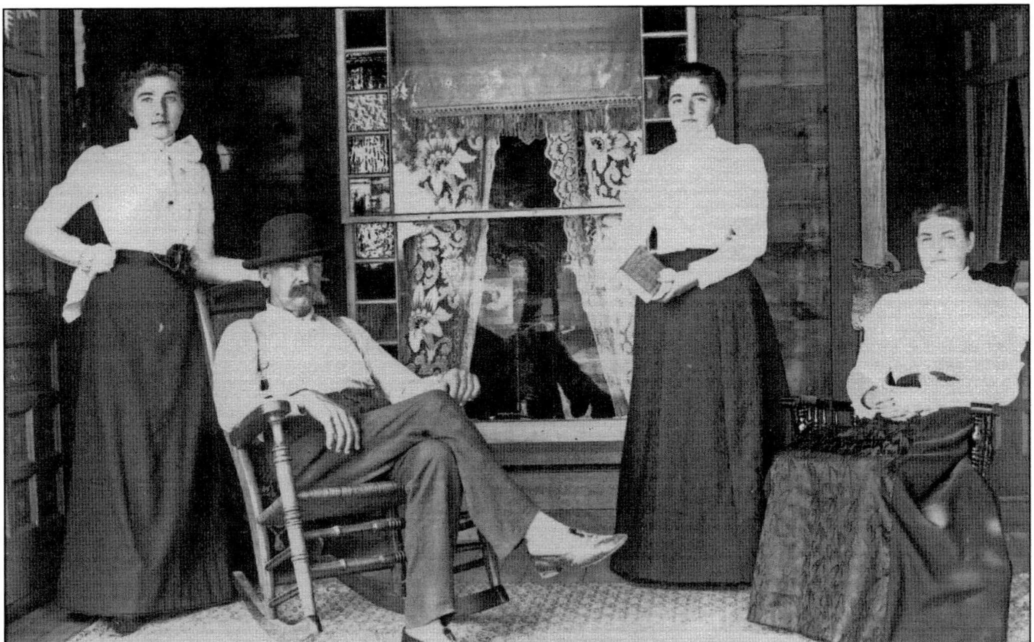

Silas Granger Dillingham was a Farmington carpenter and contractor. He is shown here relaxing on the porch with his wife, Mary, and their daughters Lula (left) and Myrtle (right). Note the fancy lace curtains in the window and the stylish stained-glass accent panes. Lula was said to be an accomplished seamstress.

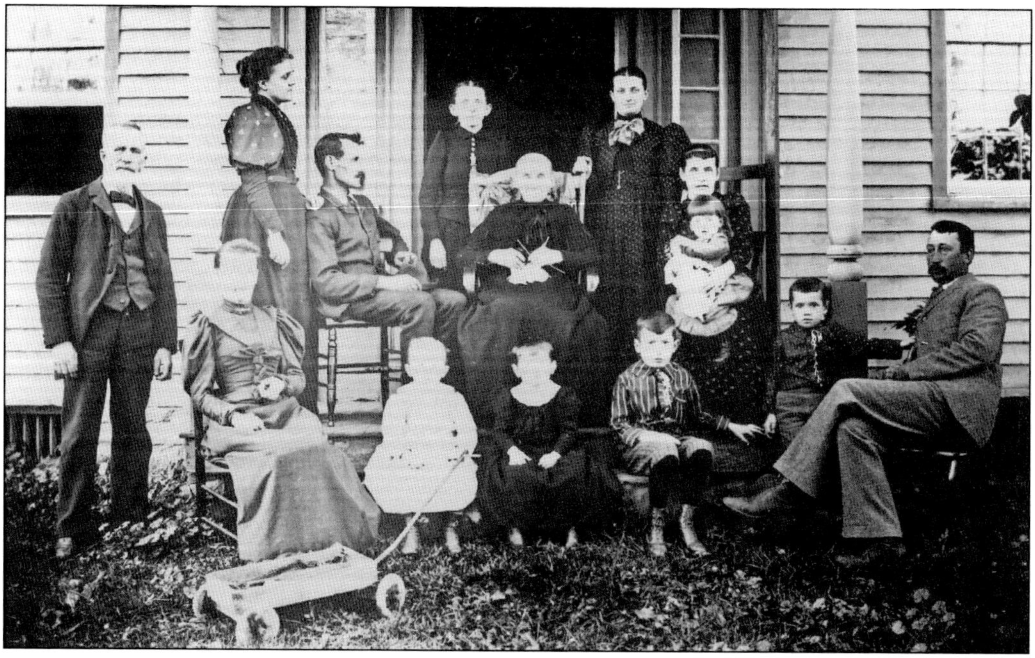

Mary Sophia Herendeen was born in Farmington in 1864. According to the inscription on this *c.* 1890 group photograph of the Calkins family, she is the one standing in the back row behind her husband, Horace Calkins. The woman in the center that is knitting is probably Mary Alice Browning Herendeen, who lived with this family in her later years.

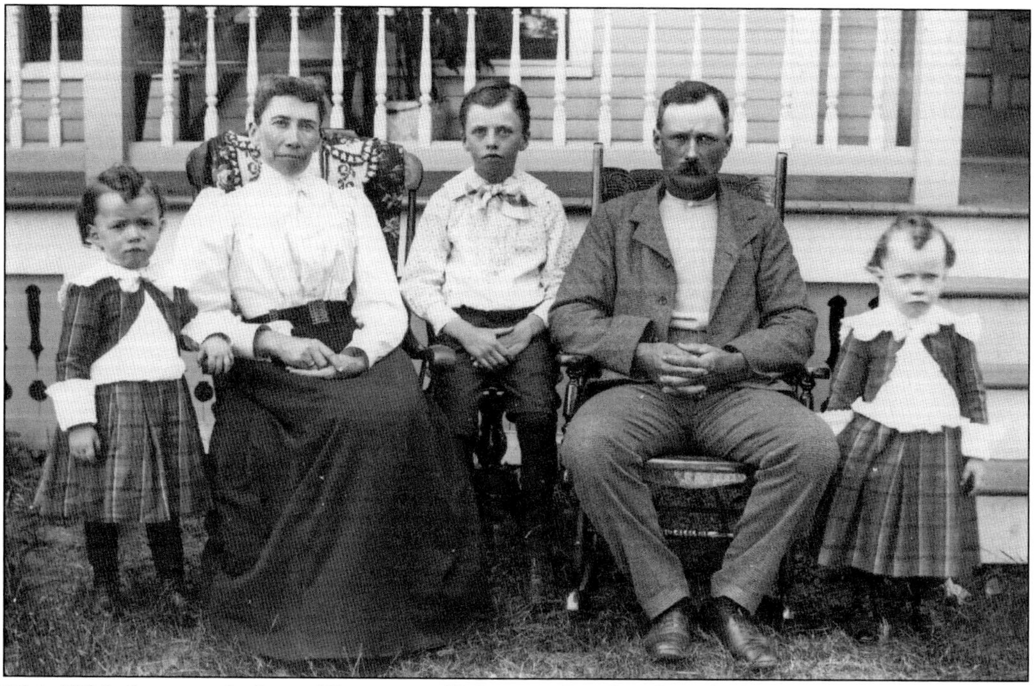

This 1900 photograph shows Thomas and Margaret Broderick with their son William and twin sons, Jerome and Joseph. The Broderick farm was on Hook Road north of the Lehigh Valley Railroad crossing at Tuttle's Corners.

A photograph postcard from 1909 shows Francis (left) and Browning Herendeen with their alert guard dog.

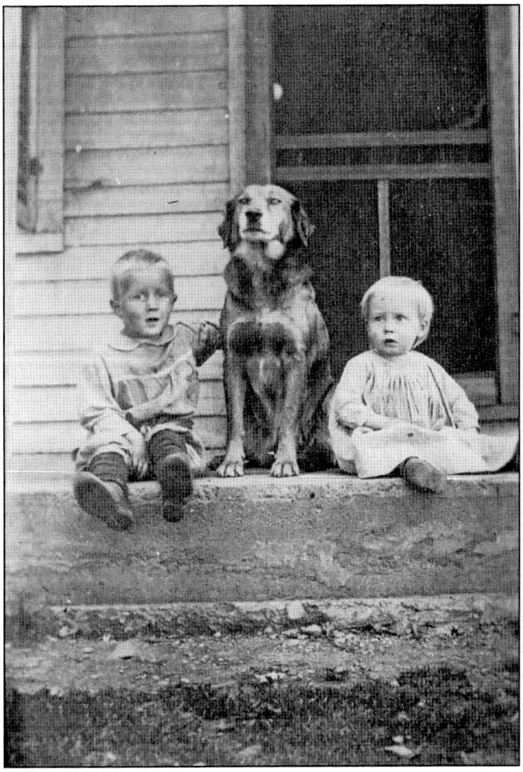

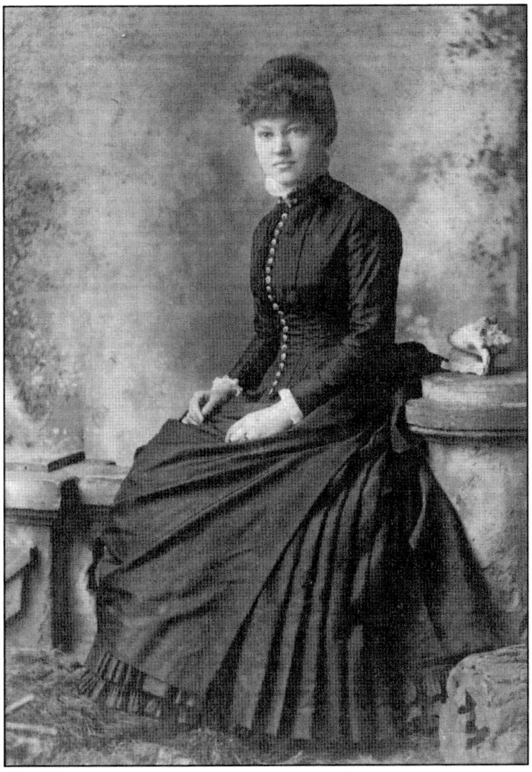

Nettie Vandenburg of Farmington sat for this portrait in 1888 before her marriage to Edwin Prosser.

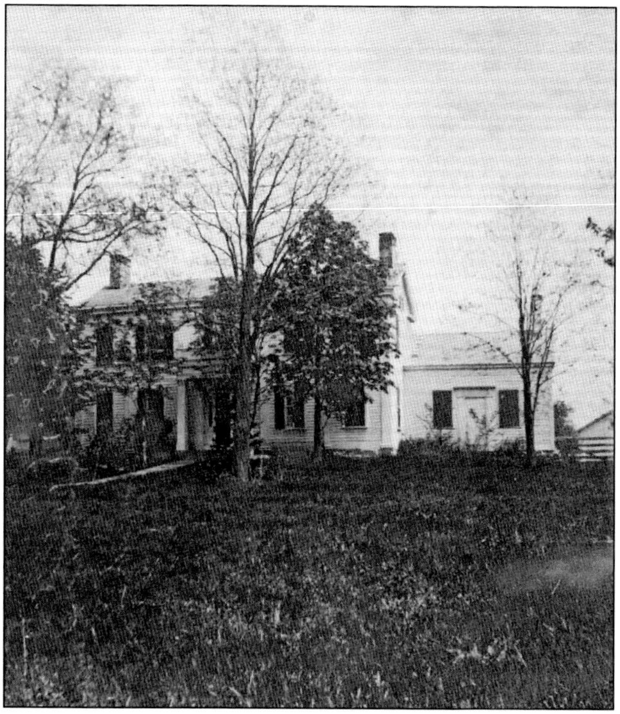

The stately home of Abiather Power, which was located near Hathaway's Corners, no longer exists. Power was one of the town's original settlers and served a term as a town tax collector. The Power family cemetery is a few hundred feet east of the intersection of County Road 41 and State Road 332; Abiather is buried there.

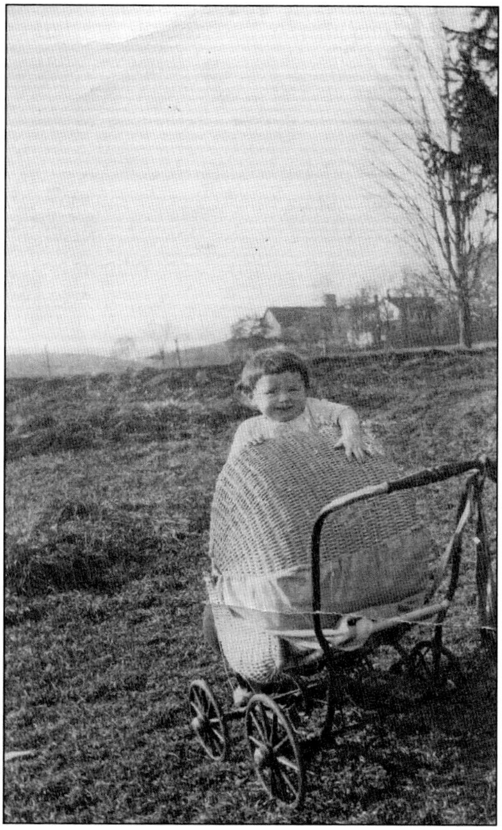

Gustavus Carson Wehrlin peeks over the top of his baby carriage in the early 1920s. Gus served the town of Farmington in many capacities over the years, most notably as town historian and town councilman. He was also a tireless advocate for the volunteer fire department. (Courtesy Barbara Wehrlin.)

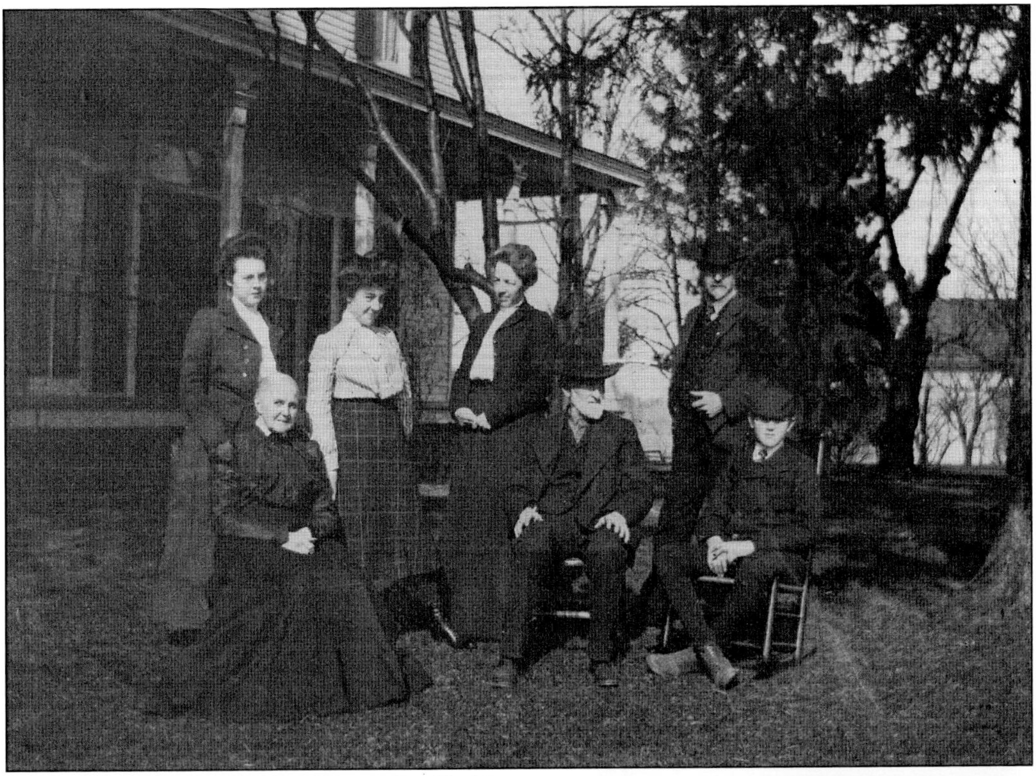

This is a 1895 photograph taken at the Sheldon homestead on the corner of Sheldon and Rushmore Roads. Pictured here are (seated) Gardner Sheldon, his wife Huldah, and grandson Albon Sheldon Jr.; (standing, from right to left) Albon Sheldon Sr., his wife Lizzie Rogers Sheldon, their daughter Mary Alice (who is Albon Jr.'s twin sister), and their daughter Evelyn. (Courtesy Miriam Sheldon Padgham.)

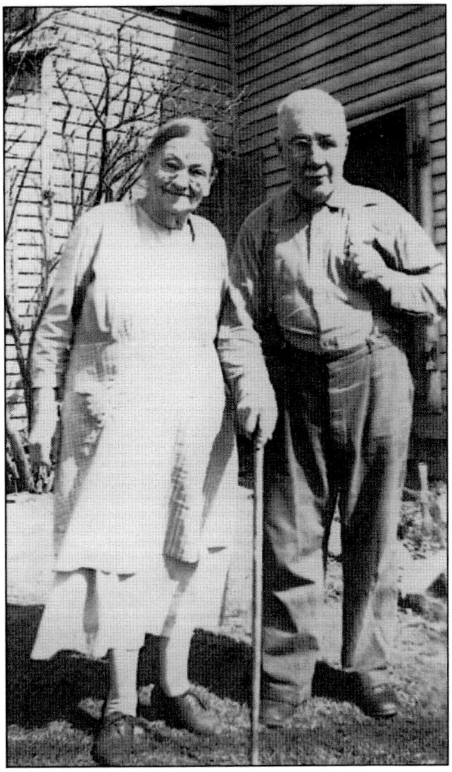

This couple, John and Jennie McFall, is pictured about 1940. The McFall family lived in the former E. J. Gardner house on Hook Road south of Pumpkin Hook. John worked for the Farmington Highway Department. (Courtesy Don Ford.)

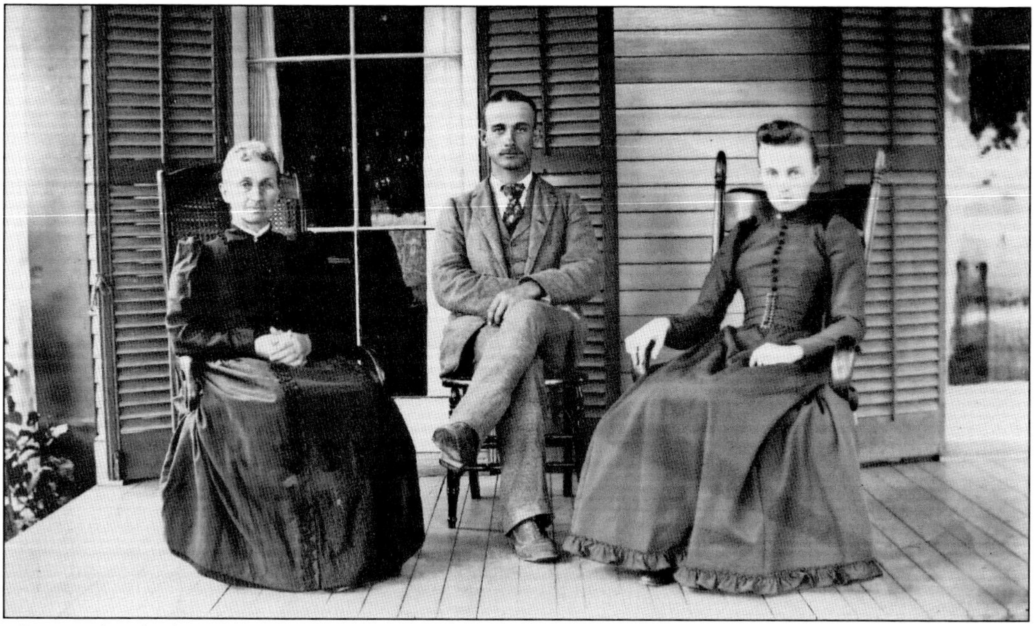

These individuals are posing here on a porch about 1900. They are Eugene Markham, Ida Markham Lombard, and their mother, Ann Eliza Markham. Eugene and his wife, Harriet Markham, lived on Hook Road in Pumpkin Hook. Ann Eliza is buried in North Farmington Friends Cemetery under a small monument she and her brother Charles H. Gardner handcrafted from Lake Ontario cobblestones. (Courtesy Diana and Rudy van der Velden.)

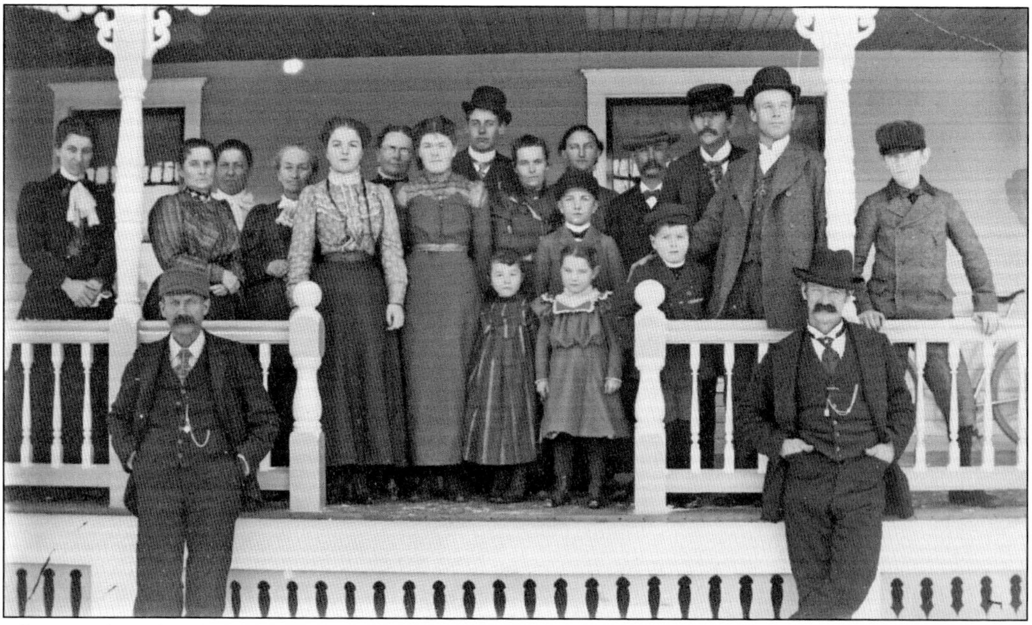

This Gardner family group gathered on the porch of C. H. Gardner's home on Hook Road around 1900. The boy on the right is Charles R. Gardner; below him is his father, Charles H. Gardner. (Courtesy Diana and Rudy van der Velden.)

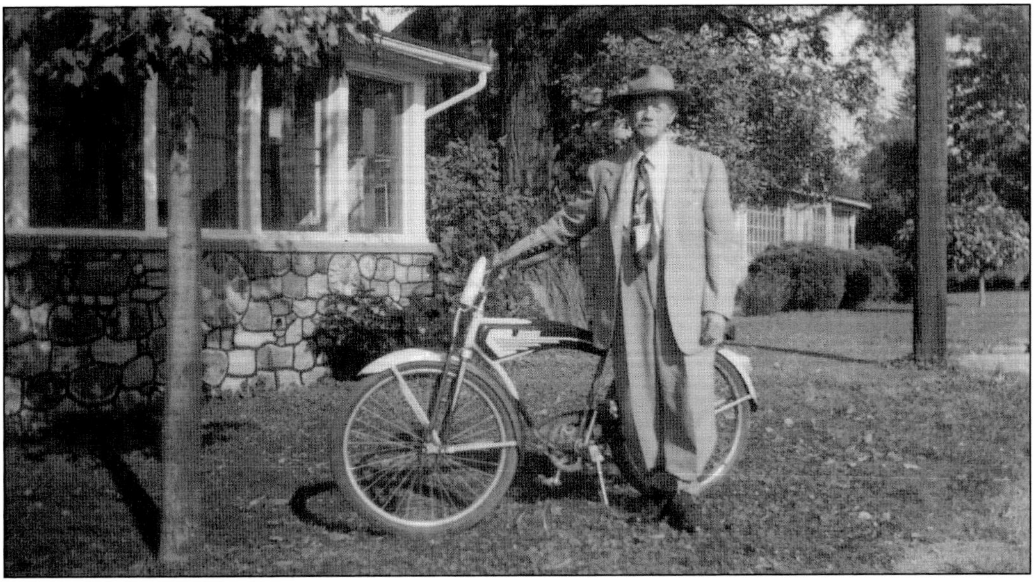

On his 92nd birthday, October 5, 1949, Charles H. Gardner posed with his bicycle, which he still rode even at such a late age. The suit he is wearing is very similar to what was called at the time a "zoot suit"—an extreme fashion style worn by young hipsters. (Courtesy Diana and Rudy van der Velden.)

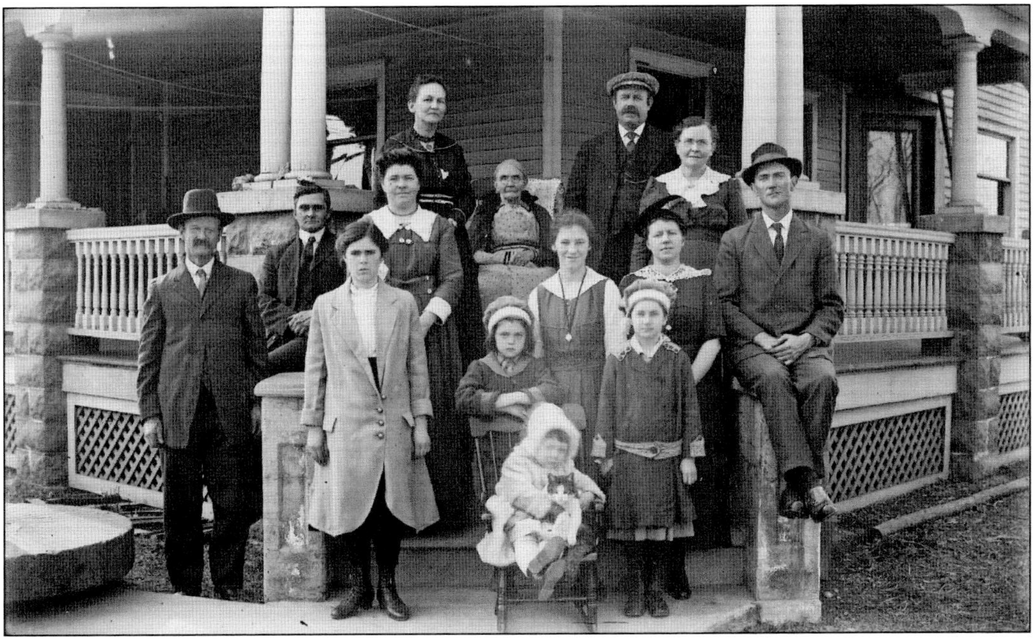

Members of the Greene, Stearman, and Gardner families pose in front C. H. Gardner's home on Hook Road sometime in the 1920s. Walter Stearman is in the back row wearing a cap, and Clara Greene Wells is in the front row wearing what appears to be an altered man's coat. (Courtesy Diana and Rudy van der Velden.)

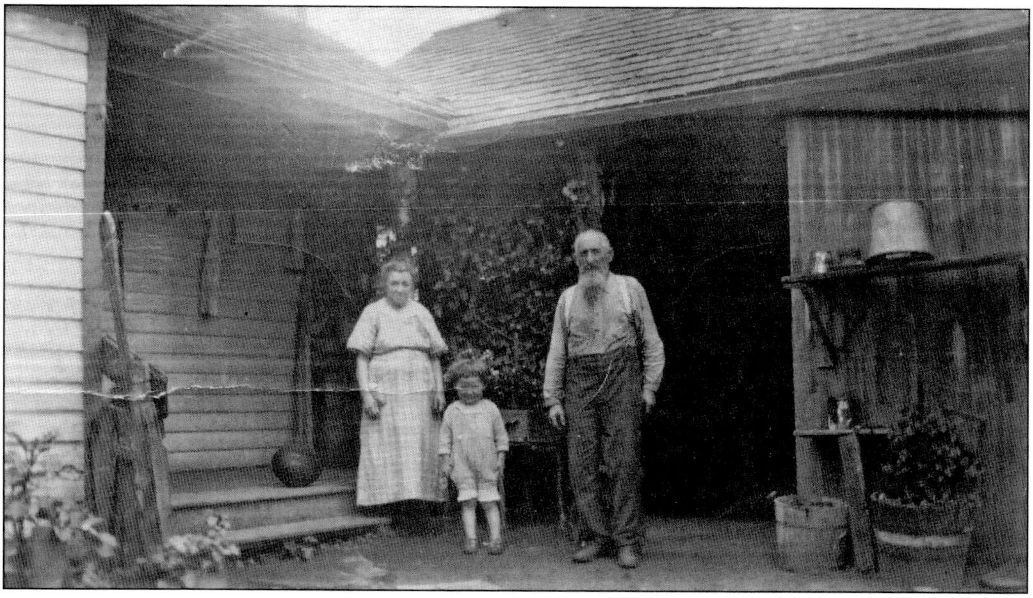

Gus Wehrlin is shown with his grandparents, Fred and Fannie Wehrlin. This photograph was taken in back of the Wehrlin house at 5576 Allen-Padgham Road in the mid-1920s. The house was built by local contractor Silas G. Dillingham and later occupied by the Arthur Herendeen family. (Courtesy Barbara Wehrlin.)

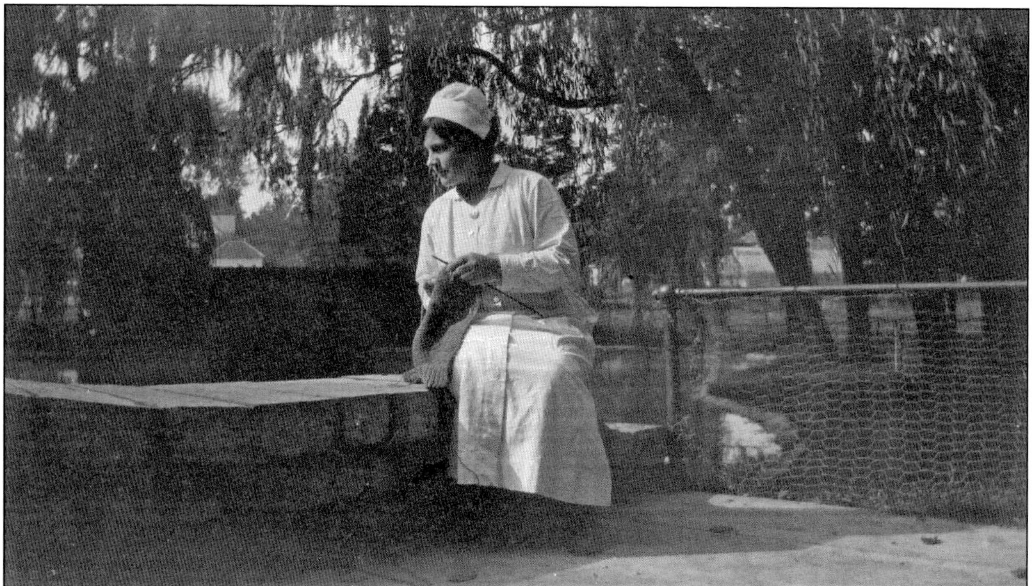

Evangeline S. McLouth was a nurse in World War I. She later worked at Clifton Springs Hospital, where this picture was likely taken about 1920. (Courtesy Barbara Wehrlin.)

Gus Wehrlin posed for this portrait around 1940. Gus's father, Edward, and his mother, Sara, each served terms as town clerk of Farmington. Gus was also the town historian for many years. (Courtesy Barbara Wehrlin.)

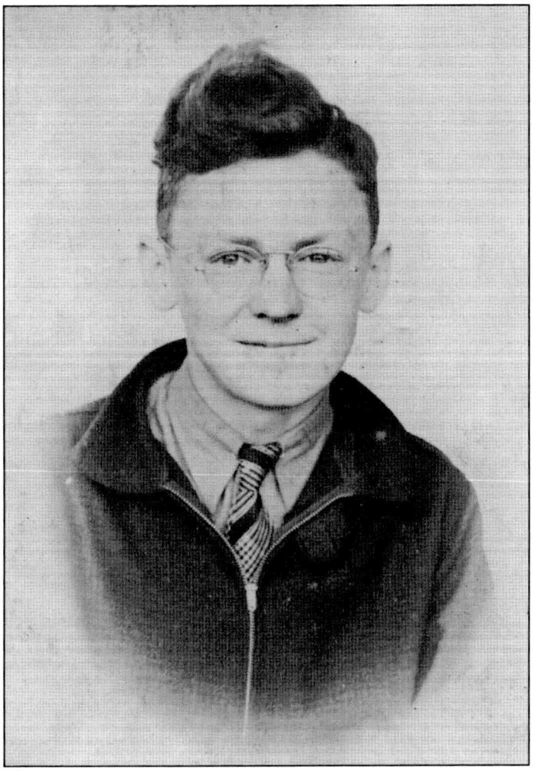

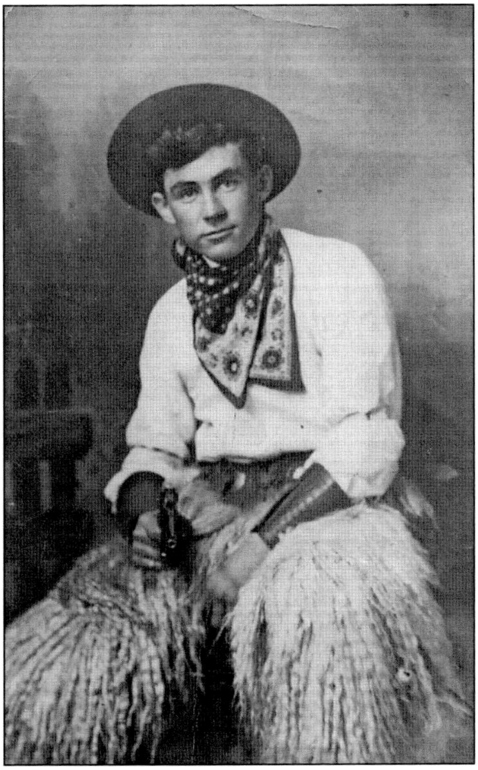

This photograph postcard of Edward J. Wehrlin in a cowboy outfit was sent to Gus Wehrlin by his mother sometime in the 1920s. Written in the message area is: "Your father will laugh when he knows I sent this. Syracuse is in first place—great news, huh? It won't be long now. Hope you received your mail e'er this. Love, Mother." This is an era when Will Rogers had popularized the cowboy image and when photograph studios often posed customers in costume. (Courtesy Barbara Wehrlin.)

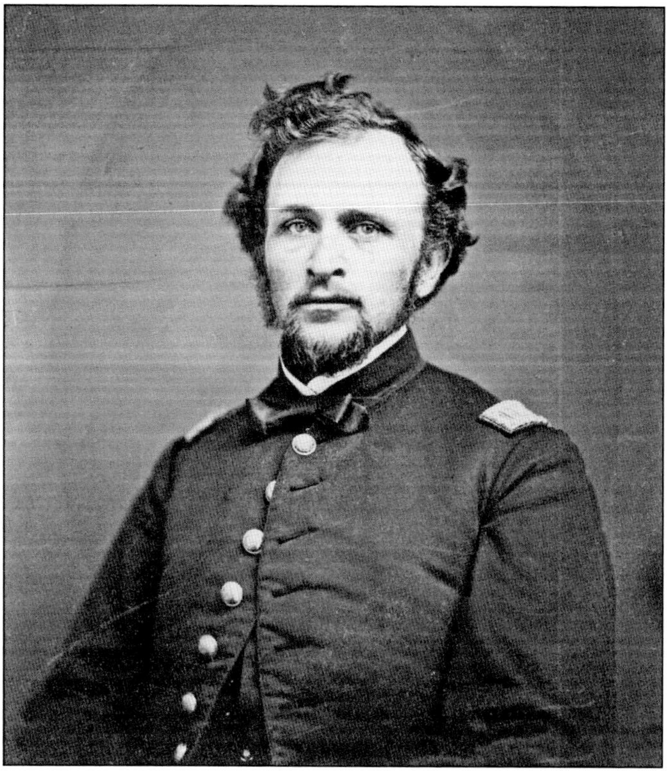

Farmington resident Edgar Whetten Dennis was born about 1834. He enlisted as a private in New York's 4th Heavy Artillery Regiment on December 27, 1861. Less than a year later, he was commissioned as an officer. By the war's end, he had been promoted through the ranks to brevet colonel. He survived the war and lived until 1878. (Courtesy Ontario County Historical Society.)

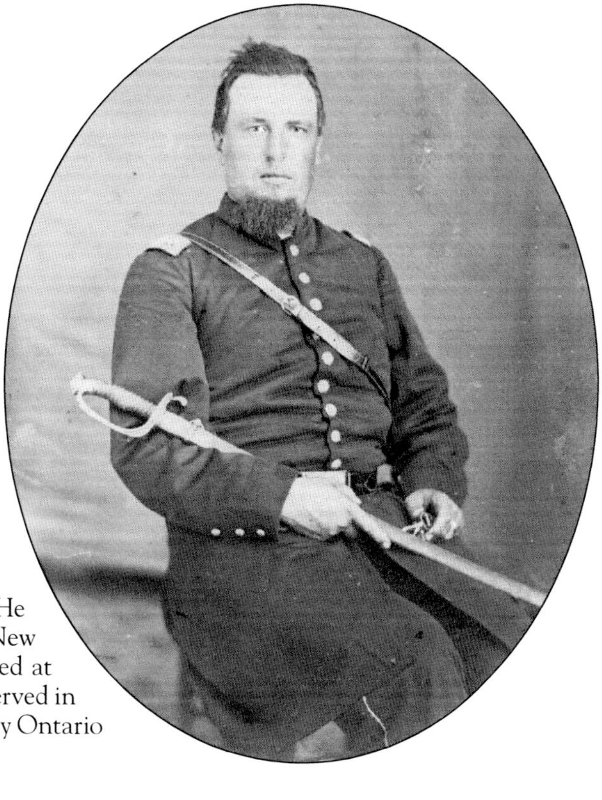

Orin J. Herendeen was born about 1835. He served in the Civil War as a captain in New York's 126th Infantry Regiment and died at Gettysburg. Farmington residents have served in every armed conflict on record. (Courtesy Ontario County Historical Society.)

# *Three*

# CHILDREN AND EDUCATION

The Quaker settlers started the first schools in Farmington. Half of their 1803 meetinghouse was for religious meetings and the other half for a school. Until schools were centralized in the mid-20th century, Farmington had as many as 13 school districts. Most of these were comprised of one-room schoolhouses and typically had a single teacher for all grades. If children could be spared from the work on the family farm, they walked to the nearest district school. Boys and girls of all ages were expected to assist their fellow students in the educational experience. Public education was only available through the eighth grade. Those students who wanted "higher" education and could afford it attended Macedon Academy or private schools in Canandaigua or Victor.

Between 1942 and 1954, Farmington school districts were gradually consolidated into those of neighboring towns. More than half of Farmington's students became part of the Victor School District. The remainder became part of Canandaigua, Red Jacket, or Palmyra-Macedon Districts, depending on which part of Farmington they lived in.

These photographs lead one to one realize that, despite the enormous differences between historic and modern daily lives, children are much the same anywhere and at any age. Their clothing styles are different, but one can easily imagine the children in these photographs interacting with their peers in many of the same ways as their own great-grandchildren of today.

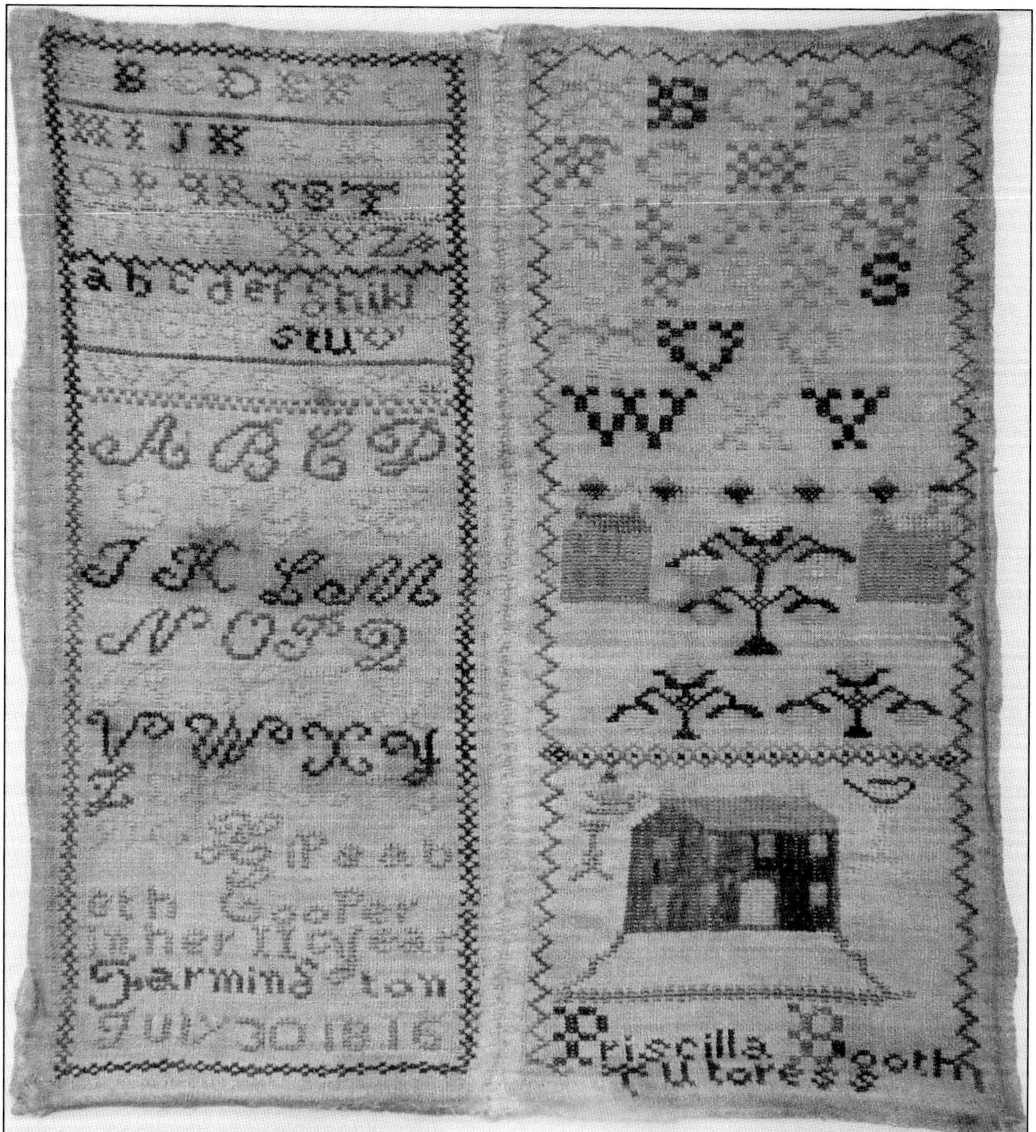


This needlepoint sampler was made by Farmington 11-year-old Hipsabeth Cooper in 1816. Samplers like this were a way for young girls to demonstrate their needlework skills and to show that they had been taught to read and write. (Courtesy Ontario County Historical Society.)

This 1920s photograph shows Joseph Earl "Mickey" McLaughlin in front of his Dillman grandparents' house at 400 Cline Road. (Courtesy Judy McLaughlin Snyder.)

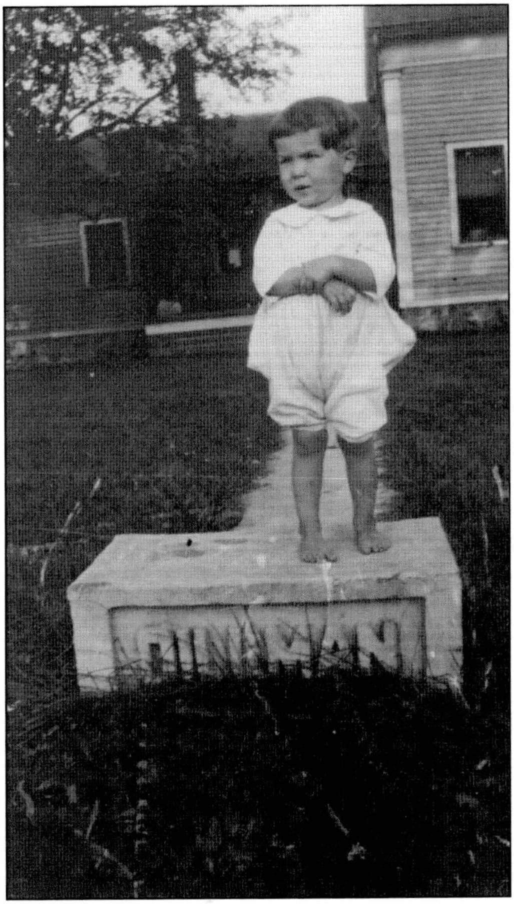

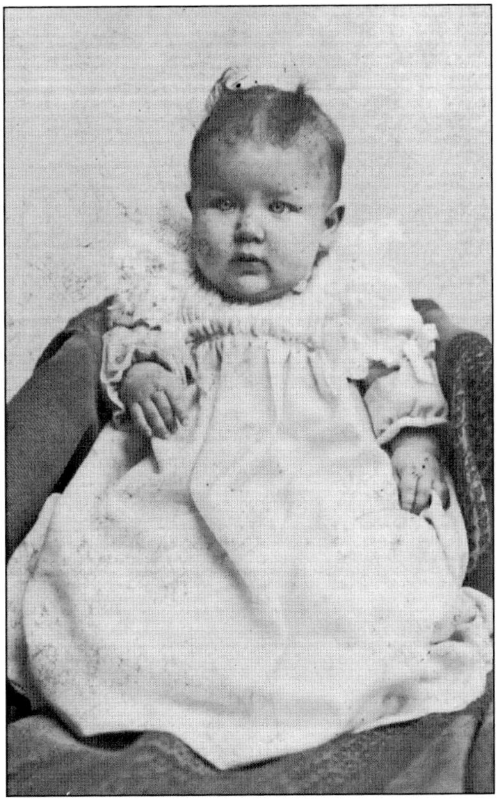

This is Alta Dillman at age four months and three weeks. She seems unaware of her demonic little hairdo. (Courtesy Judy McLaughlin Snyder.)

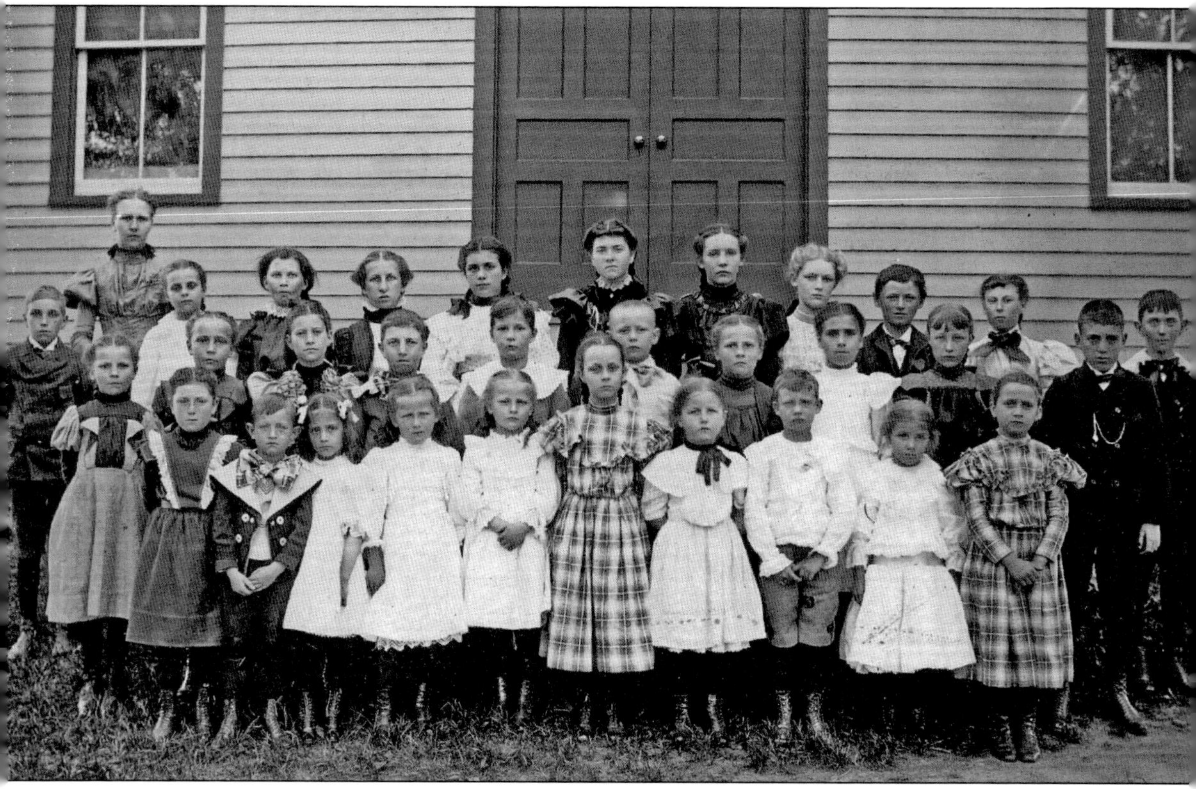

This is a group photograph of District School No. 12 students taken around 1900. Charles R. Gardner is to the far right, and Grace Gardner is in the middle of the back row. At the time of this photograph, 2 out of every 10 adults couldn't read or write, and less than six percent of all Americans had graduated from high school. (Courtesy Diana and Rudy van der Velden.)

The inscription on this photograph identifies this little girl as Ruth Dillman Reed. Not all children were so comfortable with being carefully posed and remaining still for the long exposures that a studio portrait required.

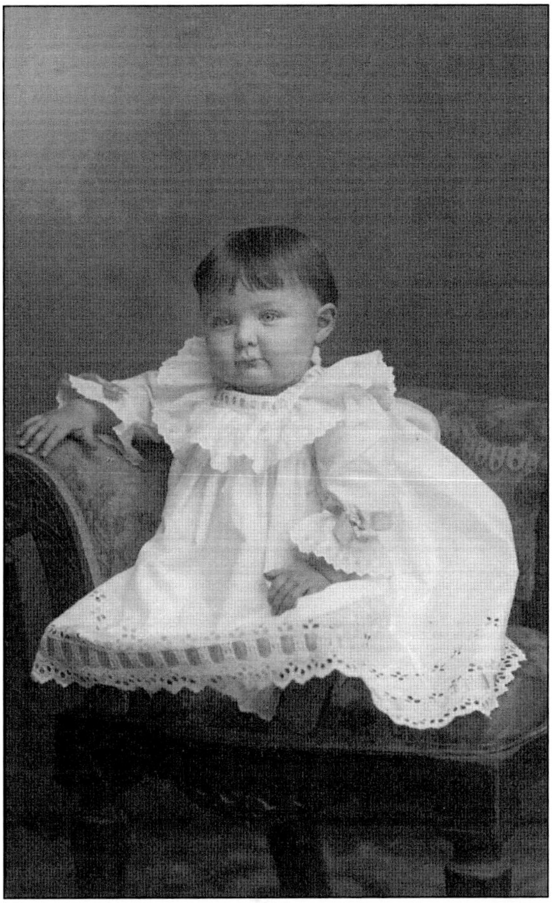

The boy in this elaborate wicker carriage is Earl Katkamier. Wicker was a very popular and stylish construction material for furniture. Katkamier's expression suggests something less than complete confidence about being involved in this photographic project. Sometimes in a posed photograph like this, the child's mother or other relative is just out of view of the camera, warning them not to move and not to get their best clothes dirty.

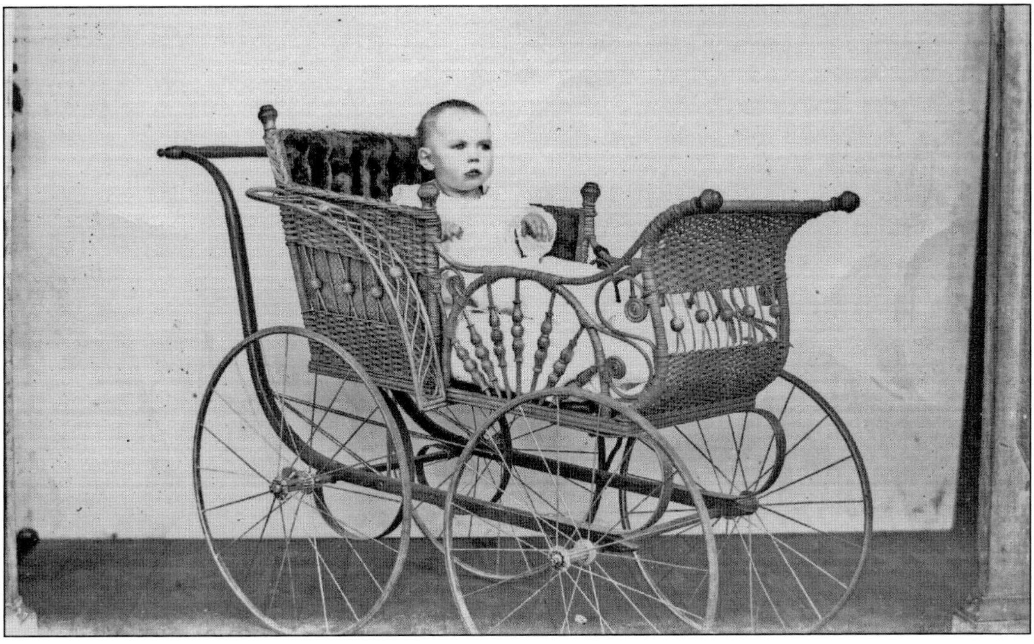

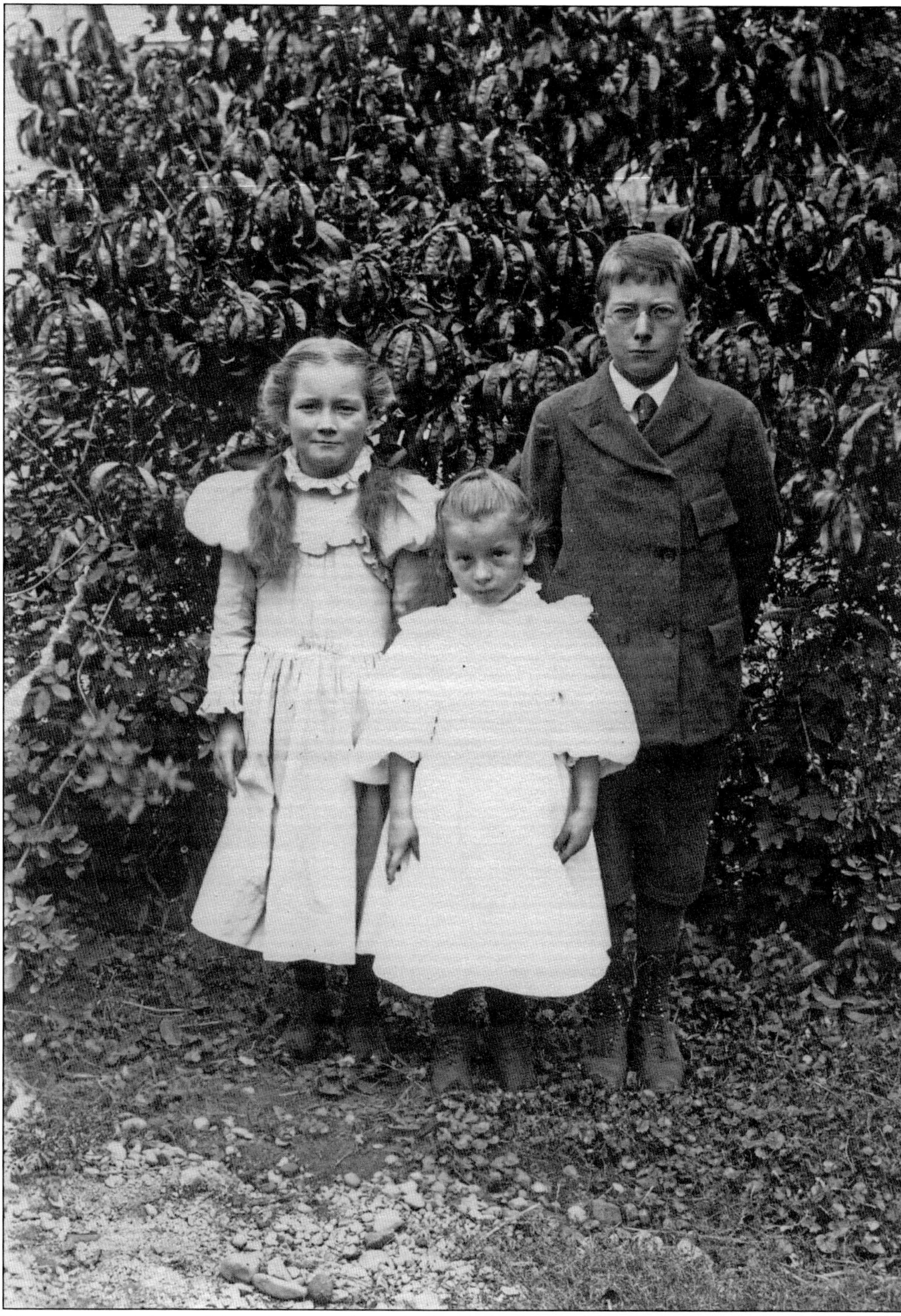

The estimated date of this photograph is about 1910. The children are identified as members of the Robbins family.

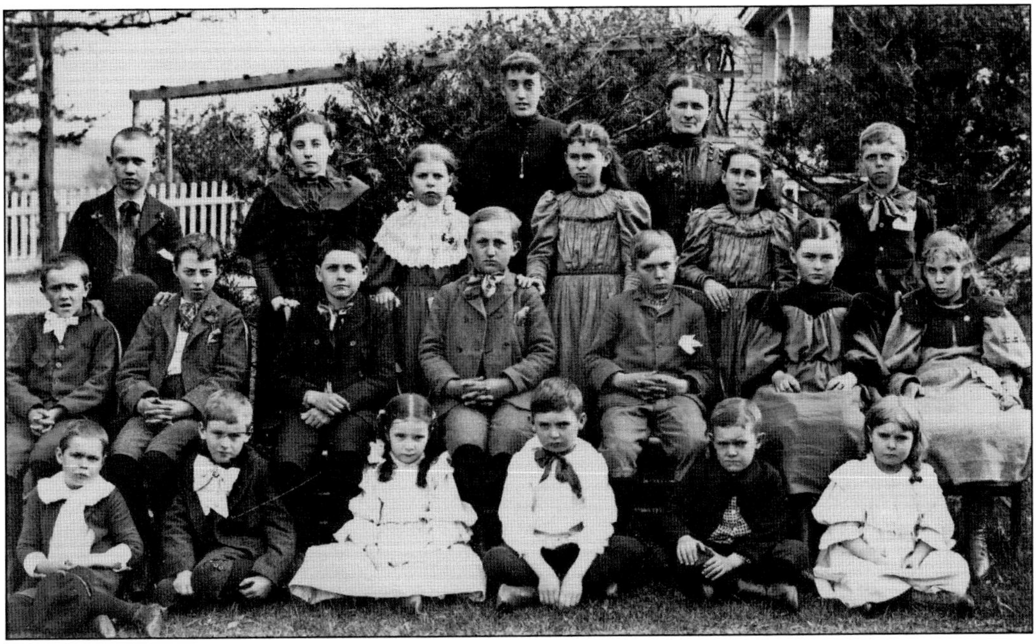

This *c.* 1910 photograph is identified as a Farmington school group, but the district number and teacher are not known.

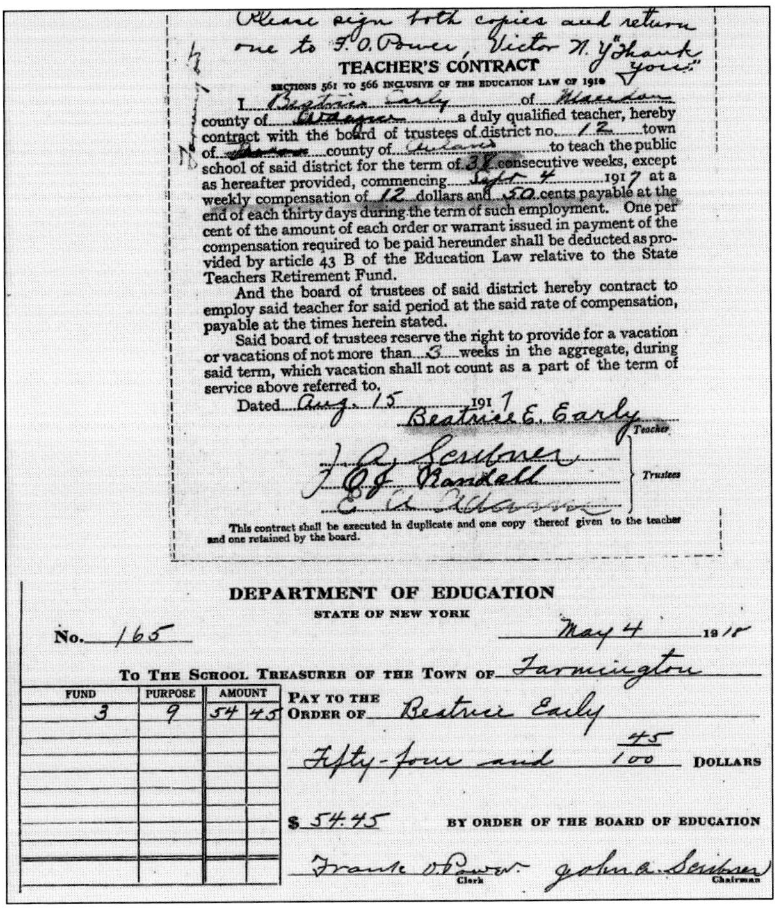

Please sign both copies and return one to F. O. Power, Victor N. Y. "Thank you."

**TEACHER'S CONTRACT**

SECTIONS 561 TO 566 INCLUSIVE OF THE EDUCATION LAW OF 1910

I Beatrice Early of Macedon county of Wayne a duly qualified teacher, hereby contract with the board of trustees of district no. 12 town of [illegible] county of Ontario to teach the public school of said district for the term of 38 consecutive weeks, except as hereafter provided, commencing Sept 4 1917 at a weekly compensation of 12 dollars and 50 cents payable at the end of each thirty days during the term of such employment. One per cent of the amount of each order or warrant issued in payment of the compensation required to be paid hereunder shall be deducted as provided by article 43 B of the Education Law relative to the State Teachers Retirement Fund.

And the board of trustees of said district hereby contract to employ said teacher for said period at the said rate of compensation, payable at the times herein stated.

Said board of trustees reserve the right to provide for a vacation or vacations of not more than 3 weeks in the aggregate, during said term, which vacation shall not count as a part of the term of service above referred to.

Dated Aug. 15 1917

Beatrice E. Early, Teacher

J. A. Scribner
[illegible] Randall
E. A. [illegible]
Trustees

This contract shall be executed in duplicate and one copy thereof given to the teacher and one retained by the board.

**DEPARTMENT OF EDUCATION**

STATE OF NEW YORK

No. 165 May 4 1918

To The School Treasurer of the Town of Farmington

| FUND | PURPOSE | AMOUNT |
|---|---|---|
| 3 | 9 | 54 45 |

Pay to the Order of Beatrice Early

Fifty-four and 45/100 DOLLARS

$ 54.45 BY ORDER OF THE BOARD OF EDUCATION

Frank O. Power, Clerk John A. Scribner, Chairman

Teacher's unions were already 50 years old in 1918 when town records show that Farmington teacher Beatrice Early was paid $12.50 per month. Early lived close by the District School No. 12 where she taught. She was required to rise early to start the fire in winter. It was also her job to draw water from a nearby well for students to drink during the school day.

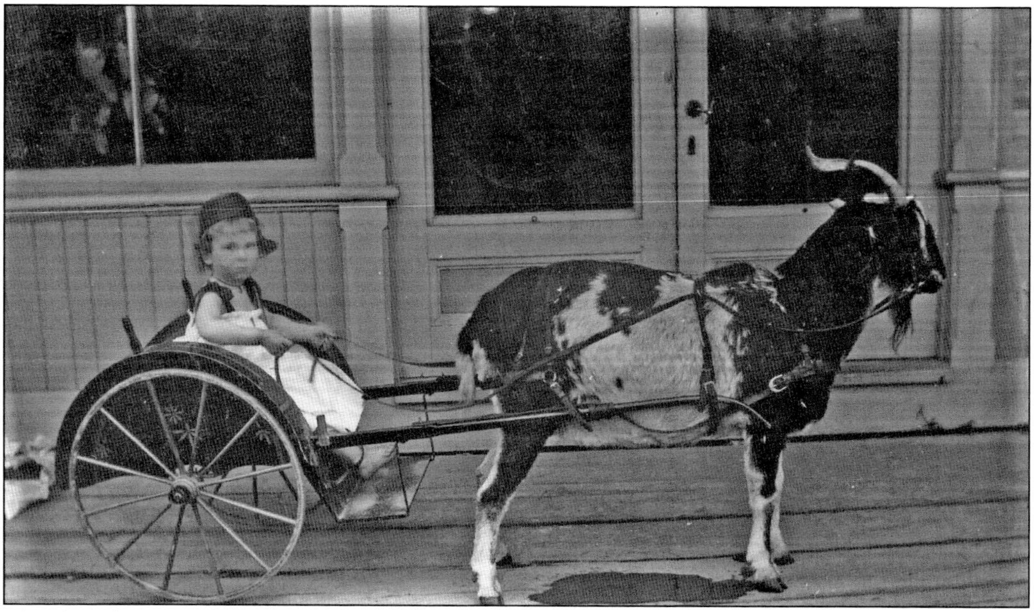

This barefoot girl is little Gussie Brundage. She was lucky enough to have her own little cart, which was drawn by a billy goat.

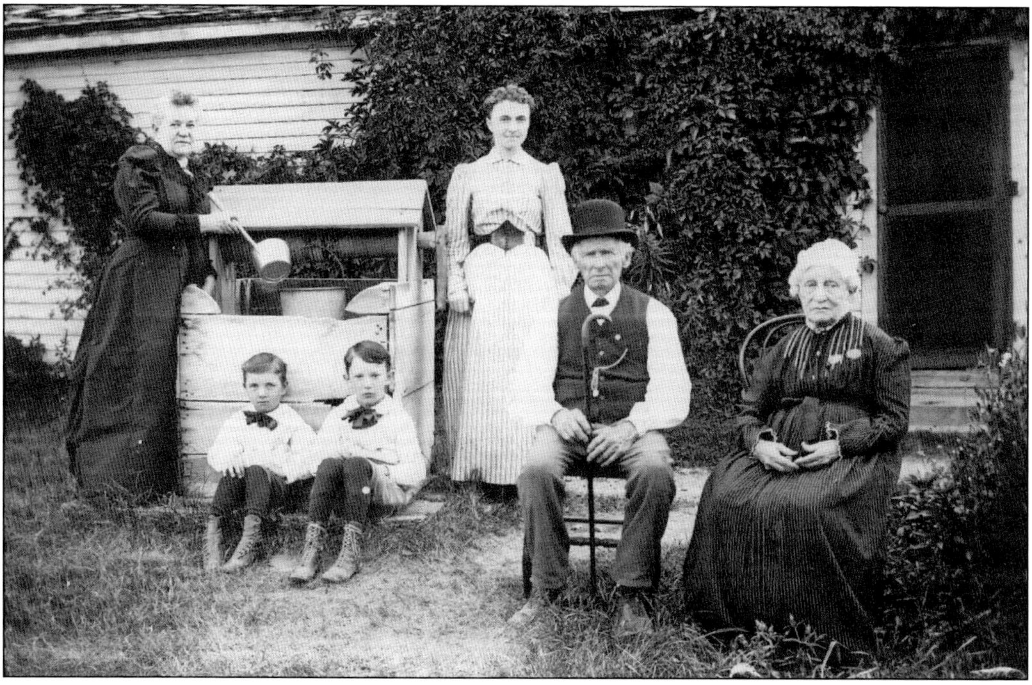

The two boys on the ground in front of the well are Lindley Gardner (left) and Willie White. The adults are identified as Mrs. White, Sarah Gardner Betz, William Holden, and Mrs. Holden. Instead of a hand pump, the well has an old-fashioned bucket and windlass. This house was located on Allen-Padgham Road just east of Hook Road.

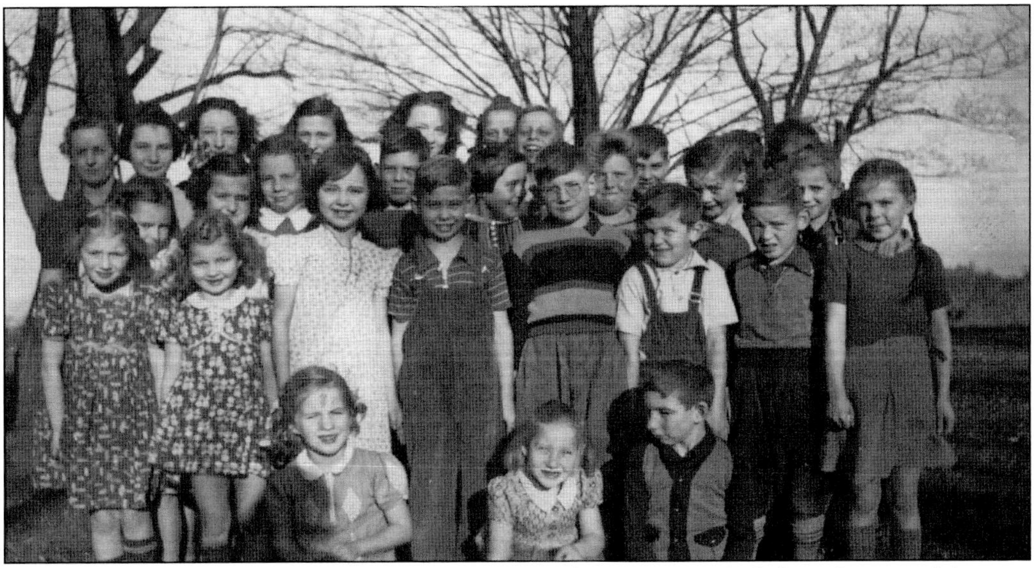

This is a snapshot of some District School No. 12 students in 1940. At left, in front, are Margaret Herendeen and her cousin Marjorie Herendeen (to the right of Margaret). Also in the photograph are Alice Herendeen, Harold Herendeen, Darwin Weigert, Robert Bowe, Betty Jane Collins, Doris and Harold Button, and several members of the Coon family.

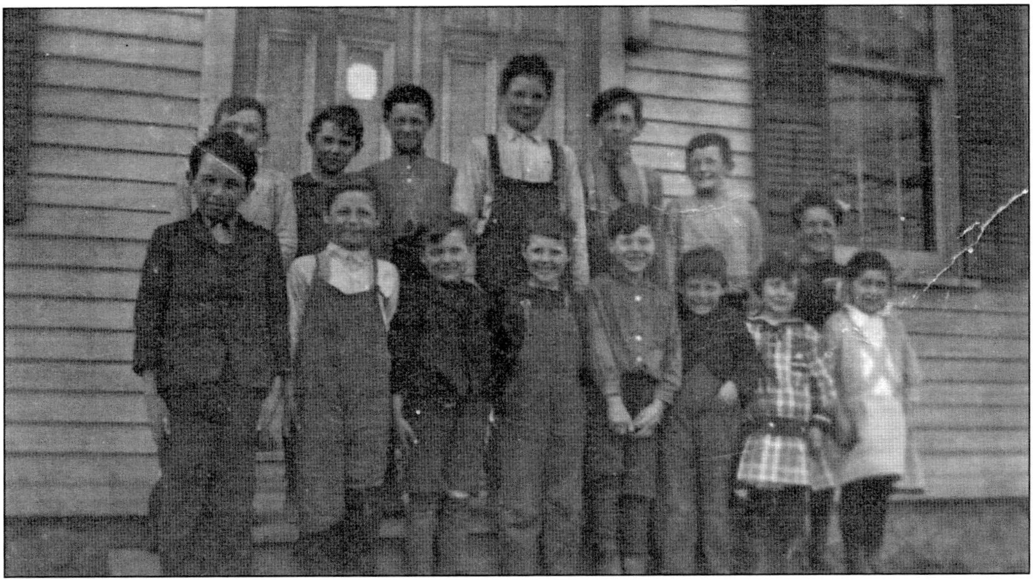

Students in School District No. 1 posed for this 1917 photograph postcard inscribed with "from your teacher, Miss Wheeler." There are lots of happy smiles. Could this have been the last day of school?

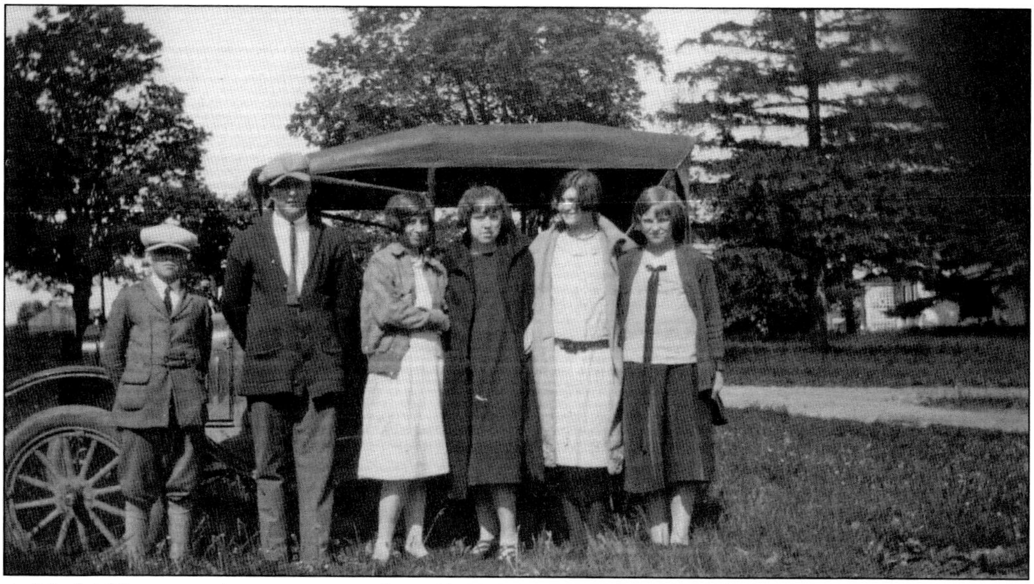

A Model T was used to transport these Farmington students to school in 1925 and 1926. The individuals are, from left to right, Leonard Padgham, Lew Pegelow (driver), Ruth Grinnel, Jennie Padgham, Gladys Greene, and Betty Padgham. Even after the advent of the automobile, most students walked to their nearest district schoolhouse.

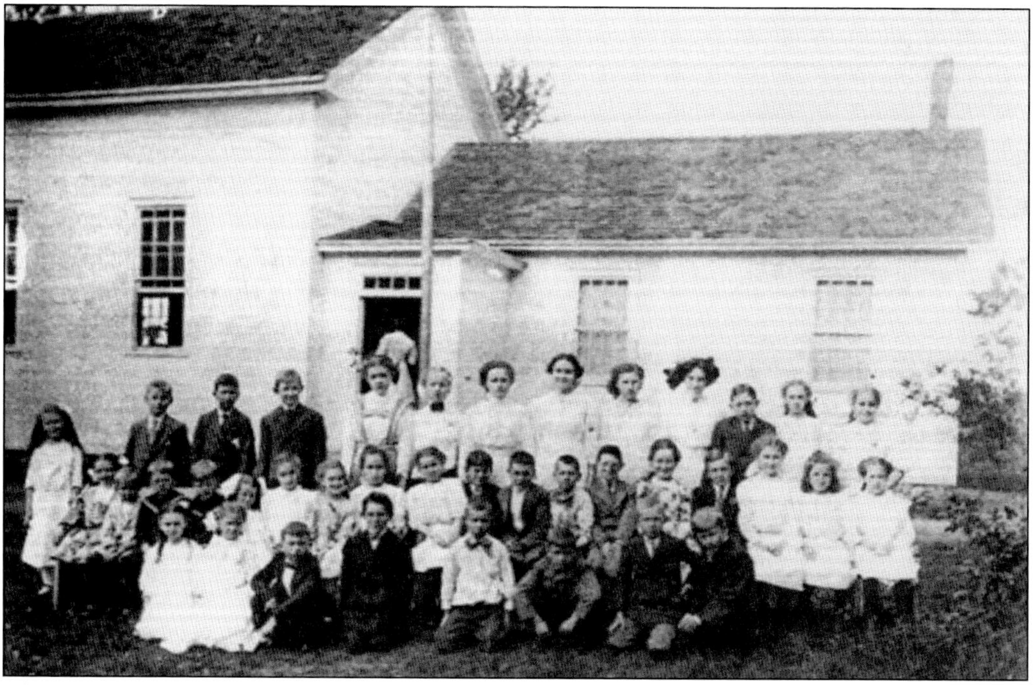

These students at the District School No. 12 schoolhouse pose for a portrait around 1910. The schoolhouse was in Pumpkin Hook. It was built in 1812 and served as a school for 142 years. It was the oldest public building in Farmington when it was destroyed in 1991.

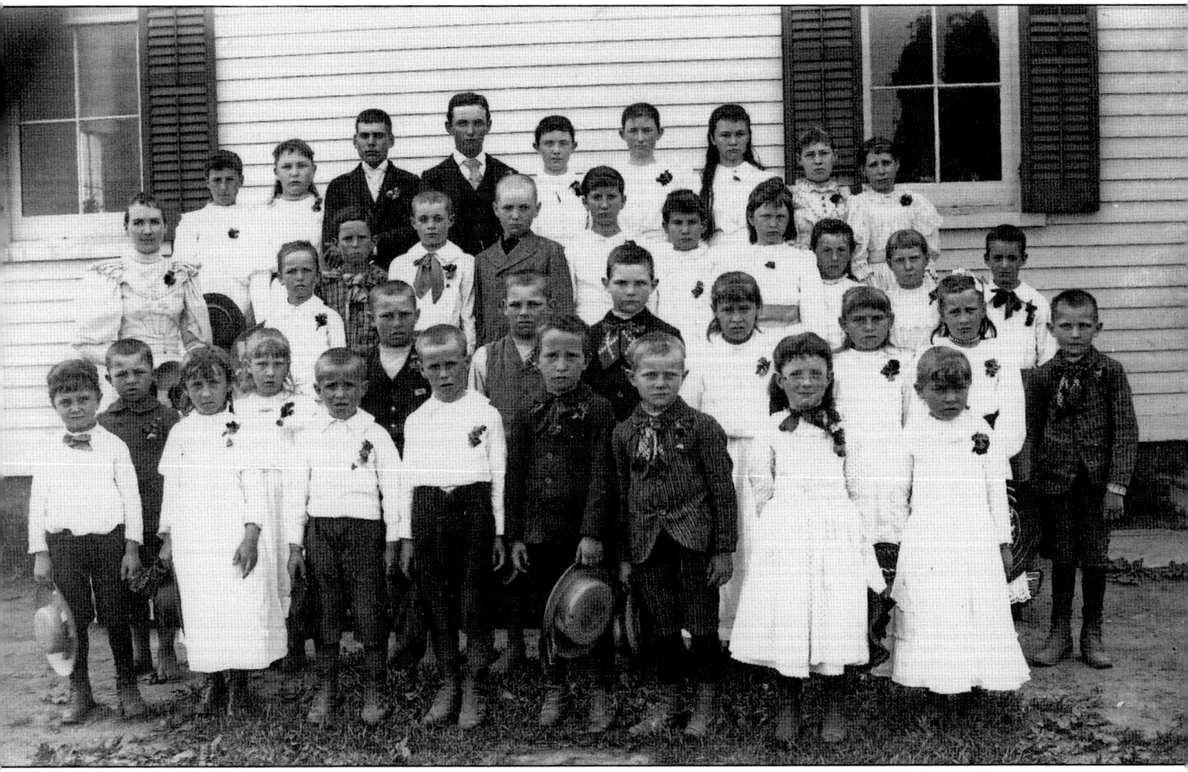

These are the students at the District School No. 5 schoolhouse in 1901. Florence Bowerman was the teacher. The school was located at the intersection of Weigert Road and Loomis Road, which ceased to exist when the New York State Thruway was constructed in the early 1950s. Everyone in this photograph seems to be dressed up, suggesting that this is a graduation or moving-up celebration.

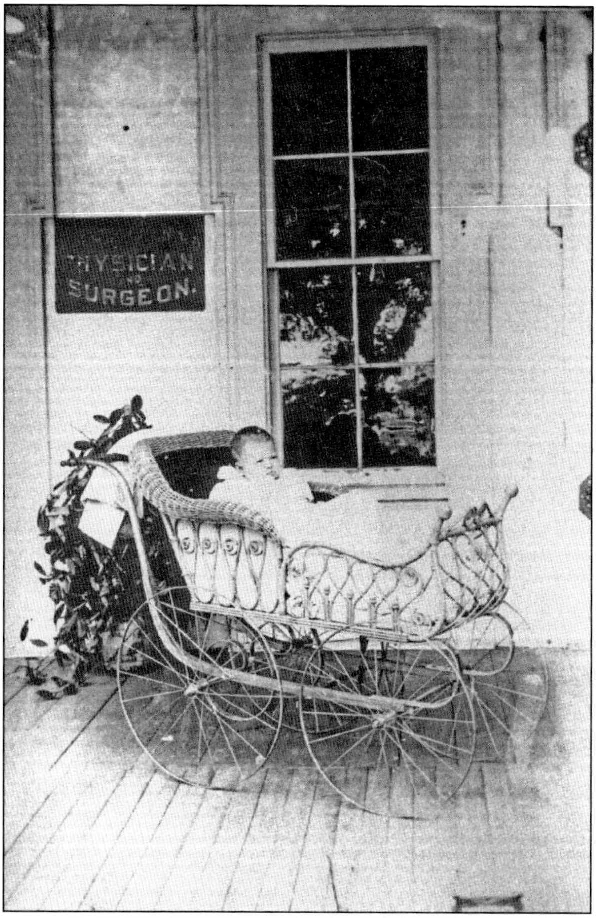



Ruth Clapper is pictured on the porch of her father's office around 1897. Dr. William Clapper was a Farmington physician and surgeon.

Two unidentified Farmington girls pose with what appears to be the same baby carriage as in the previous photograph. These antique carriages are nothing like a modern stroller. They needed large-diameter wheels to navigate rough dirt paths, and they had no cushions or safety harnesses. They also didn't need an instruction manual to explain how to fold or unfold them, because they weren't designed to do that.

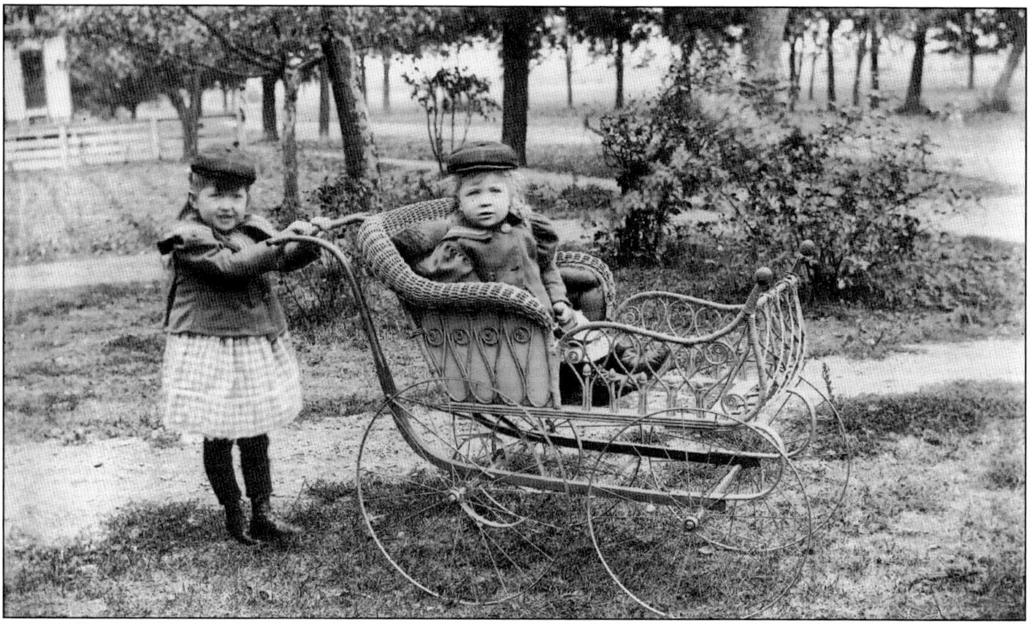

The boy in this Victorian chair is Herman Betz. Giant floppy ties were the neckwear of choice for little boys in 1903. For many years, the Betz family operated a store at 5654 Allen-Padgham Road. The store was built in 1866 as a shoe store and repair shop.

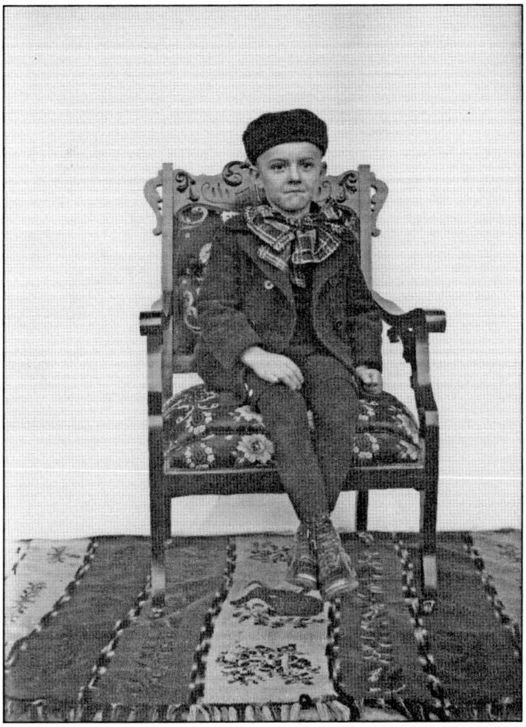

A slight discontinuity in the center of this *c.* 1891 photograph is the only clue that this is a trick shot. The same child is on both sides of the teeter-totter.

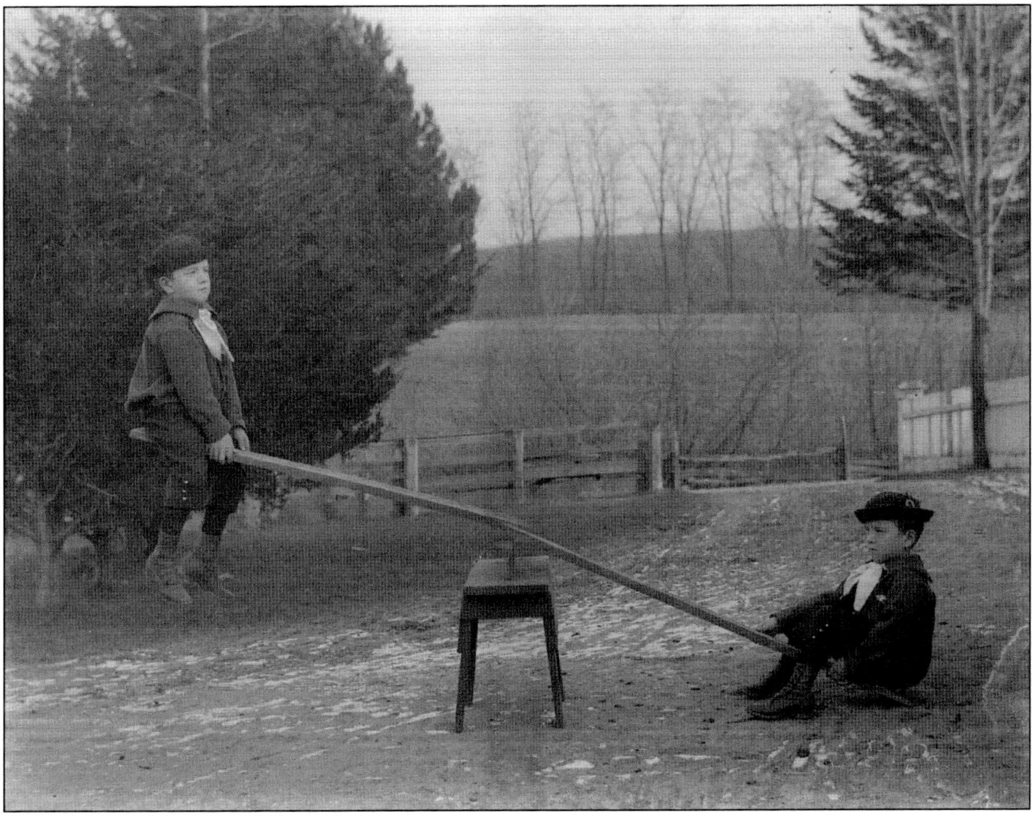

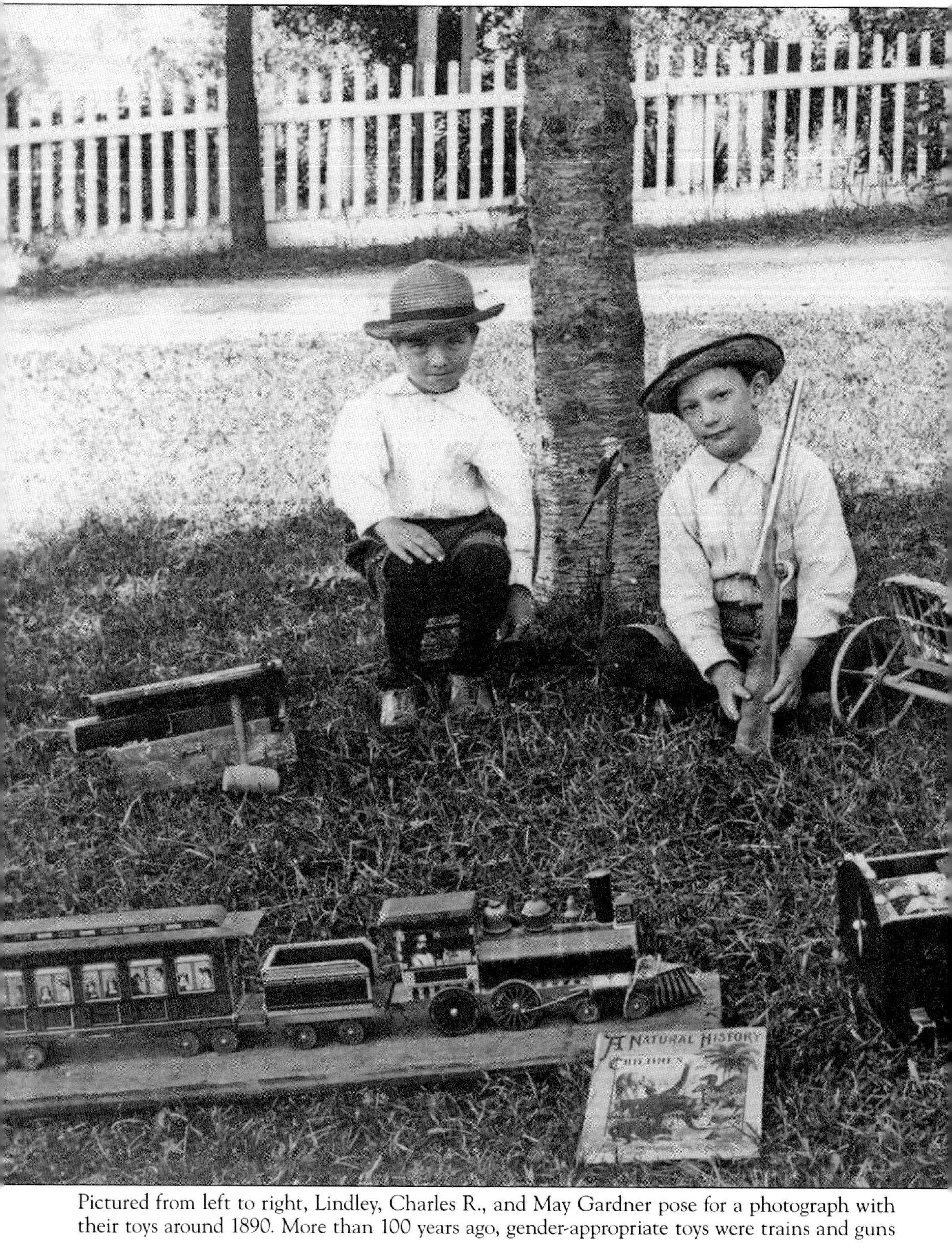


Pictured from left to right, Lindley, Charles R., and May Gardner pose for a photograph with their toys around 1890. More than 100 years ago, gender-appropriate toys were trains and guns

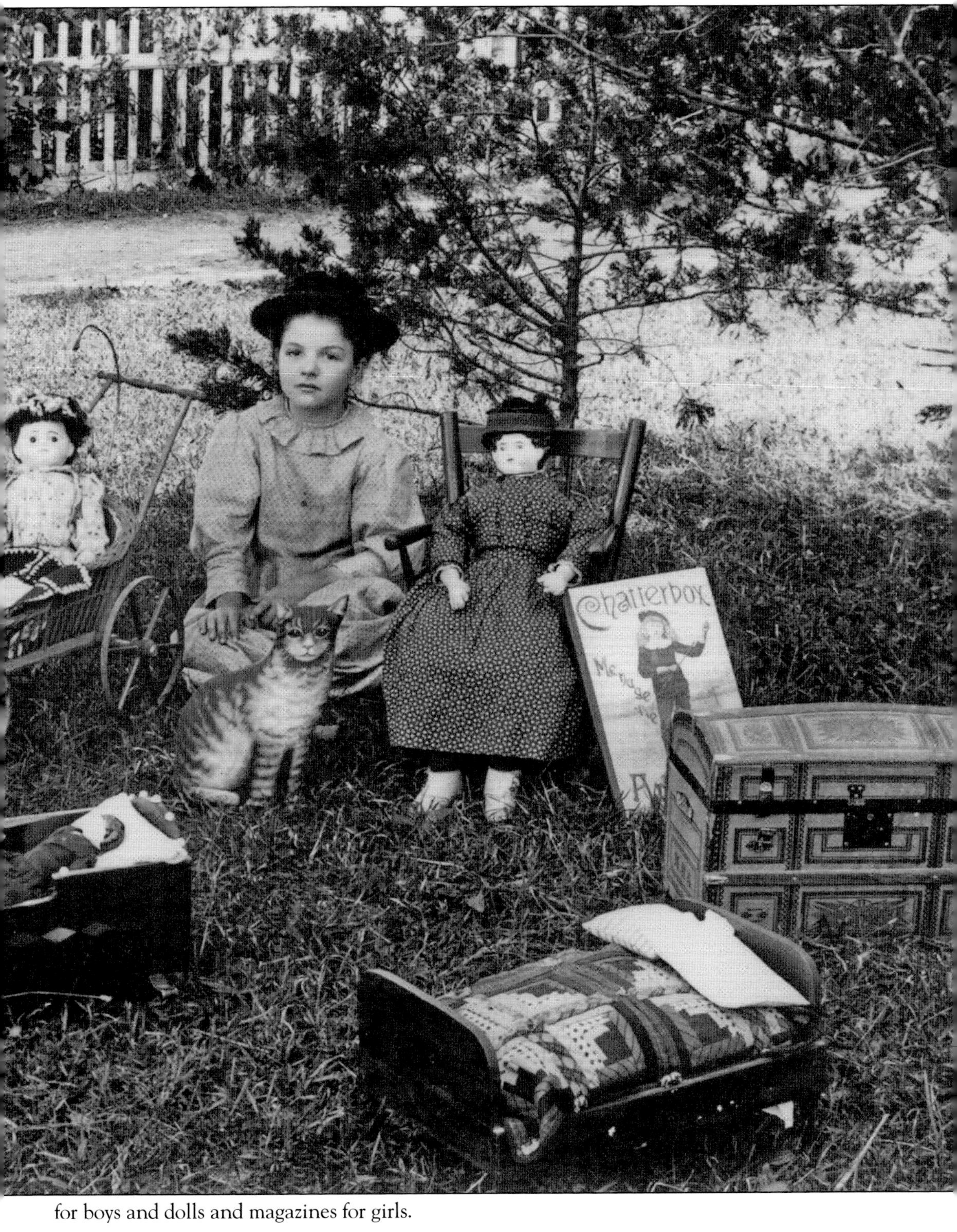


for boys and dolls and magazines for girls.

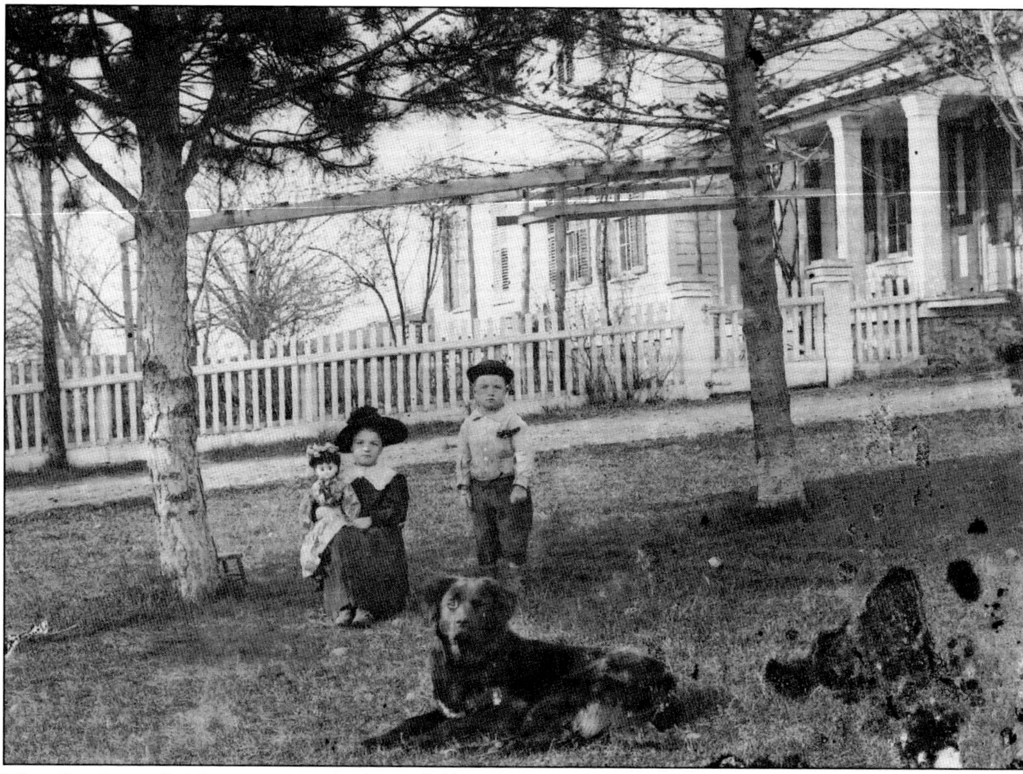

The Gardner children pose with their doll and dog in front of the Gardner home about 1889.

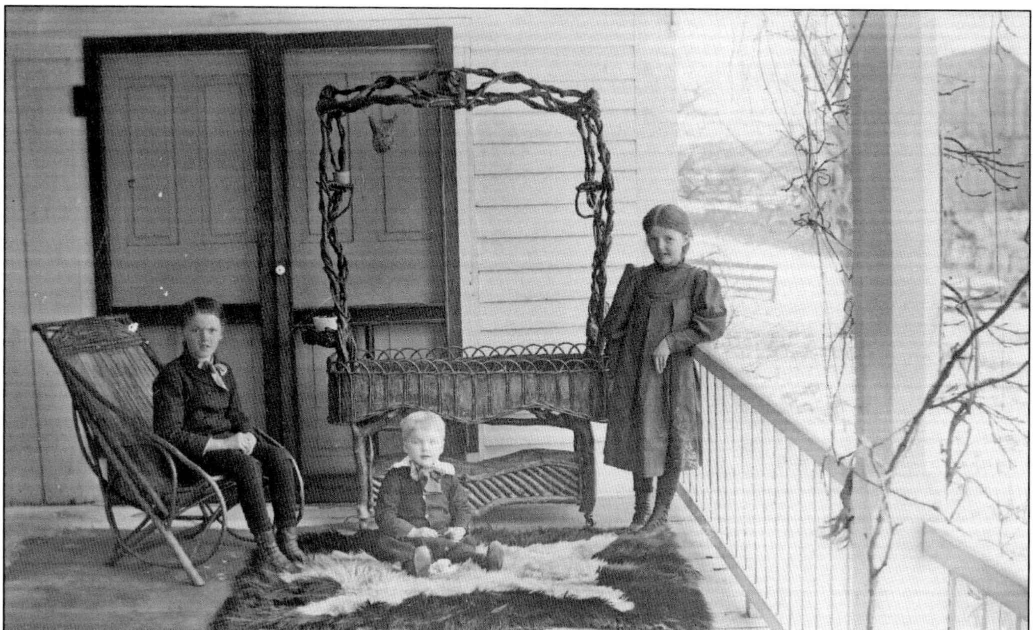

This photograph, taken at about 1893, shows Charles Gardner (left) with cousins Lindley (on rug) and May Gardner. Behind them is what appears to be a rustic planter. These planters were often handmade from local materials, and this one appears to be mounted on casters.

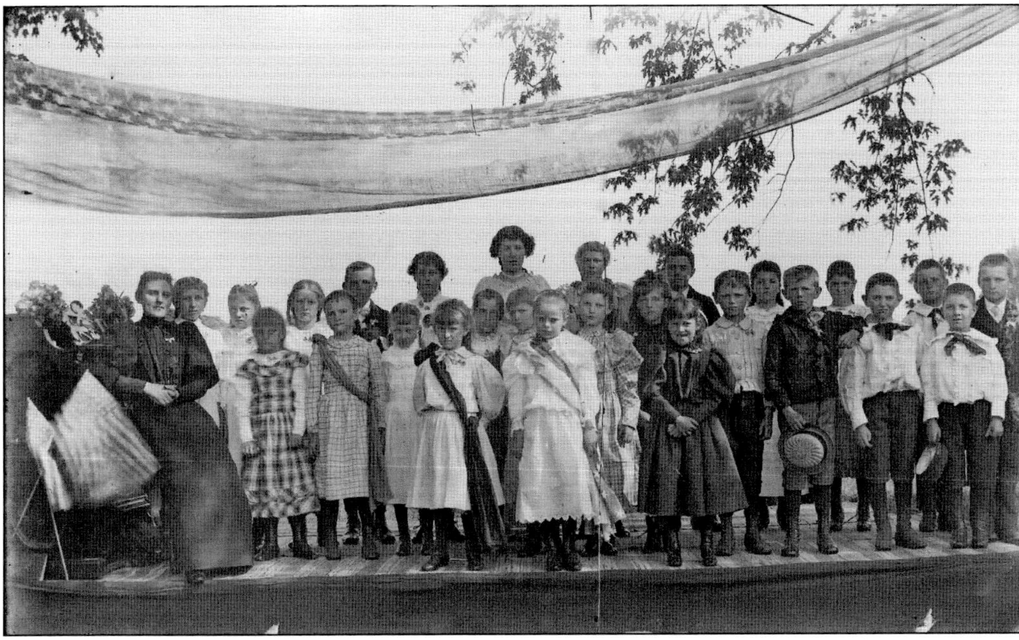

This panoramic photograph shows a commencement exercise at District School No. 12 around 1890. There is a flag banner overhead, and two of the girls are wearing flag-themed sashes. The woman on the left is sitting on the bench of a pedal-operated organ, whose music stand is just visible at the top.

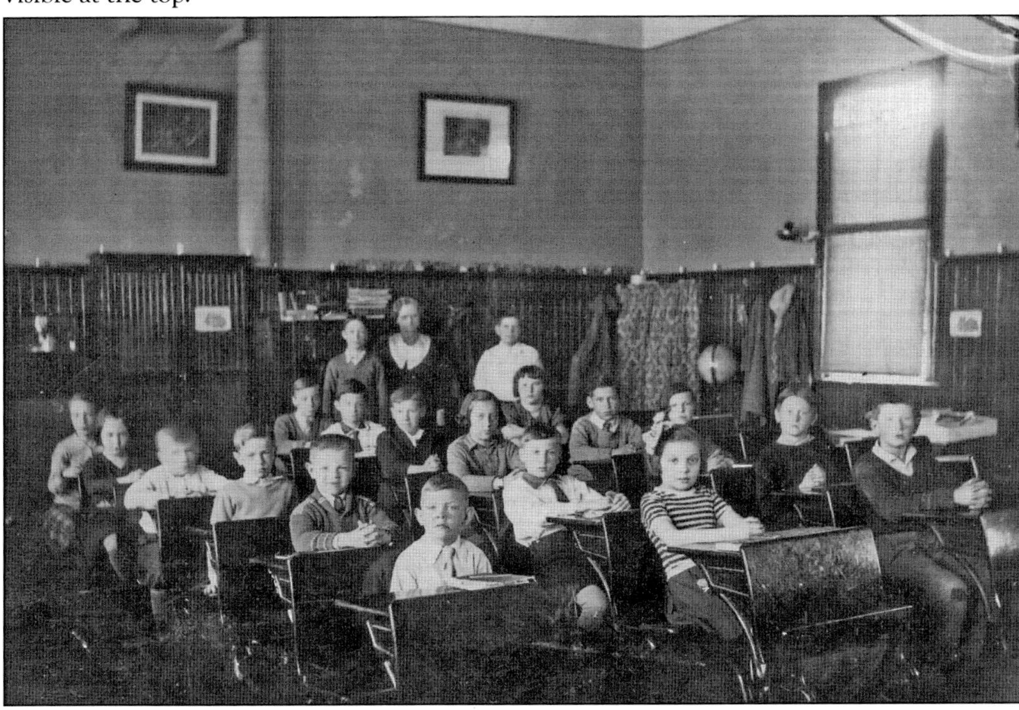

Teacher Beatrice Early presides over students at District School No. 12 school around 1935. This was one of Farmington's largest one-room district schoolhouses, and it operated until 1954. (Courtesy Diana and Rudy van der Velden.)

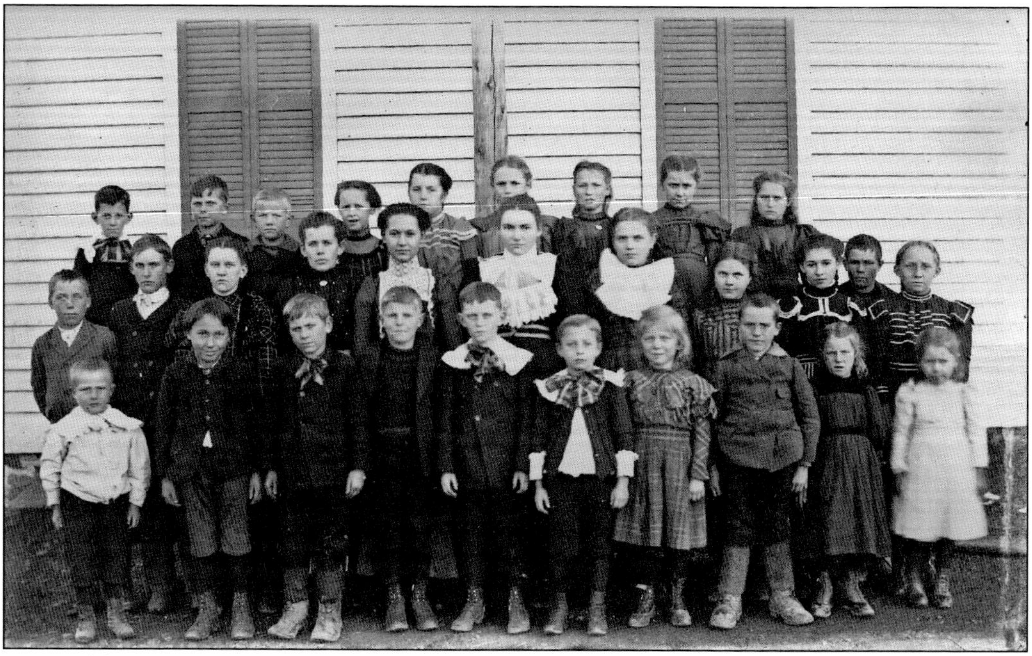

Pictured here are Hattie Fish and her District School No. 11 pupils. This school district was located in the northeast corner of the town near the intersection of Fox Road and County Road 28. (Courtesy Diana and Rudy van der Velden.)

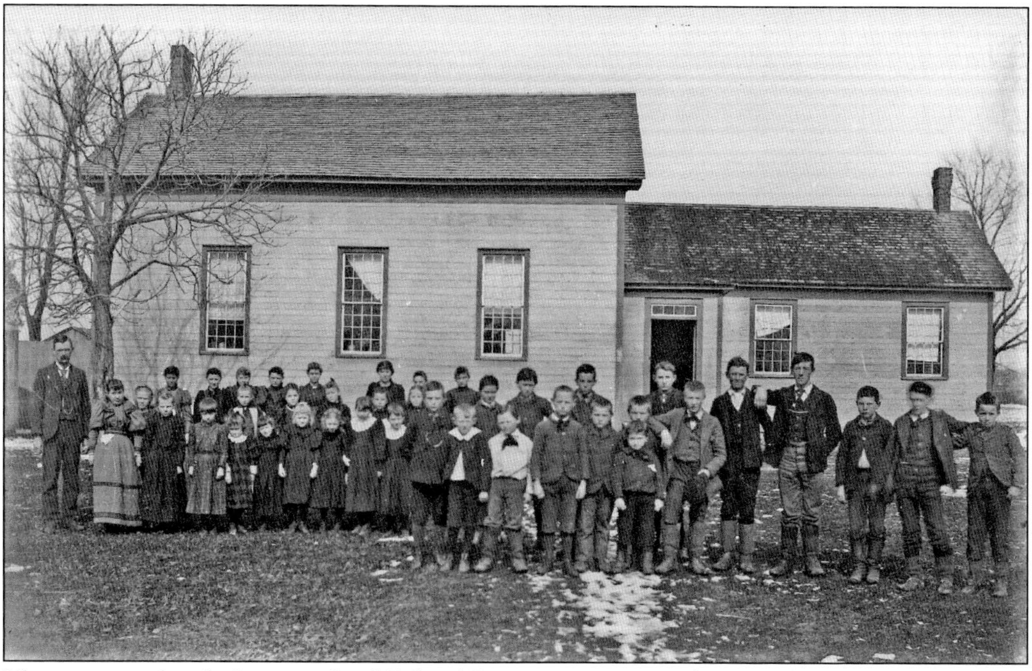

This is an undated photograph of School District No. 12 students with their teacher, Mark Mathewson. This view of the building, looking west, gives a good picture of the large main classroom fronting Hook Road and the woodshed, or privy, at the rear. (Courtesy Diana and Rudy van der Velden.)

# *Four*

# Community Life in Old Farmington

Many of these photographs are of a Farmington that predates the dominance of the automobile. Horses and horse-drawn conveyances were the customary means of getting around. Compared to today, a much larger proportion of the population lived on family-owned farms.

Everyone participated in parades, festivals, and socials. There was no competition from radio, television, movies, or the Internet, and community life was centered in the immediate neighborhood where everyone knew everyone else. The family doctor was probably a neighbor and visited patients at home when they were ill. If patients didn't have enough money to pay the doctor for his services, he often accepted produce or livestock instead.

Most Farmingtonians spent their entire lives within a few miles of the spot where they were born. The local church and school were the dominant cultural resources. While in many ways this was a simpler time, it was no paradise. Until antibiotics were invented in the 1940s, an astonishing number of people died from infections that would be trivial to treat today. Before the widespread adoption of safety equipment and regulations, farm machinery was dangerous and responsible for many gruesome accidents.

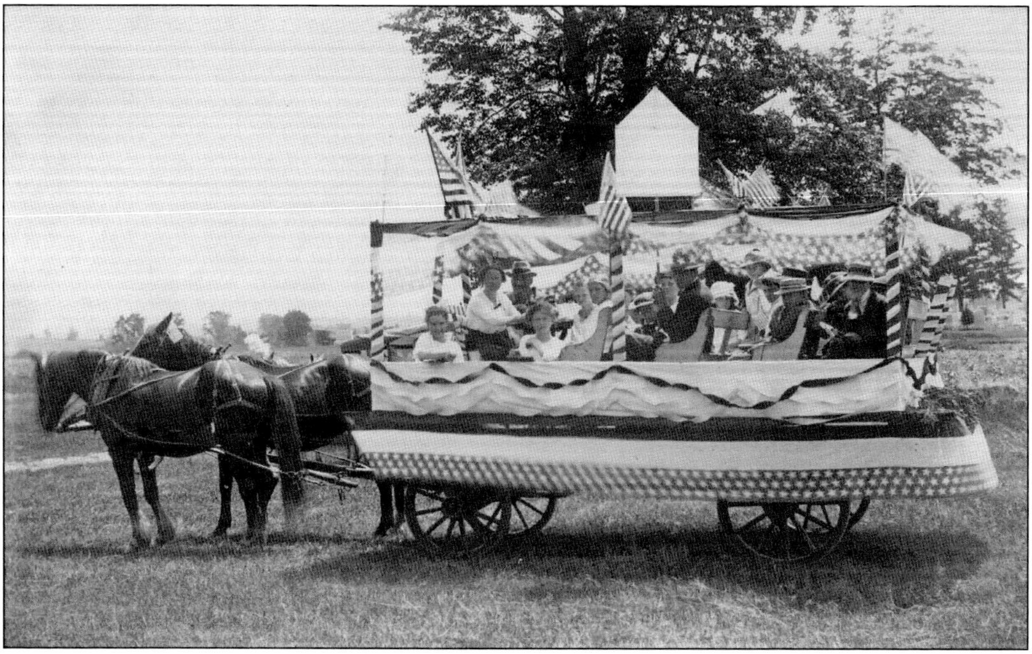

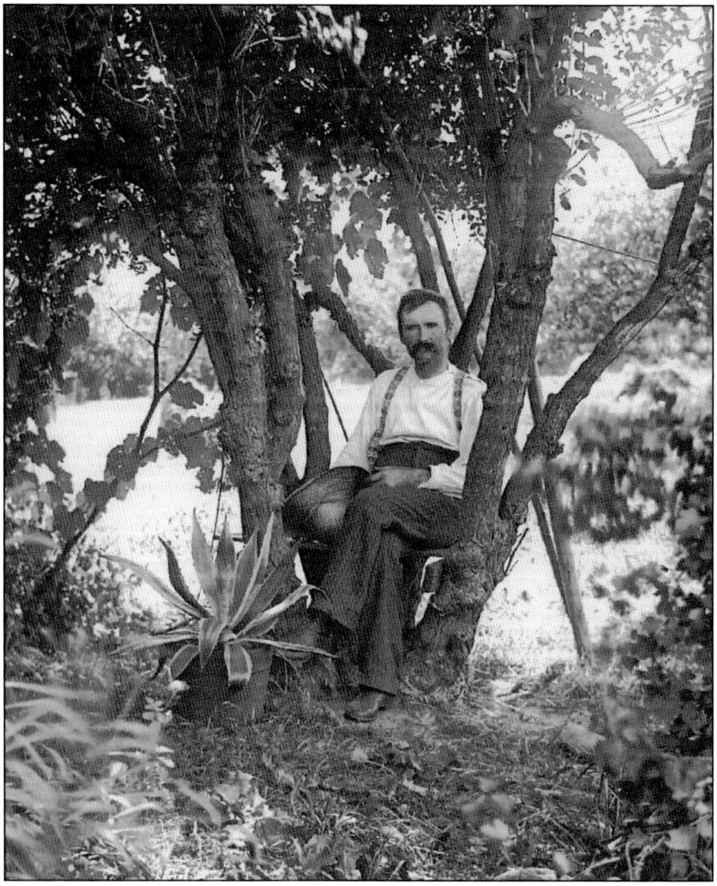

This horse-drawn float was in Farmington's Fourth of July parade around 1900. Benches were installed on the bed of a wagon to seat nearly 20 people. This was an era when the Fourth of July was not just another three-day weekend, it was the major national holiday. Farmingtonians expressed their patriotism in celebrations that brought out the whole community. Parades and speeches drew huge crowds.

In a simpler time, recreation could mean just sitting in a secluded garden spot and relaxing.

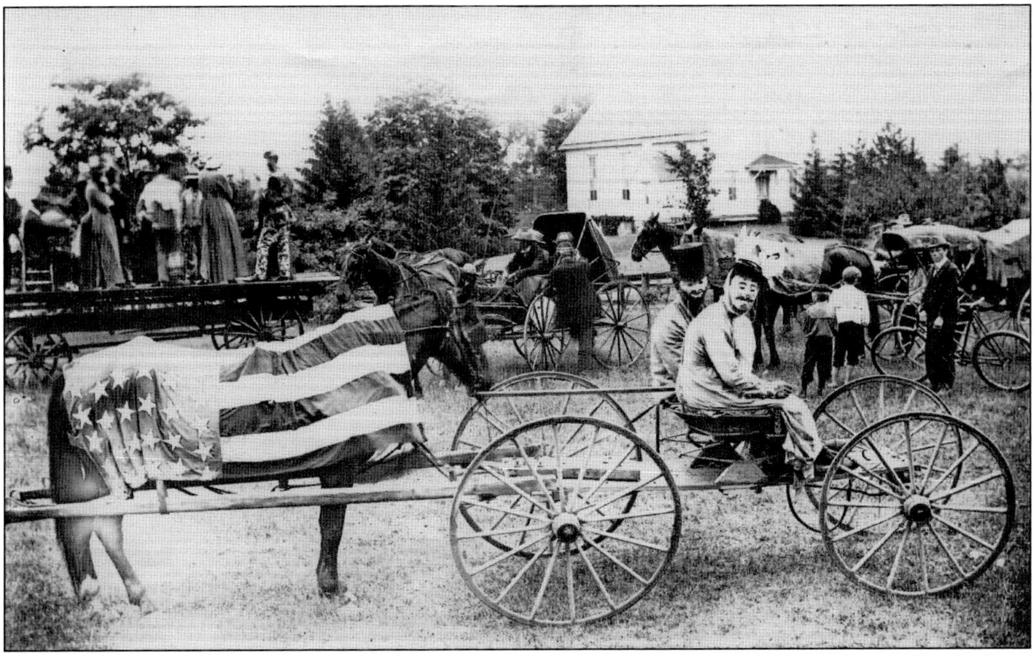

The inscription states that this is a "horseless carriage" and identifies these two individuals as Harry Warlow and William Bowerman. Apparently some sort of joke is intended. The horse is harnessed to the wagon backwards, and the men are in costume. The Farmington Friends Church can be seen in the background.

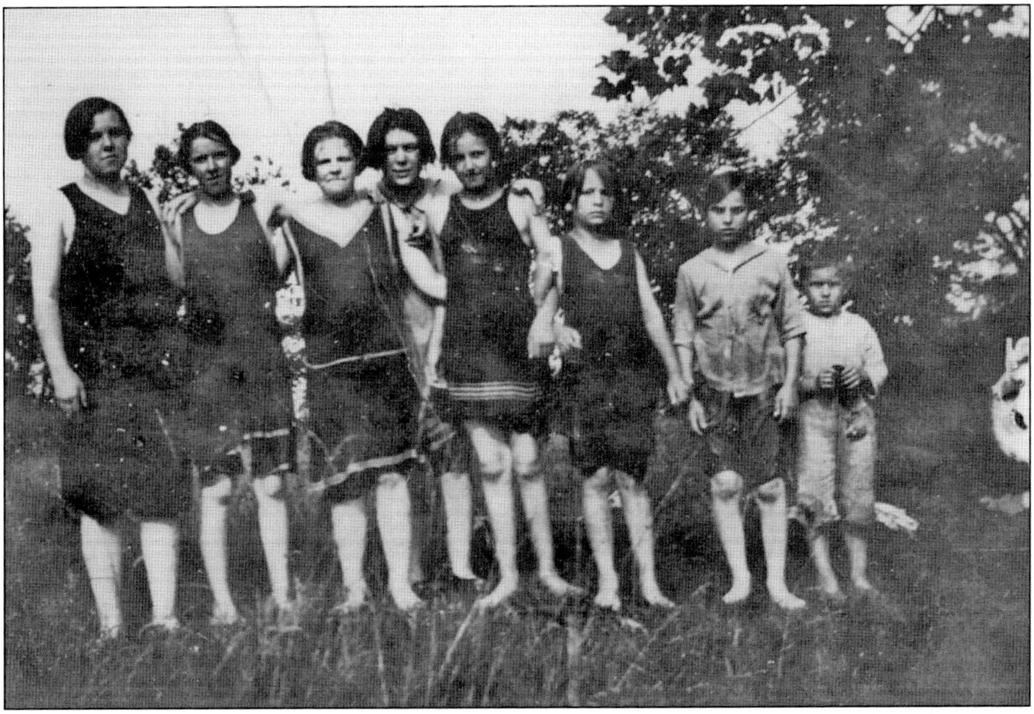

One of the women in this August 1924 photograph is Jane Effie Herendeen Gourlay. There were many popular swimming holes on Farmington's Mud Creek.

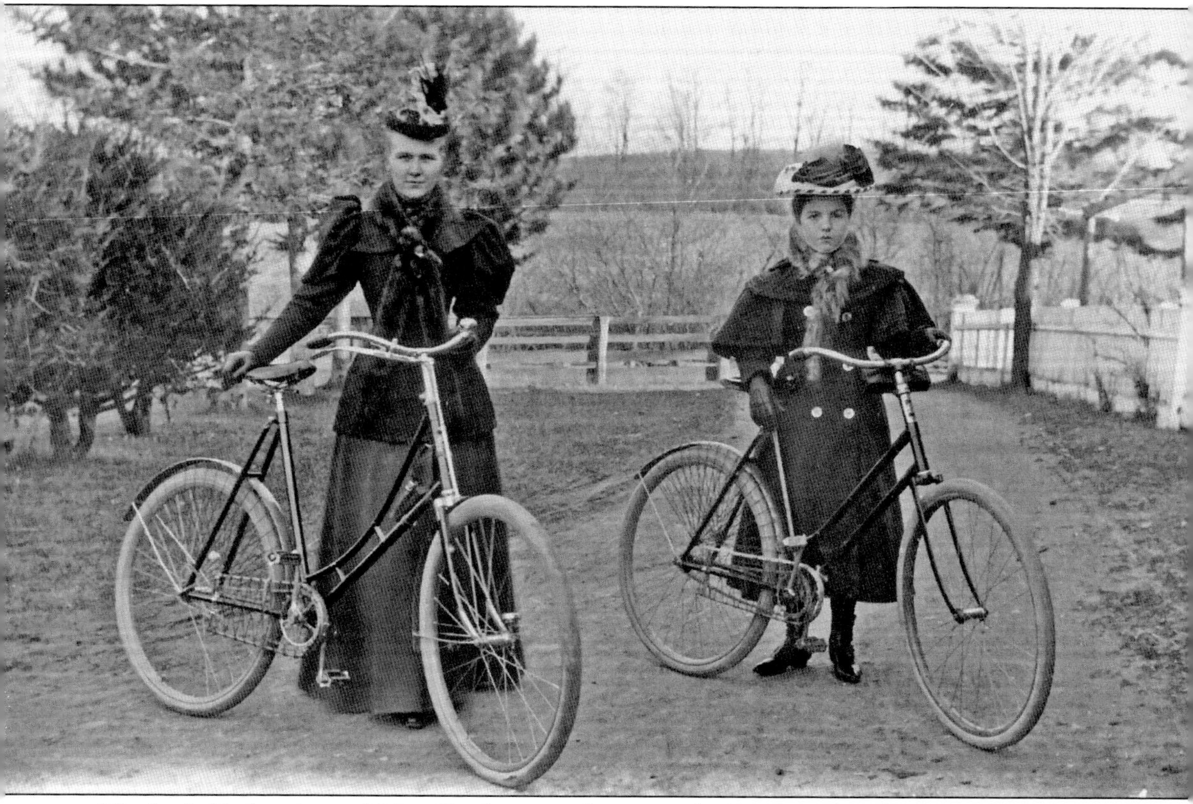

Elizabeth Katkamier and May Gardner are shown with their bicycles about 1895. This was a time period when a fur stole and fancy hat were considered perfectly appropriate for bicycling. Note the extensive wire guards to keep skirts from getting caught in the machinery. Katkamier's bicycle has a lever-operated "spoon" brake on the front wheel. The "coaster" brake operated by the pedals would not be invented for decades yet.

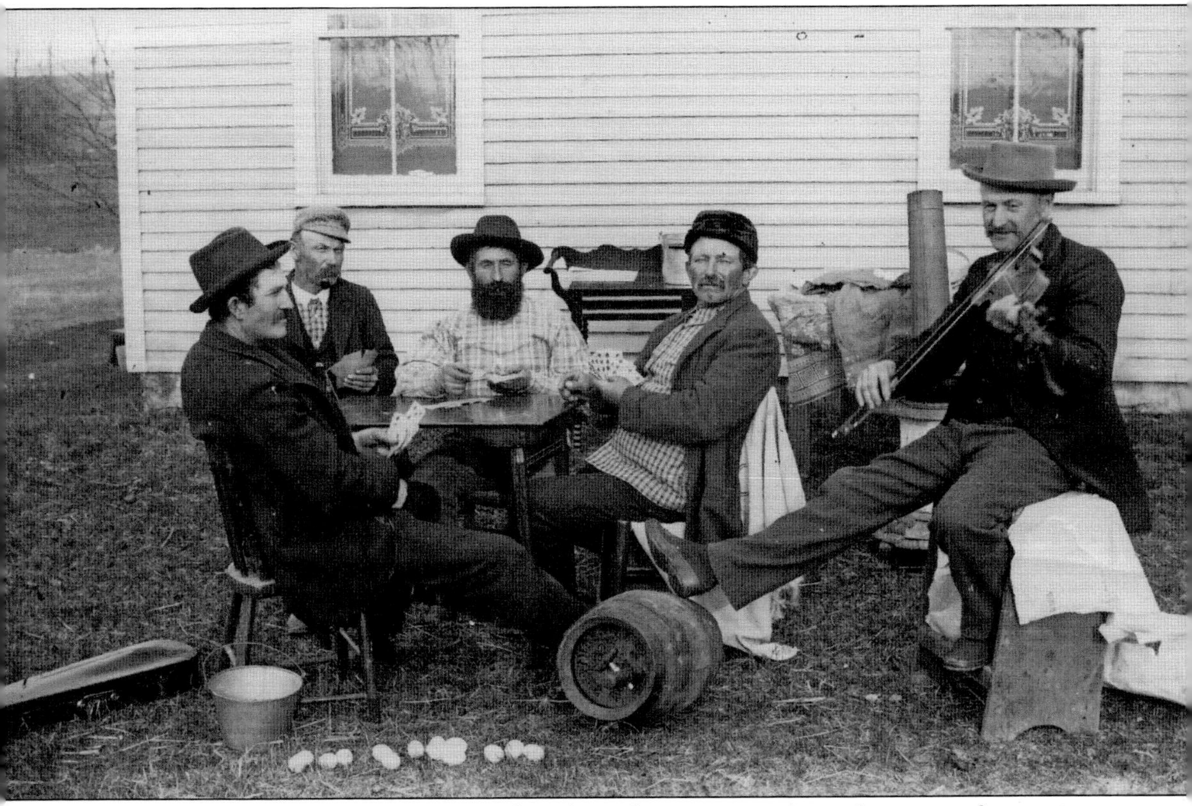

Never let it be said that Farmingtonians don't know how to enjoy themselves, even if it requires carting their furniture outdoors to play cards. A keg of beer from the Bartholomay Brewery in Rochester, some hard-boiled eggs, and a little fiddle music were part of having a good time. A pot-bellied stove behind the fiddler may have helped to keep everyone warm. The inscription states that the location of this photograph is outside the Betz home on Allen-Padgham Road. The men are, from left to right, Frank Rauch, Leonard Gardner, Fred Wehrlin, Frank Kemp, and Charles Cotton.

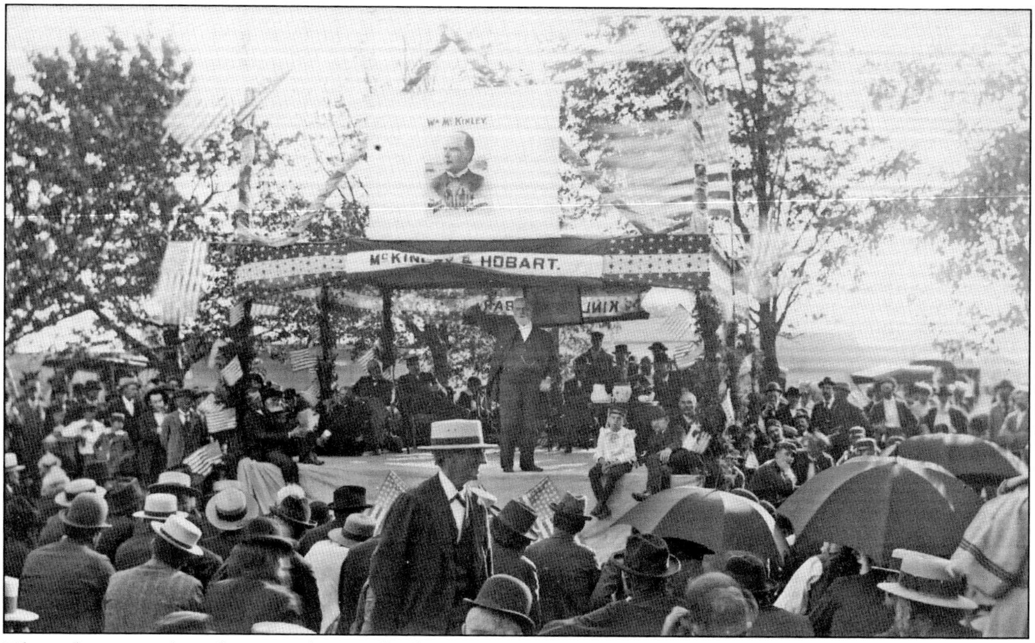


This photograph, taken in the yard of District School No. 12, shows Farmington Republicans rallying for candidate William McKinley, who defeated William Jennings Bryan for the presidency in 1896. Four years later, McKinley was reelected. When McKinley was assassinated in 1901, Vice President Theodore Roosevelt succeeded him. These flags were not up to date, as the standard flag for the time would have had 45 stars instead of the 42 stars on these flags.

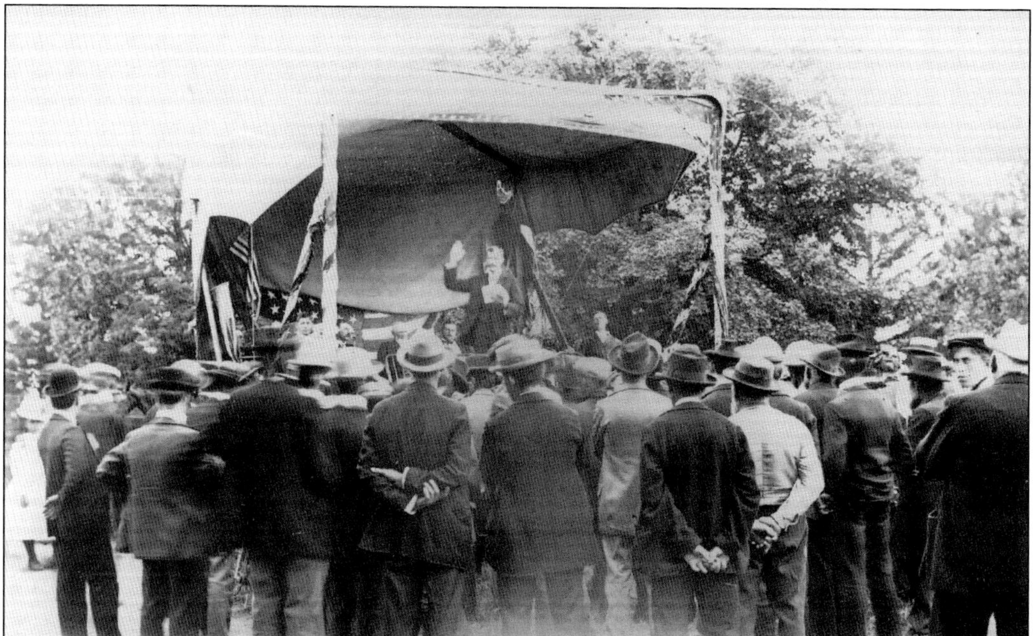

Anson Gardner is the featured orator at this Farmington Fourth of July celebration. He addresses the crowd from a makeshift stage. Anson had to have a powerful speaking voice, because there were no public-address systems in those days.

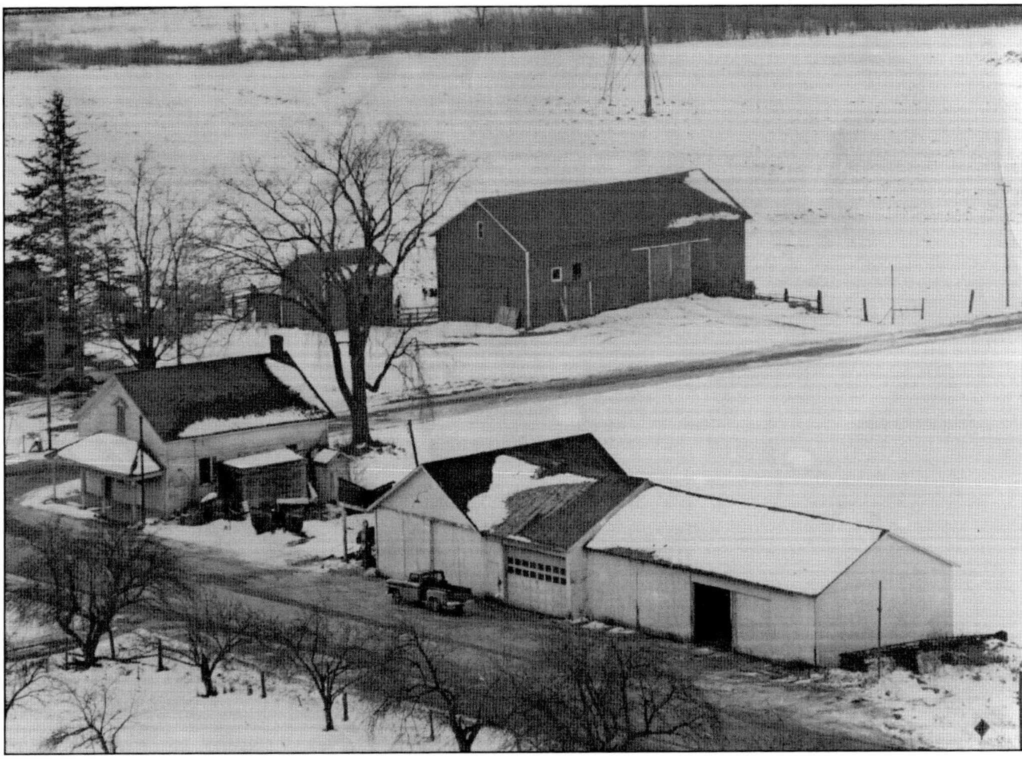

This is an aerial view of the old Farmington Town Hall and garage, looking southwest, sometime in the 1950s. Collett Road runs horizontally across the photograph, and County Road 8 is in the foreground. The old town hall was built in 1832. On May 12, 1966, it was sold to Ontario County for $1,100 and was demolished six months later. From this same viewpoint, the new town hall, built from 1978 to 1979, would be about 200 yards behind the vantage point and off to the right.

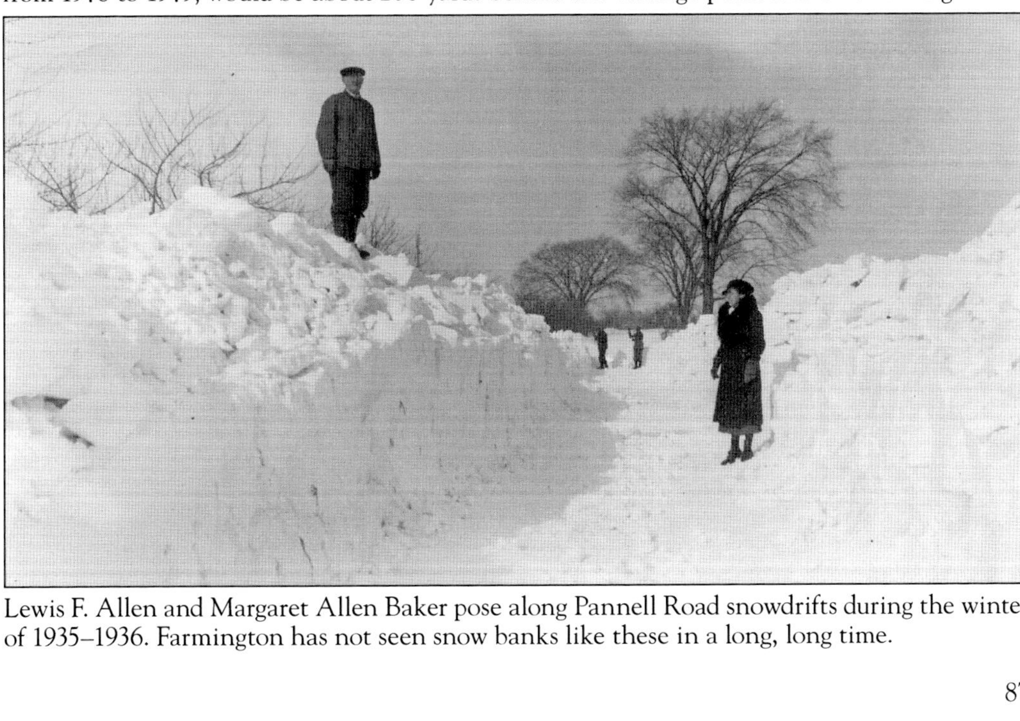

Lewis F. Allen and Margaret Allen Baker pose along Pannell Road snowdrifts during the winter of 1935–1936. Farmington has not seen snow banks like these in a long, long time.

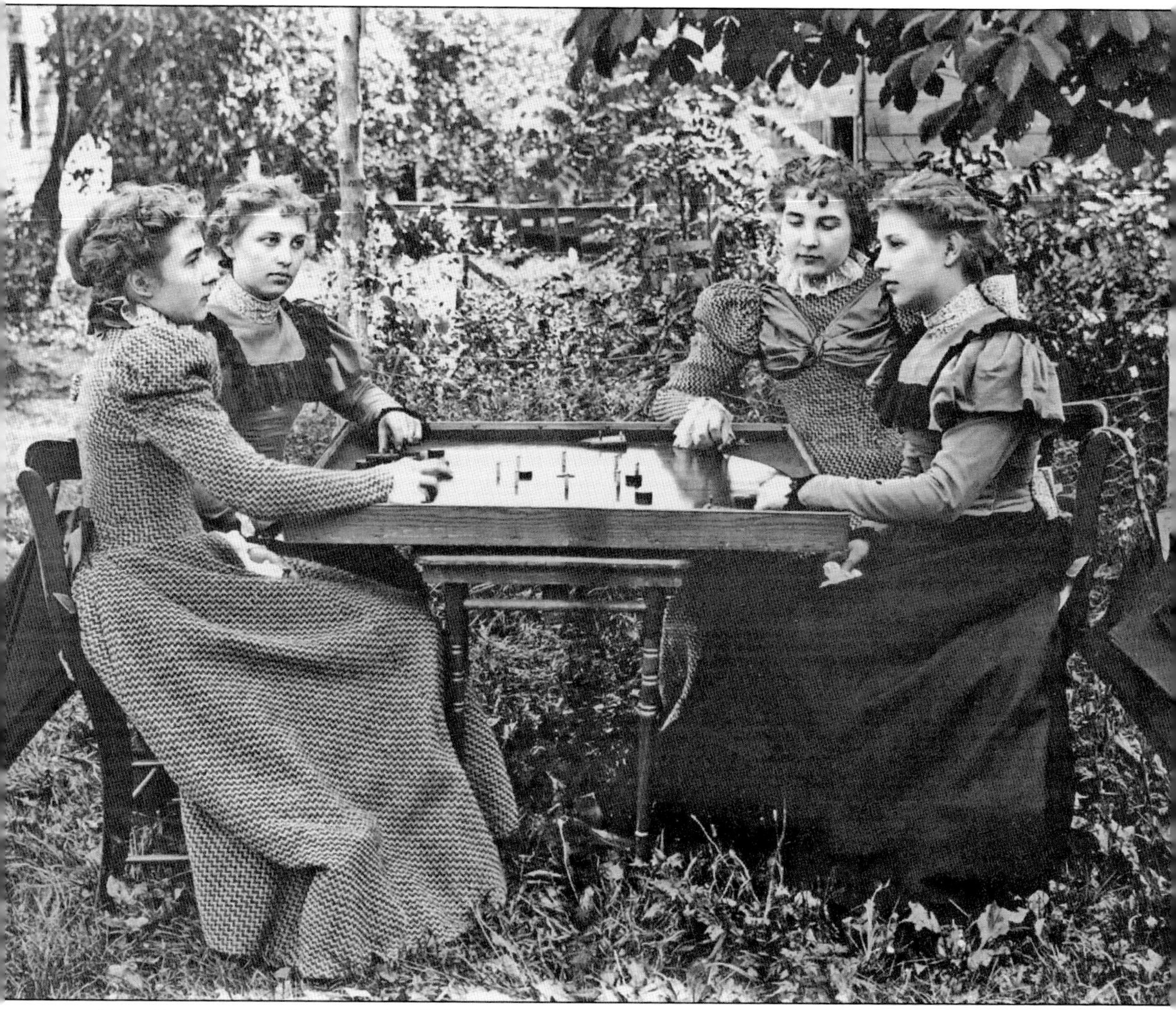

Here Farmington photographer E. J. Gardner has captured neighbors Lulu Dillingham (herringbone dress) and Hattie Chilson Collett from two different angles. At that time, nearly 100 years before Photoshop, he used some camera and darkroom trickery to combine the two views into one photograph. Notice the umbrella hanging from the back of the chair. The girls appear to be playing an early version of a pinball game.

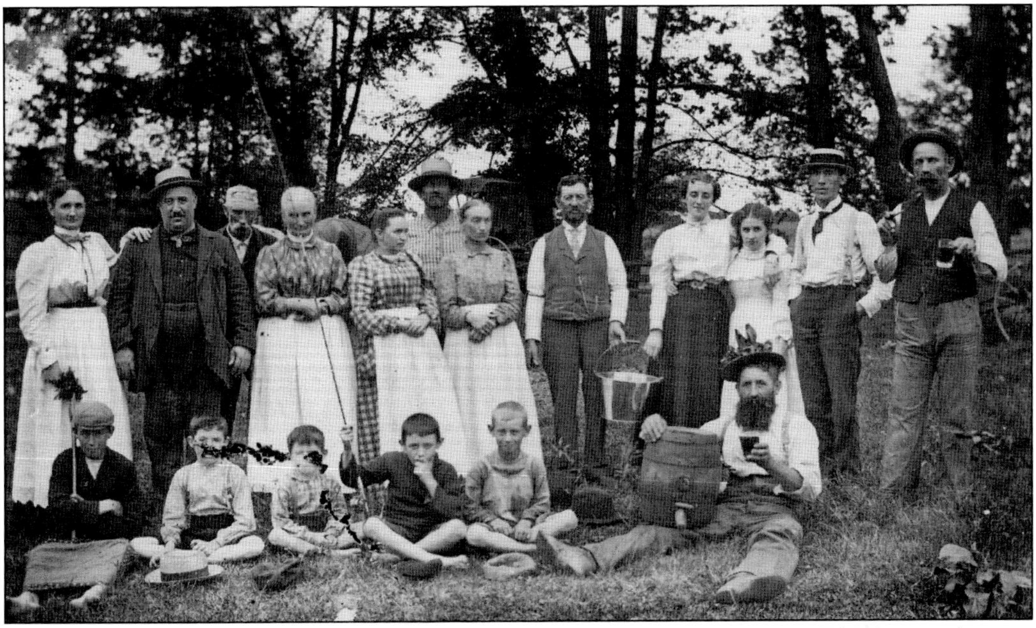

The Wehrlin, Cotton, and Chilson families enjoy a summertime picnic. The boy in front is holding a fishing pole; the lady holding one side of the bucket is smiling at the seated man, who appears to be wearing her hat.

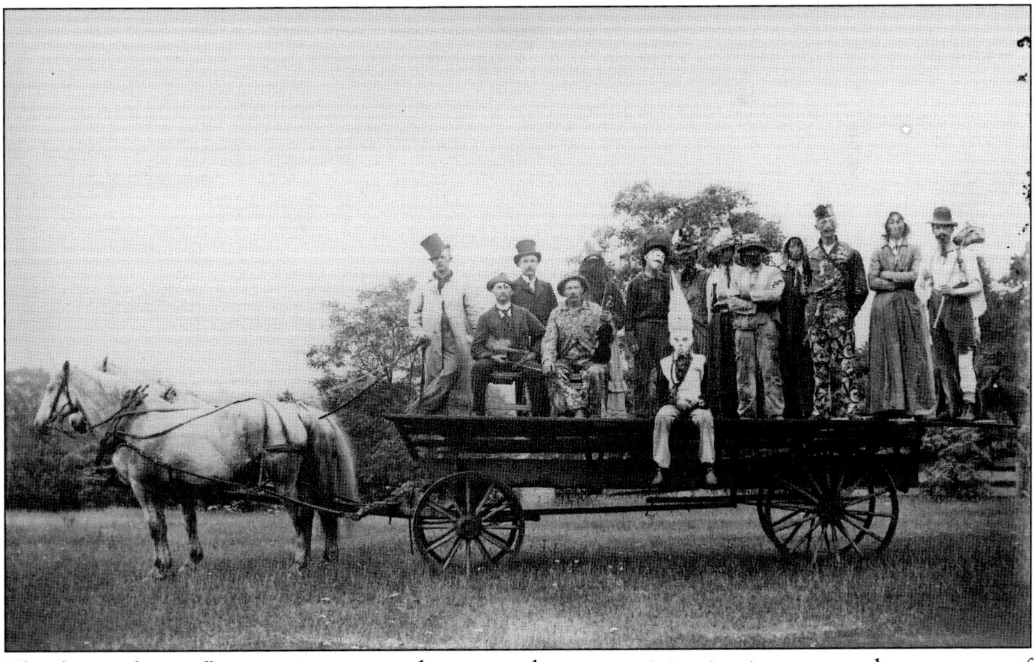

This horse-drawn float carries men and women who are participating in a square dance as part of a 1900 Fourth of July parade. They are dressed in a wide variety of costumes, perhaps to represent various ethnic groups.

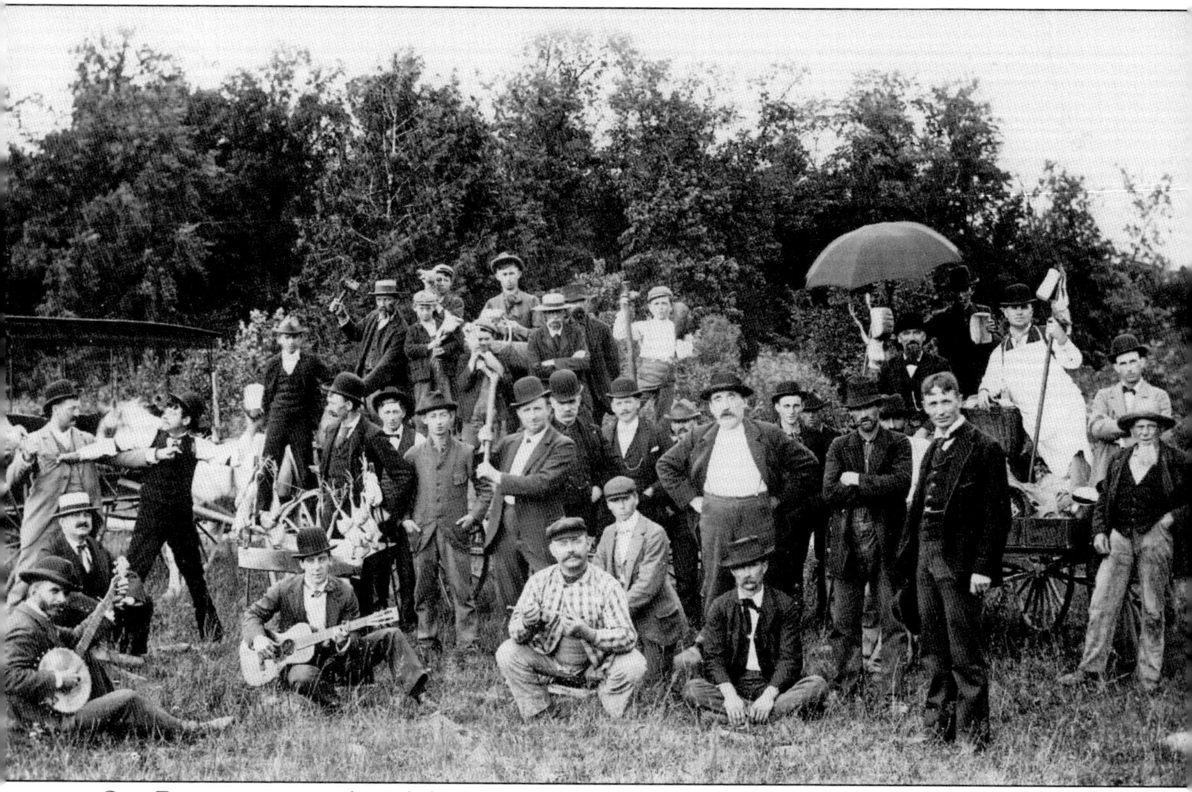

One Farmingtonian is brandishing an axe, perhaps ready to decapitate the chickens, and two men on the left seem to be using the chickens as weapons. No ladies are present, so this may be a fraternal organization outing. The man under the umbrella is hoisting a pint with one hand and holding a loaf of bread with the other. Musicians are playing banjo and guitar, and a boy in the back is holding up a baseball bat and catcher's mitt.

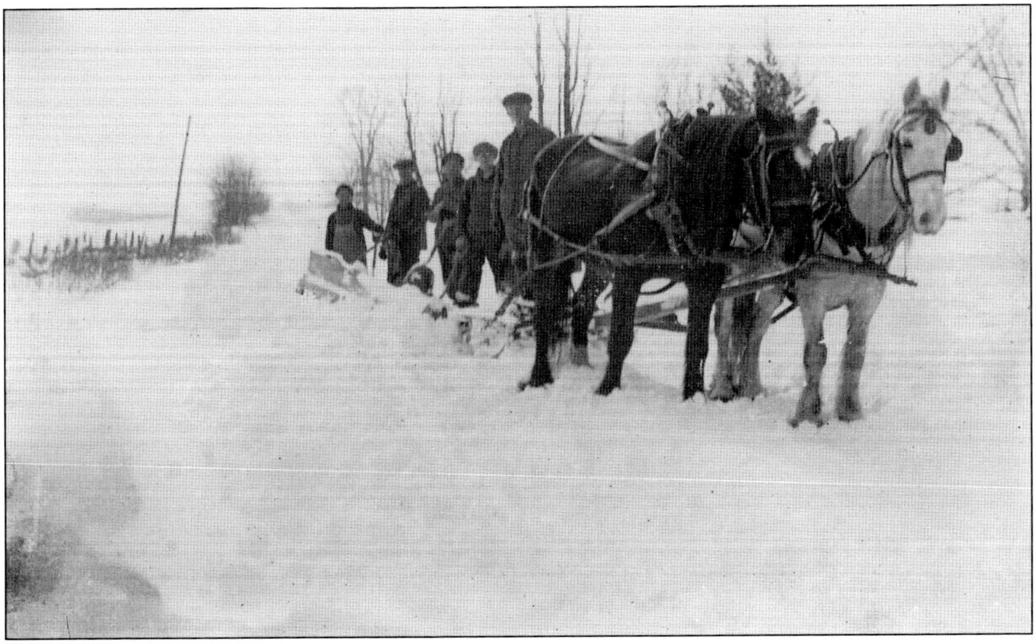

This photograph shows how Farmington roads were cleared in the winter of 1910, with a two-horsepower plow; Charles H. Gardner is supervising the crew. The average wage in the United States that year was 22¢ an hour.

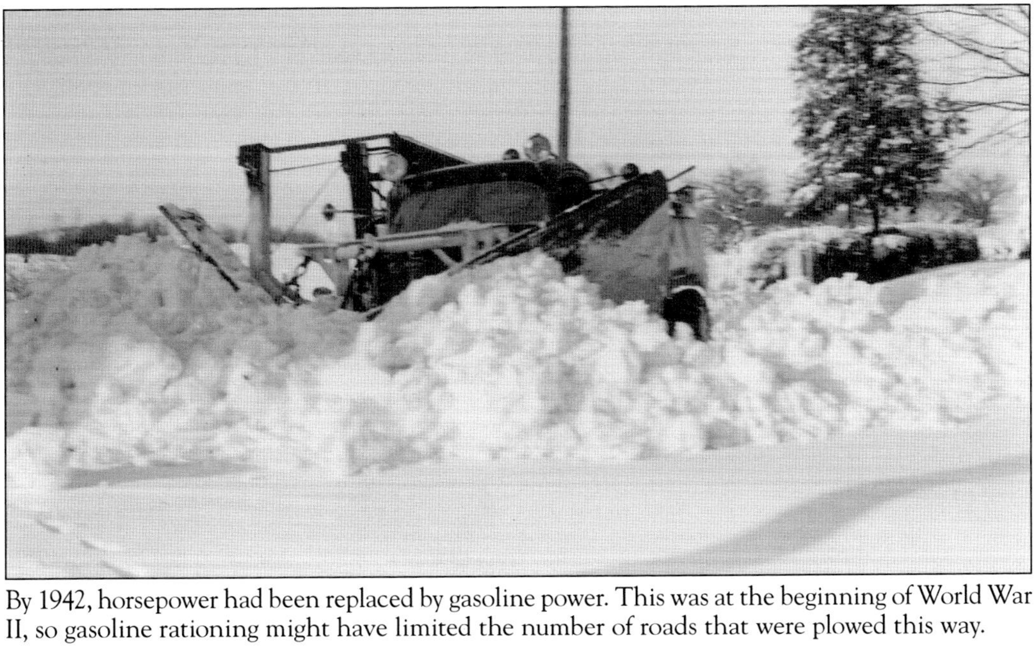

By 1942, horsepower had been replaced by gasoline power. This was at the beginning of World War II, so gasoline rationing might have limited the number of roads that were plowed this way.

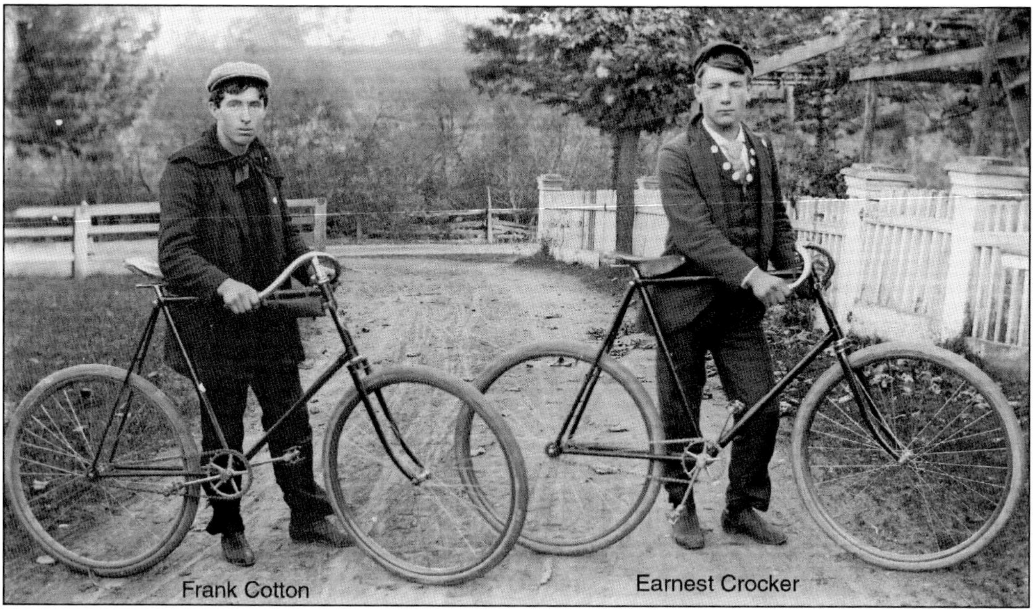


Frank Cotton and Earnest Crocker are with their "wheels," as they were called. The bicycle craze that began in the 1890s captured the public imagination much like the Internet craze of the 1990s. This photograph was taken about 1911.

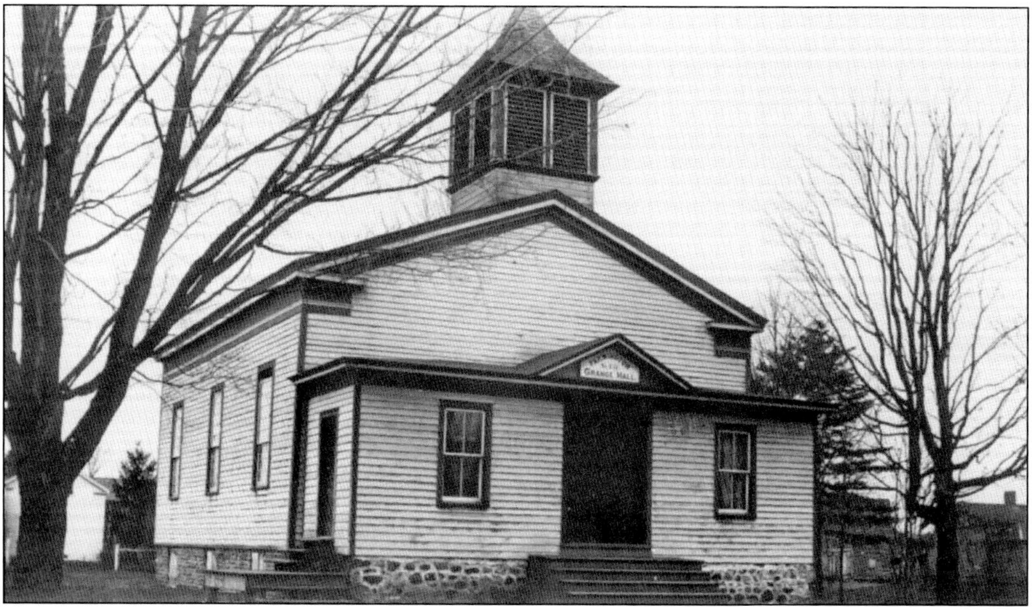

This building on Hook Road, pictured in 1890, was originally a Wesleyan Methodist church; about the time of this photograph it became Farmington Grange No. 431. The grange still owns the building. Over its long history it has been used by several local church groups and has been an election district polling place. Currently it is a Baptist Bible School. Farmington has also been home to Lutheran, Quaker, Faith Baptist, Maranatha Fellowship, and Baha'i Faith churches.

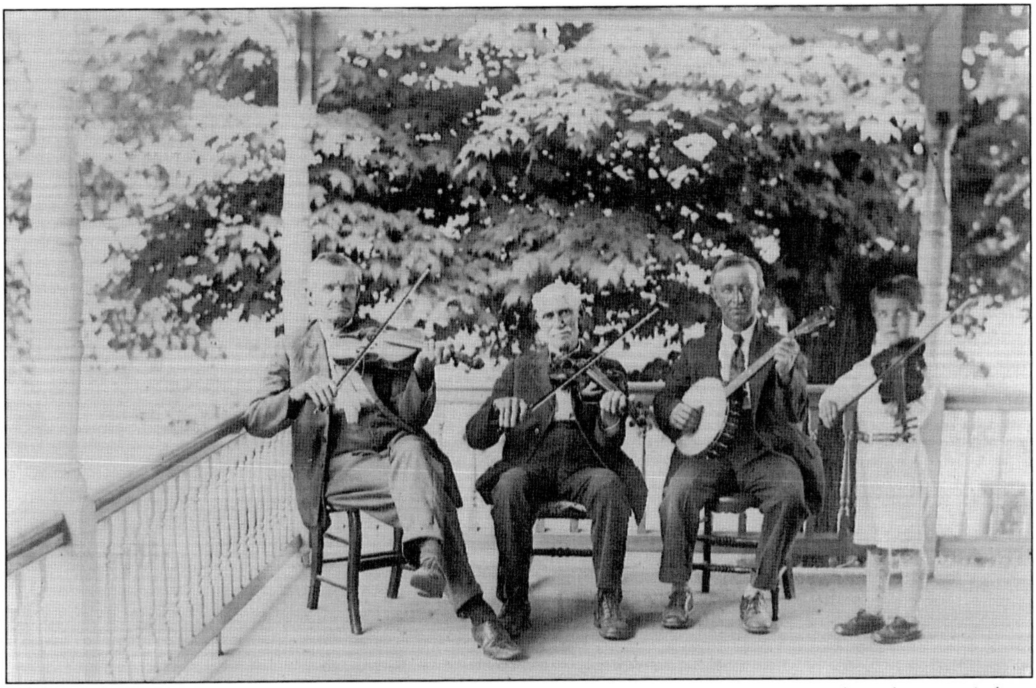

Unidentified musicians prepared for a concert on the porch of the E. J. Gardner home. A boy and two men play fiddles, while another man holds a banjo. Spontaneous local amusements were the rule, and commercial entertainment was the exception.

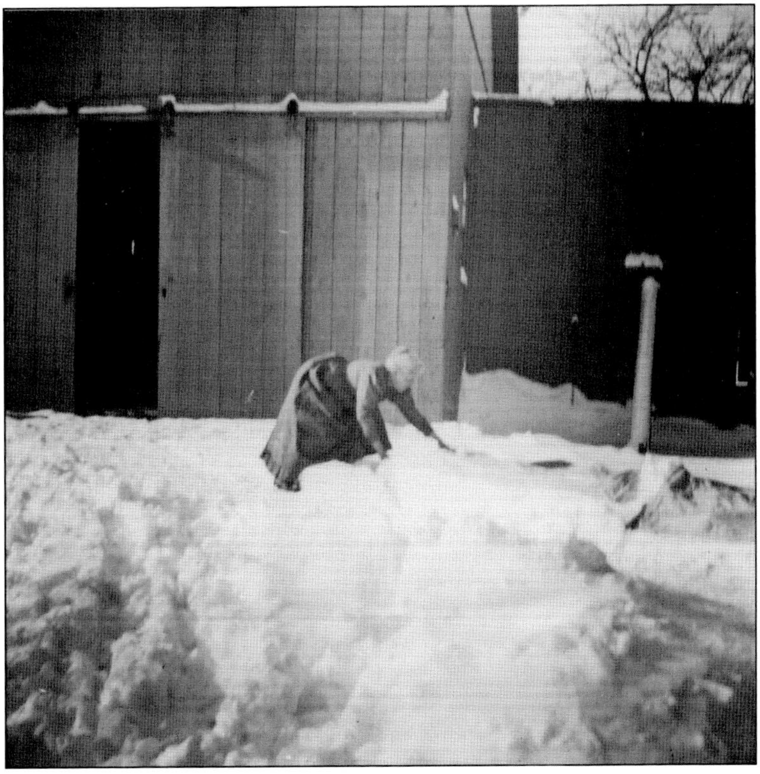

This undated photograph shows Alice Hoag spreading sheets on the snow to bleach. This was a common practice and certainly much more environmentally friendly than using toxic chemicals.

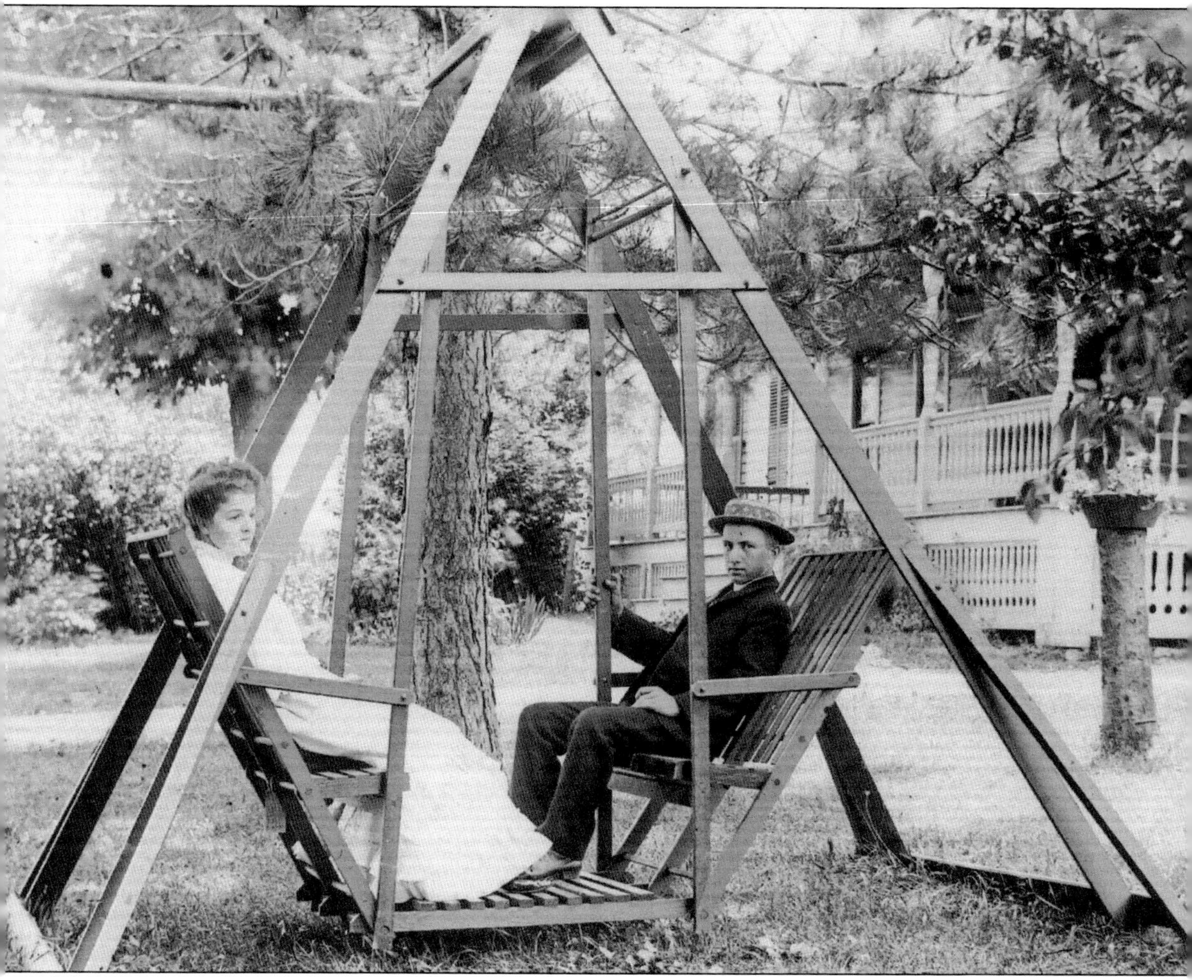

The Gardner children are relaxing in a lawn swing in front of their Hook Road home around 1900. This style of lawn swing was very popular in the early 20th century and is still seen today.

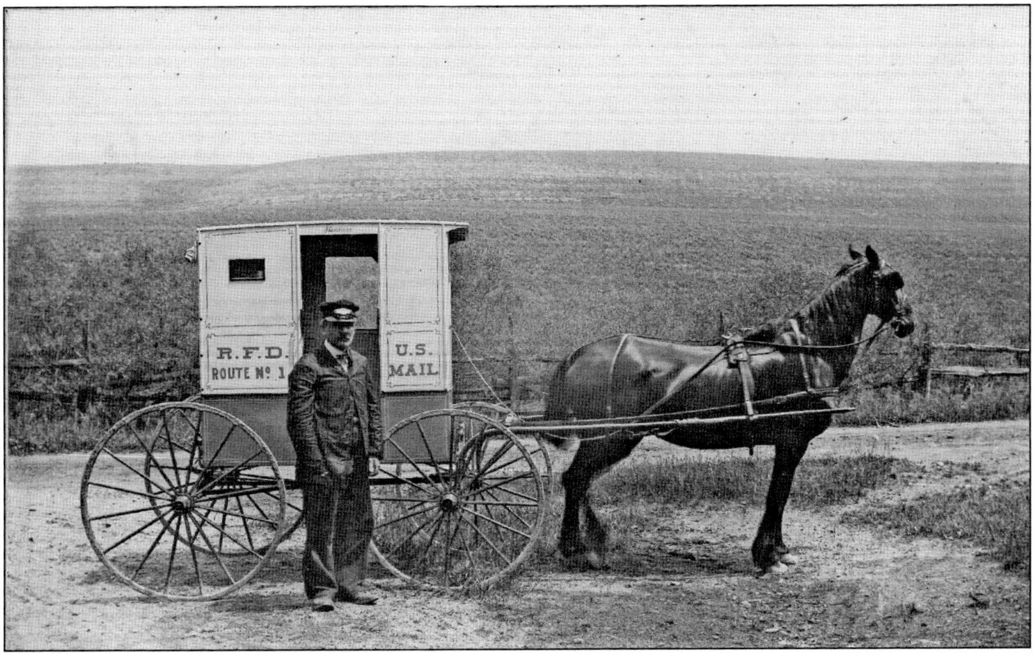


This picture is captioned, "The first R.F.D. in Farmington, Walter Willcox, Carrier." U.S. postal services like rural free delivery and parcel post mail were partly a result of national lobbying by farmers through the grange. RFD began in New York state about 1898 and in Farmington on February 1, 1902.

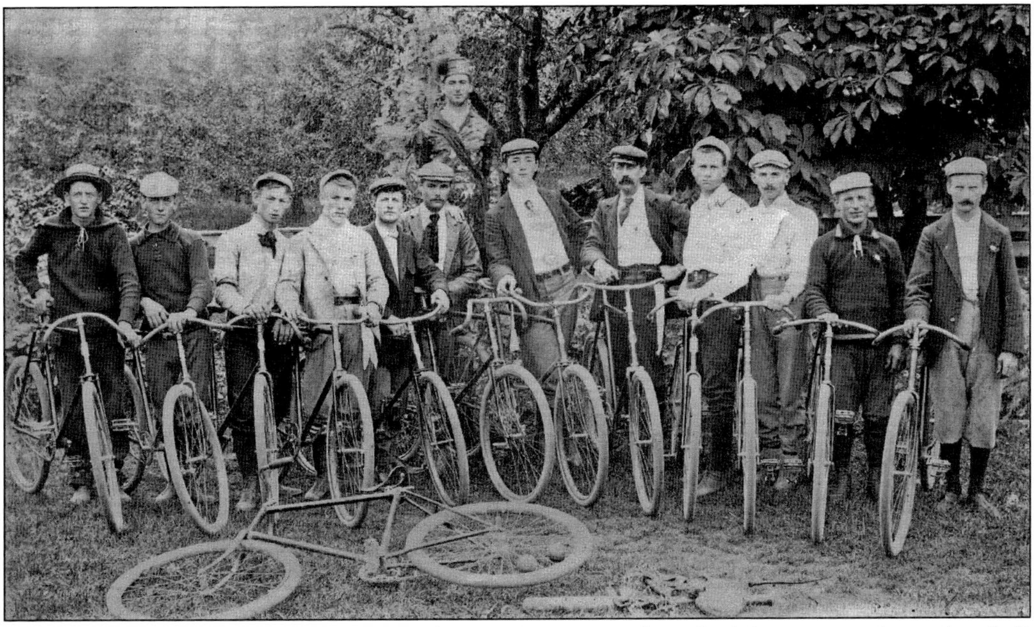

This photograph from the Gay Nineties shows a Farmington bicycle club returning from a baseball game. Pictured from left to right are Red Dillman, unidentified, William Chilson, Ernest Crocker, Francis Nussbaumer, unidentified, Henry Gardner (in back), John Coniff, Edward Betz, Sunderland Gardner II, two unidentified, and Marvin Brown. (Courtesy Diana and Rudy van der Velden.)

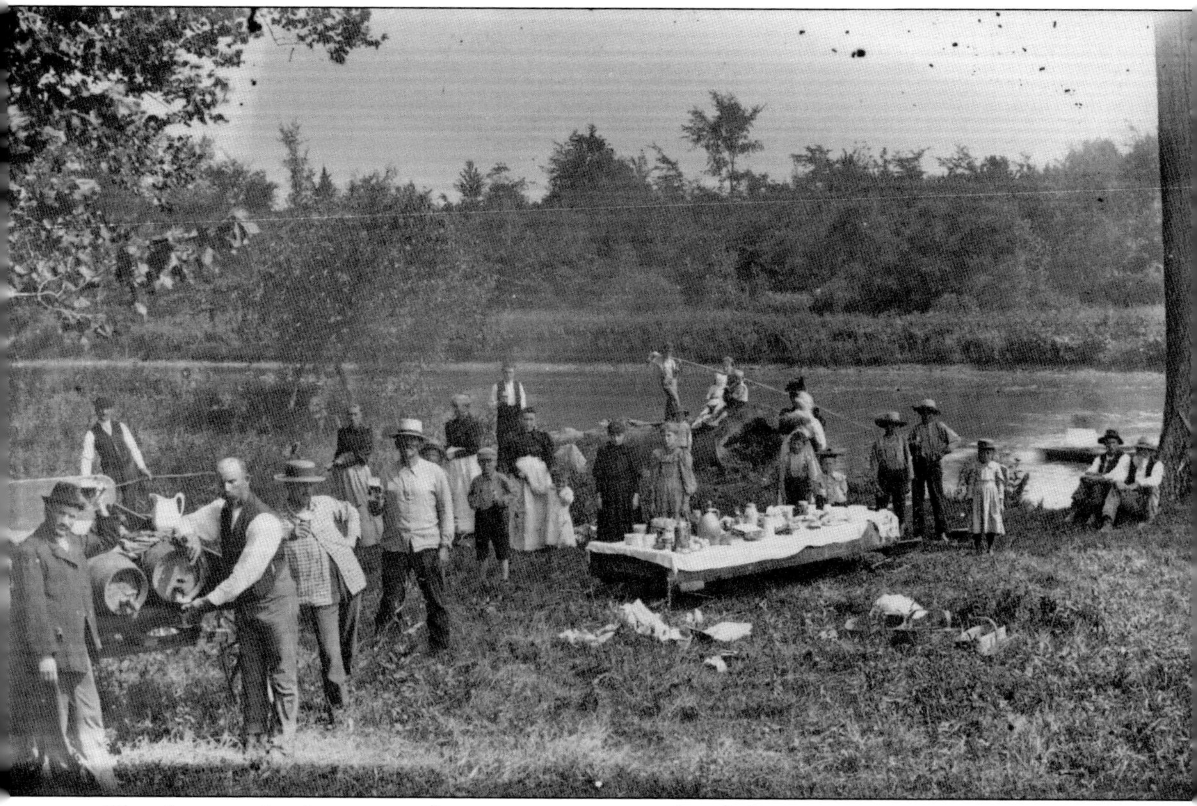

The photographer has captured a summertime picnic beside Farmington's Ganargua Creek. The picnic baskets have been unloaded, and the table is nicely laid. One man appears to be poling a raft on the creek. During the time of this photograph, the creek provided power for the Red Mill. The caption identifies this as one of Cassius V. "Lot" Chilson's parties.

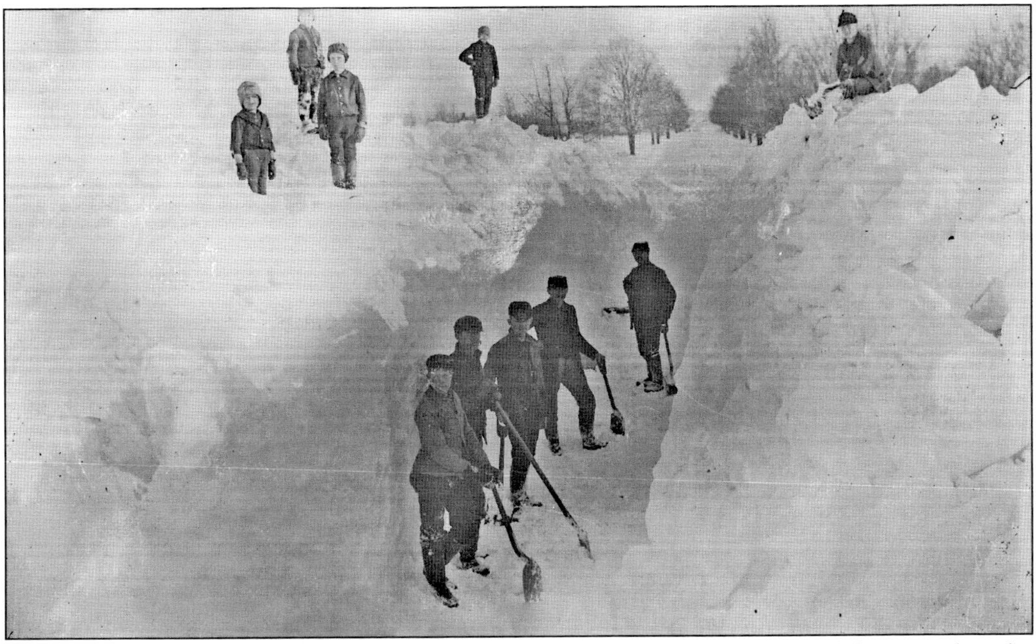

A record-setting storm hit the nation on February 15, 1895. Snow fell in Alabama and at the mouth of the Mississippi River. Twenty-four inches fell in Dallas, Texas, and dumped 43 inches on the Rochester area. The next day, February 16—when this photograph was taken on a glass-plate negative—drifts like these in Farmington were impossible to clear with horse-drawn plows. Men and boys attacked them with sheer manpower.

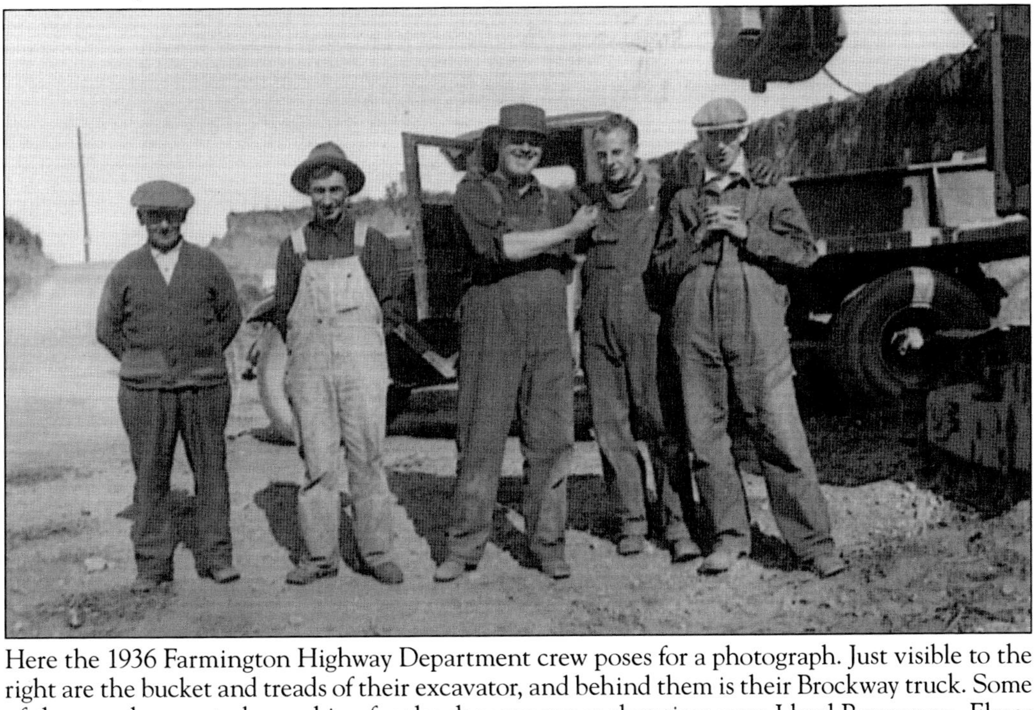

Here the 1936 Farmington Highway Department crew poses for a photograph. Just visible to the right are the bucket and treads of their excavator, and behind them is their Brockway truck. Some of the men known to be working for the department at that time were Lloyd Bowerman, Elmer Holtz, Dave Dennie, Chet Mincer, Claude Cheesman, and Bussy (or Albert) Keefe.

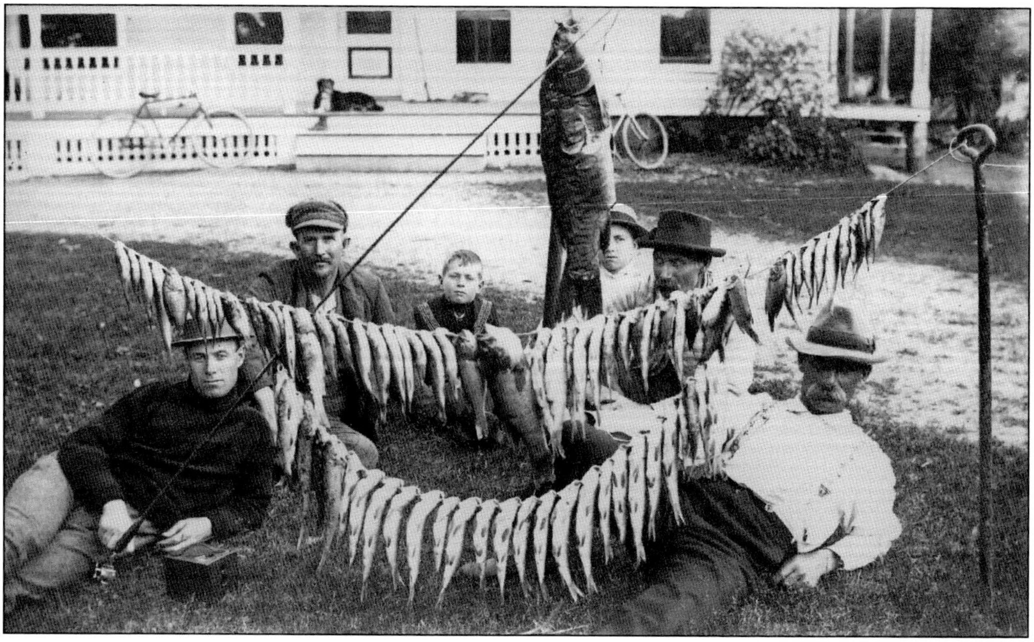

This photograph of an impressive catch of fish was taken around 1900. The individuals are, from left to right, Leslie Gardner, Leonard Gardner, Cortland Gardner, Lindley Gardner, Frank Rauch, and Eugene Markham. Notice the box camera on the ground in front of Leslie. (Courtesy Diana and Rudy van der Velden.)

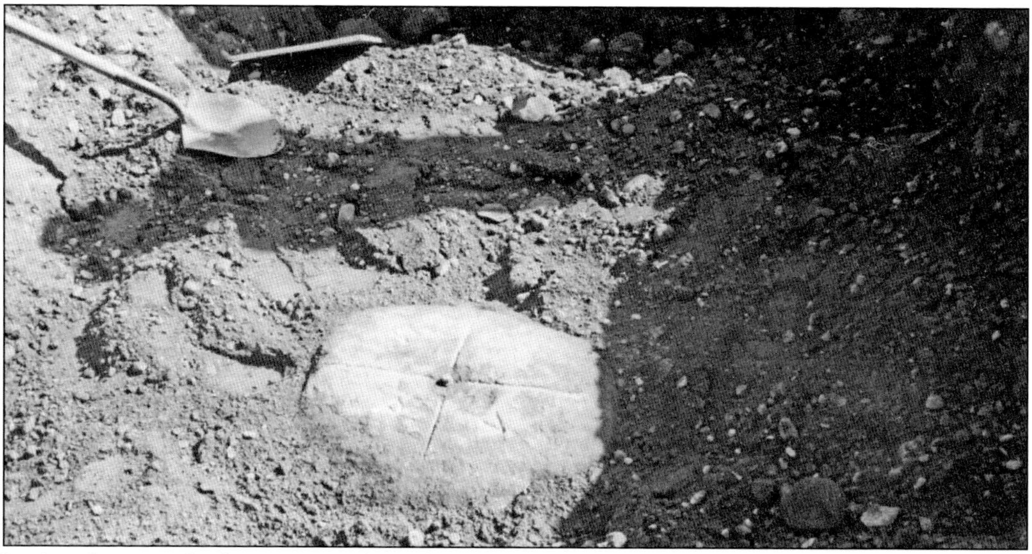

In this photograph, the very top of a multi-ton boulder is visible after a protective manhole cover was removed. The boulder was buried at the northwest corner of Farmington. The perpendicular lines mark the intersection of the towns of Farmington, Perinton, Victor, and Macedon. Around 1881, teams of horses drew the giant boulder to this spot to replace an earlier monument established by Hugh Maxwell for Oliver Phelps and Nathaniel Gorham, the original purchasers of the land. All town surveys had used this marker as a starting point. At various times in its history, the boulder had been accidentally covered and its location lost. Now there is a historic marker at the side of Cline Road marking the location.

# *Five*

# Agriculture, Commerce, and Transportation

Many of the historic locations in Farmington were once active hamlets with their own stores, rail and trolley stations, mills, livestock markets, produce exchanges, creameries, and forges. Some of the names survive—Norton's Mills, Brownsville, Mertensia, Hathaway's Corners, Blacksmith Corners—but today they are only crossroads where the casual traveler sees no clue of these formerly flourishing locales.

At its peak, Pumpkin Hook boasted hotels, taverns, several stores, and factories. The largest district school was located there, and most of the town officers lived there. It was home to a tannery, a blacksmith shop, and manufacturers of brooms, hats, shoes, wagons, and farm implements. Its mills served a wide surrounding area, its churches drew parishioners from nearby towns, and its calendar of social events was attended by residents from all over Ontario and Wayne Counties. The Hook's iris farm supplied fancy perennials to flower lovers and vendors all over the world.

The arrival of the New York State Thruway in the early 1950s and the Finger Lakes Race Track in the early 1960s changed the face of Farmington. In 2010, Farmington's family farms are still important, but they are far fewer in number. The total number of farms in the United States has dropped to a third of the number that existed in 1910, while the average acreage has increased by a factor of three. The amount of land used as farmland has stayed about the same, but the percentage of the U.S. labor force that works on farms is about one-twentieth what it was in 1910.

In 2010, businesses are concentrated along Routes 332 and 96. In 2002 (the most recent year for which U.S. census data is available), the largest categories of employment for Farmington residents were wholesale and retail trade; professional, technical, and scientific services; and accommodation/food services.

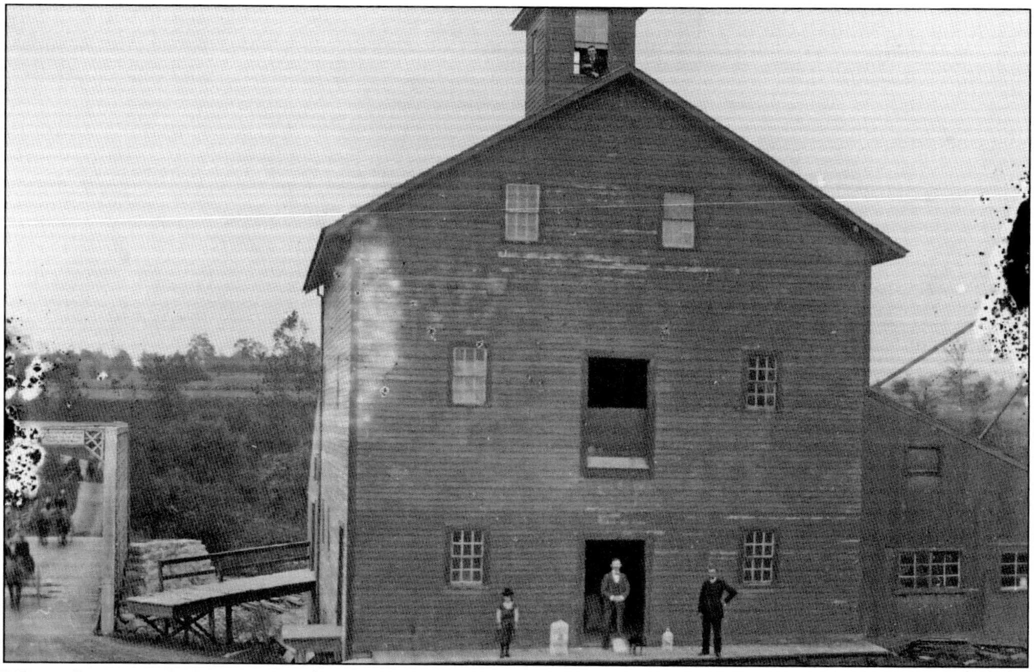

This photograph from 1895 shows two men and a girl in front of the Red Mill, which was built in 1813 by Sunderland Pattison. It was located at the intersection of Allen-Padgham and Pannell Roads, on the north side of Ganargua Creek. Notice the man looking out from the cupola, and the horse-drawn buggies crossing the bridge. A sign over the bridge warns of a fine for anyone crossing at "faster than a walk."

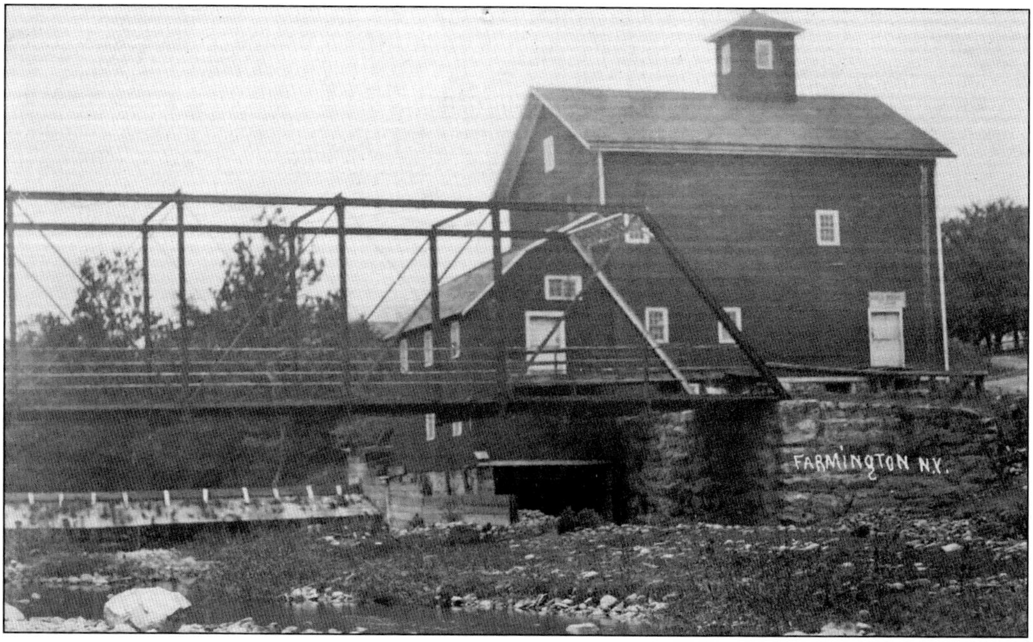


This is a 1913 photograph postcard of the old Red Mill looking upstream. In the message area of the card it reads, "E. F. Allen, Macedon NY. Dear father: That you may live to see many happy returns of your birthday is the wish of your son and daughter. Mr. & Mrs. L. F. Allen. 1843–1913."

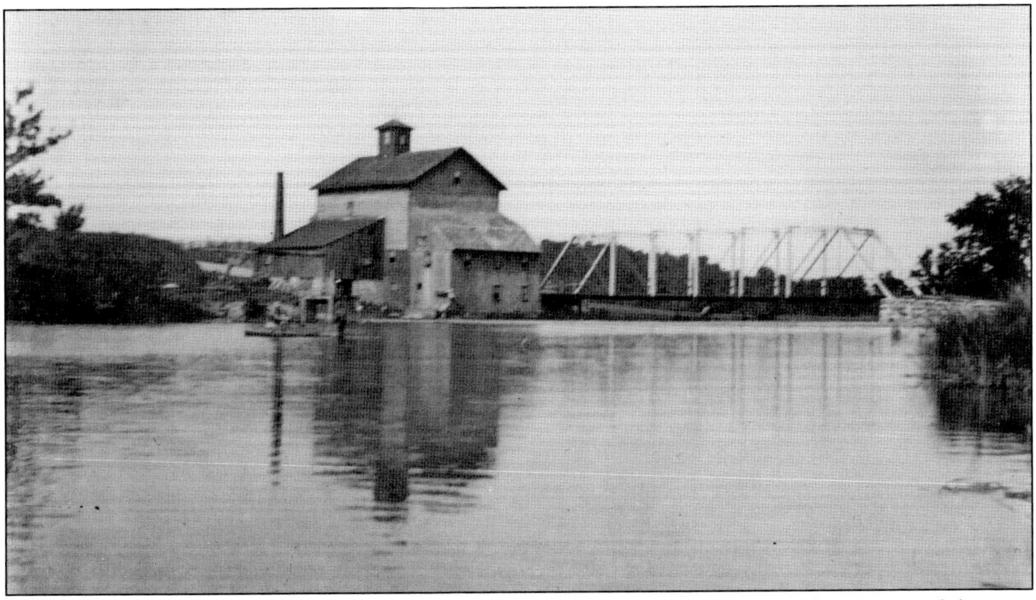

This rare photograph of Sunderland Pattison's mill viewed from upstream shows part of the vast millpond impounded by the dam. In addition to being a miller, Pattison contracted to build a section of the Erie Canal in the early 1820s. He employed several teams of men for that project. The Red Mill burned on February 4, 1945, in the middle of a blizzard.

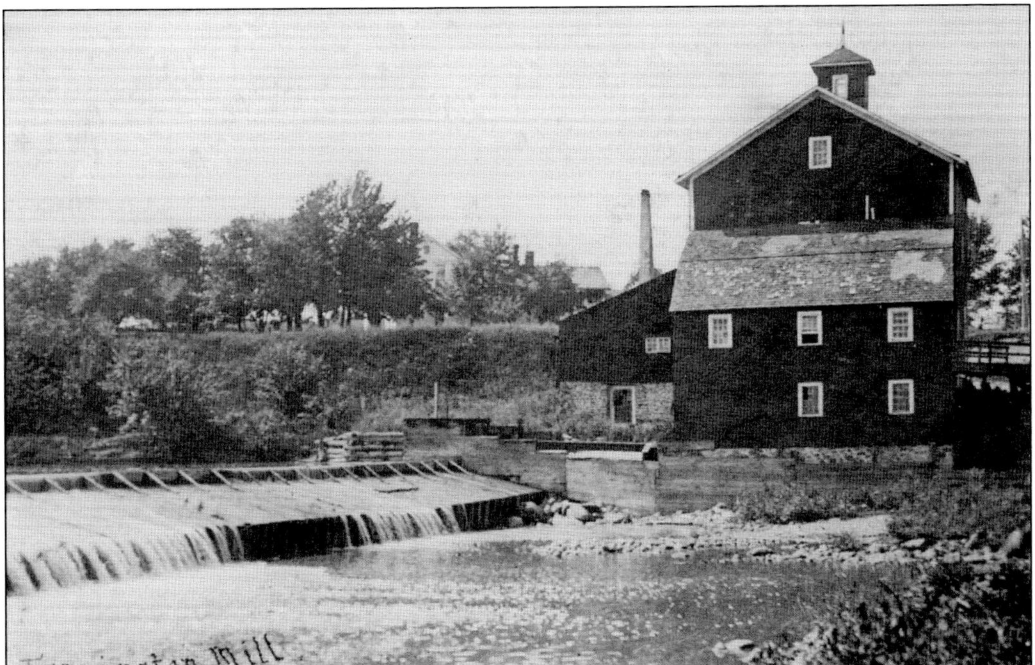


This is the dam and the Pattison mill viewed from the south side of the creek. Through the 1800s, this mill was the principal source of flour for the vicinity. There was also a sawmill at this site. Later Pattison built a canal boat to ship his flour to Albany, New York City, and other localities. The boat was built in Farmington and hauled several miles north to the canal with 40 yoke of oxen.

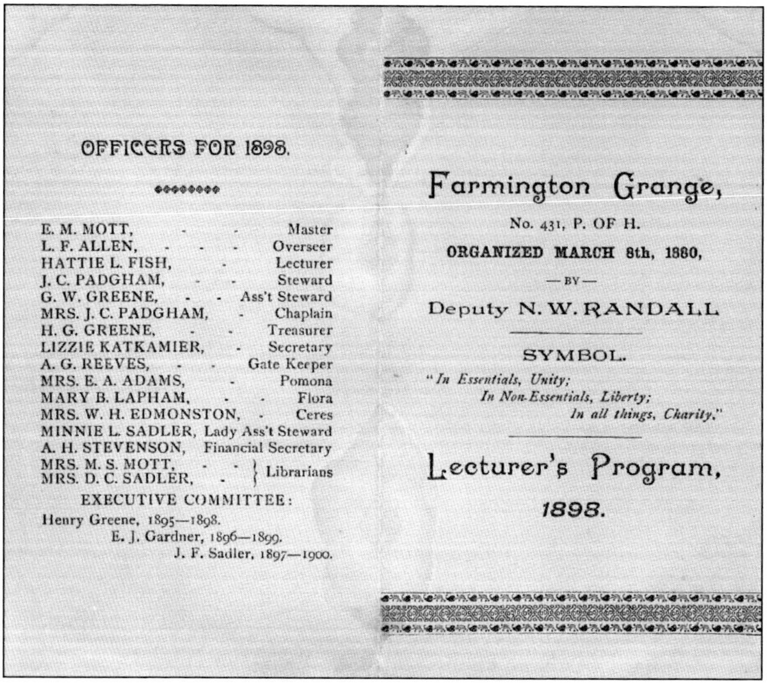

OFFICERS FOR 1898.

| | |
|---|---|
| E. M. MOTT, | Master |
| L. F. ALLEN, | Overseer |
| HATTIE L. FISH, | Lecturer |
| J. C. PADGHAM, | Steward |
| G. W. GREENE, | Ass't Steward |
| MRS. J. C. PADGHAM, | Chaplain |
| H. G. GREENE, | Treasurer |
| LIZZIE KATKAMIER, | Secretary |
| A. G. REEVES, | Gate Keeper |
| MRS. E. A. ADAMS, | Pomona |
| MARY B. LAPHAM, | Flora |
| MRS. W. H. EDMONSTON, | Ceres |
| MINNIE L. SADLER, | Lady Ass't Steward |
| A. H. STEVENSON, | Financial Secretary |
| MRS. M. S. MOTT, MRS. D. C. SADLER, | Librarians |

EXECUTIVE COMMITTEE:

Henry Greene, 1895—1898.
E. J. Gardner, 1896—1899.
J. F. Sadler, 1897—1900.

Farmington Grange,

No. 431, P. OF H.

ORGANIZED MARCH 8th, 1880,

—BY—

Deputy N. W. RANDALL

SYMBOL.

*"In Essentials, Unity;*
*In Non-Essentials, Liberty;*
*In all things, Charity."*

Lecturer's Program,

1898.

This is the printed program for the Farmington Grange's activities in 1898. Events included instruction on agricultural methods, music, debates, and readings from current and classical writers. Topics varied from "What is Happiness And Where Can It Be Found" to "Housekeeping versus Homekeeping" and "Should Farmers Take a Vacation?" The grange was a major social force in rural areas.

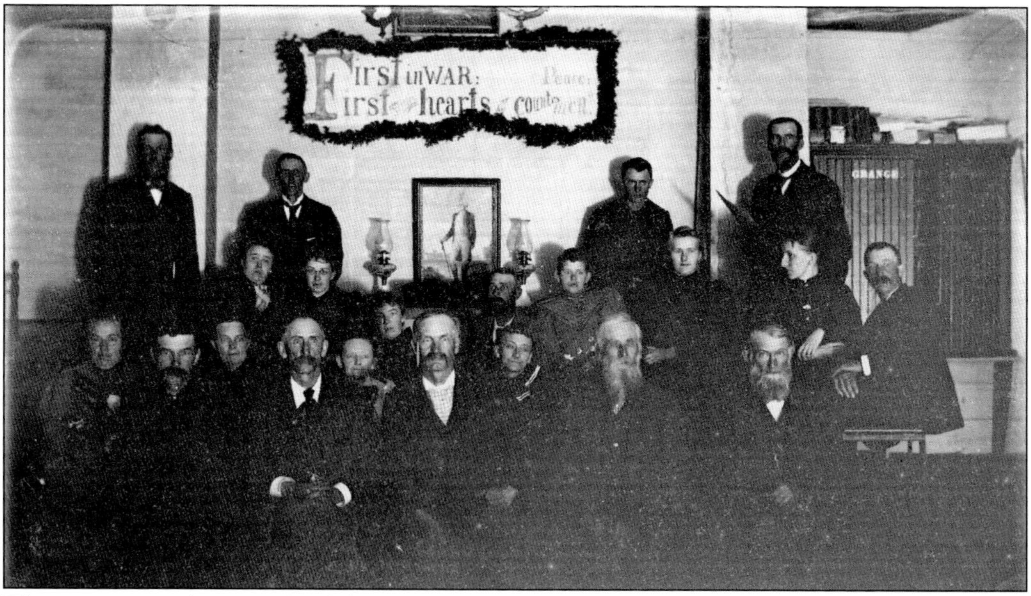


This is a group photograph of the members of the Farmington Grange around 1900. Among those in the image are Bert Stevenson, Hattie Fish, George Greene, and Matie Lapham. Note the framed portrait of George Washington and the related Henry Lee quote on the wall behind the group.

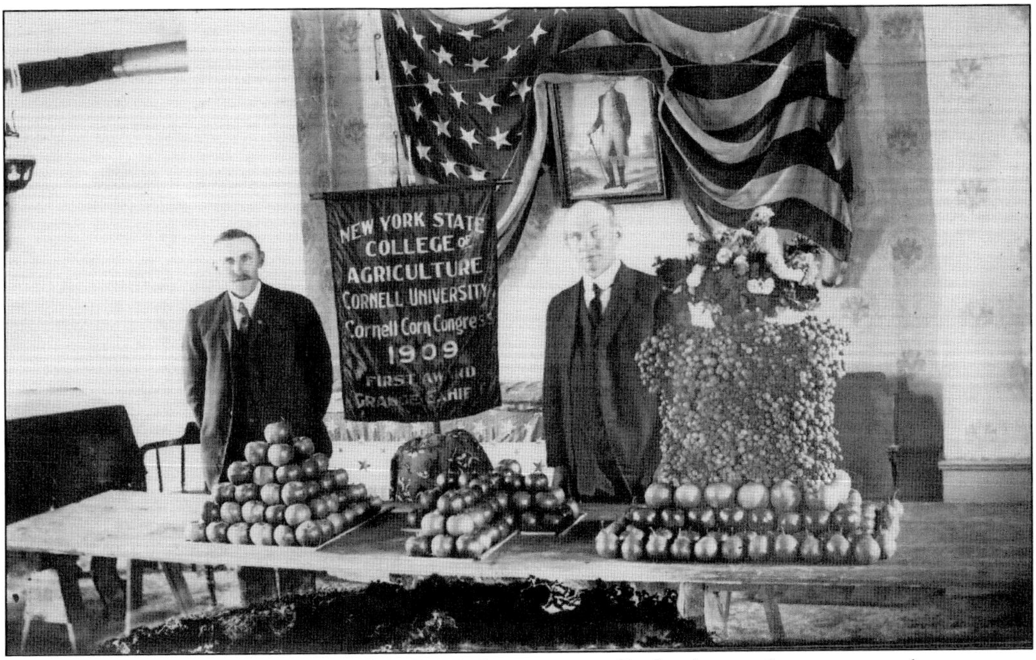


Lewis F. Allen, grange master, and A. B. Katkamier proudly display apples, pears, and grapes at a 1909 exhibit of the Farmington Grange. Behind them is a prize banner from the New York State College of Agriculture at Cornell University.

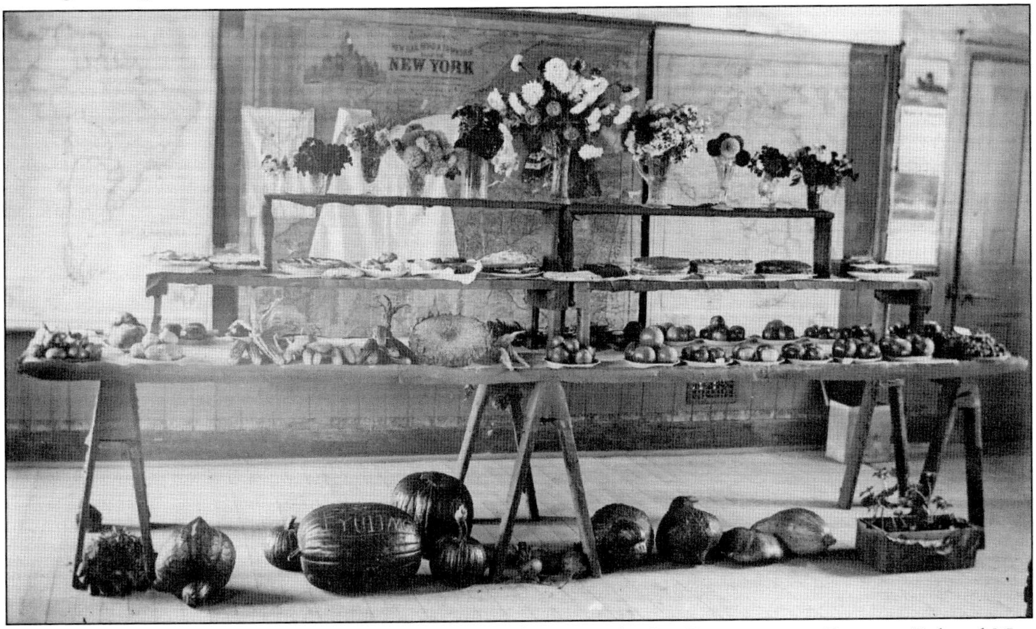


This photograph shows a grange display of produce inside the Farmington District School No. 12 school. One of the large squashes has been engraved with the name of the farm it came from. The grange (also known as the Patrons of Husbandry) was founded by farmers in 1828 in nearby Chautauqua County. Its mission was to act as an organized political and commercial force for farmers. By 1876, there were 30,000 local granges across the country, with nearly 2.5 million members.

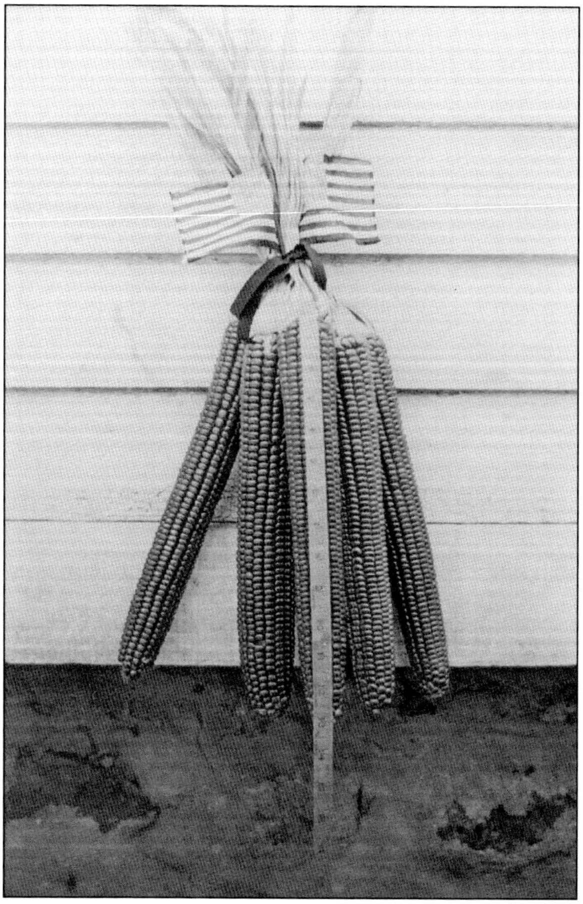

These are Farmington's prizewinning ears of corn, with a silk ribbon awarded by the "Corn Congress" at the New York State College of Agriculture in 1909. The tape measure in front shows one ear to be 13 inches long.

This early cobblestone building was popularly known as the Stone Shops and was erected by the Hathaways around 1820. At various times it housed a wagon shop, a paint shop, and a factory for the production of all kinds of edged tools such as axes, shovels, and chisels. A grindstone 4 feet in diameter and 8 inches thick was turned by a horse-powered sweep for sharpening implements. The building stood north and east of the current Lutheran church in the Pumpkin Hook area. After a long period of deterioration, the building was demolished. Some of the stones were recycled and used in road construction.

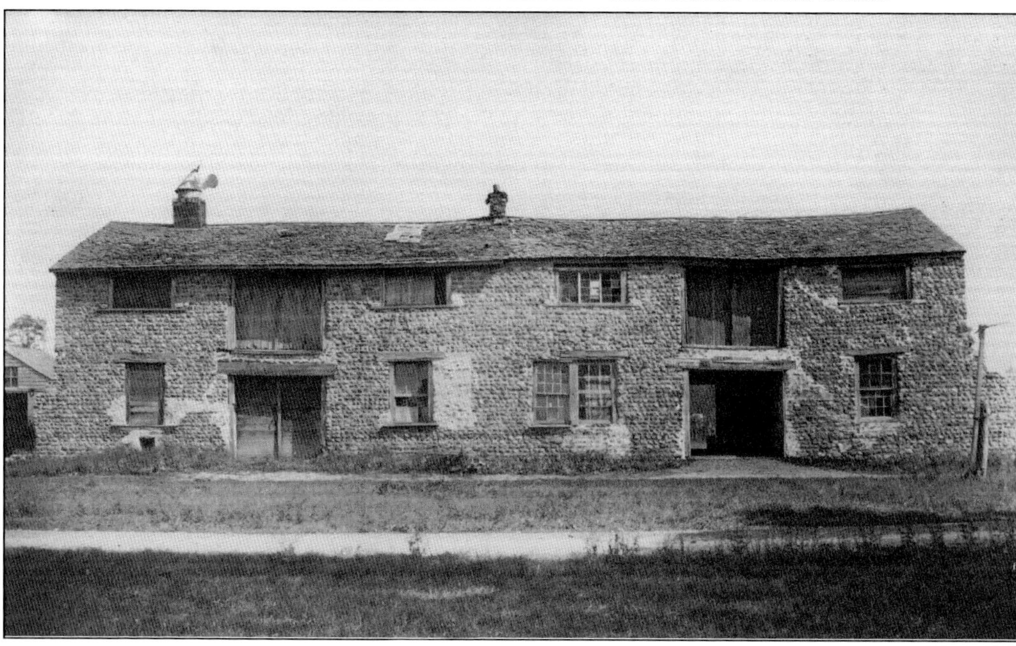

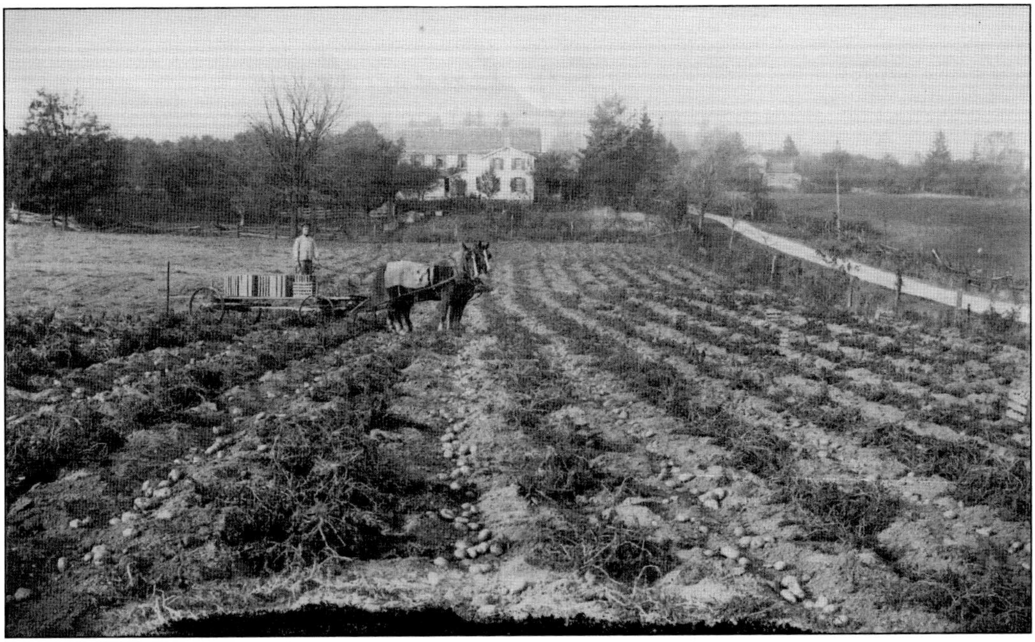

Lindley Gardner and his horse-drawn wagon collect an abundant potato harvest. Several crates of potatoes are already on the wagon. Before modern harvesting equipment was developed, harvesting potatoes and most other ground crops was backbreaking manual labor. The Gardner home at 238 Hook Road is visible in the background.

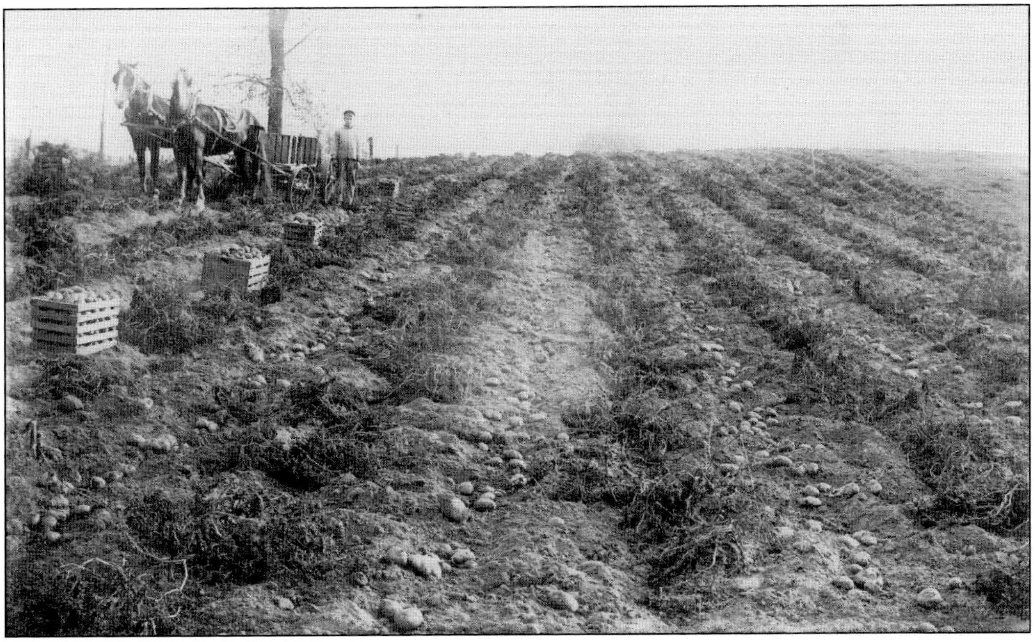

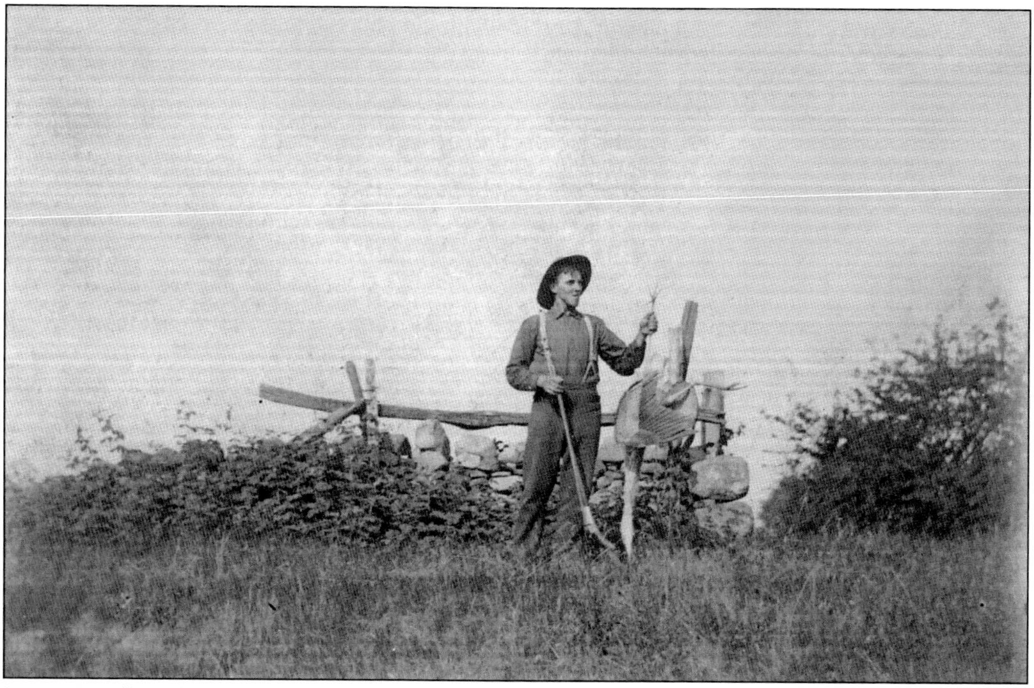

Lewis F. Allen shows off the result of a successful hunt for a wild goose about 1900. In 2010, Farmington still has open spaces that support a native game population, especially in the eastern part of town.

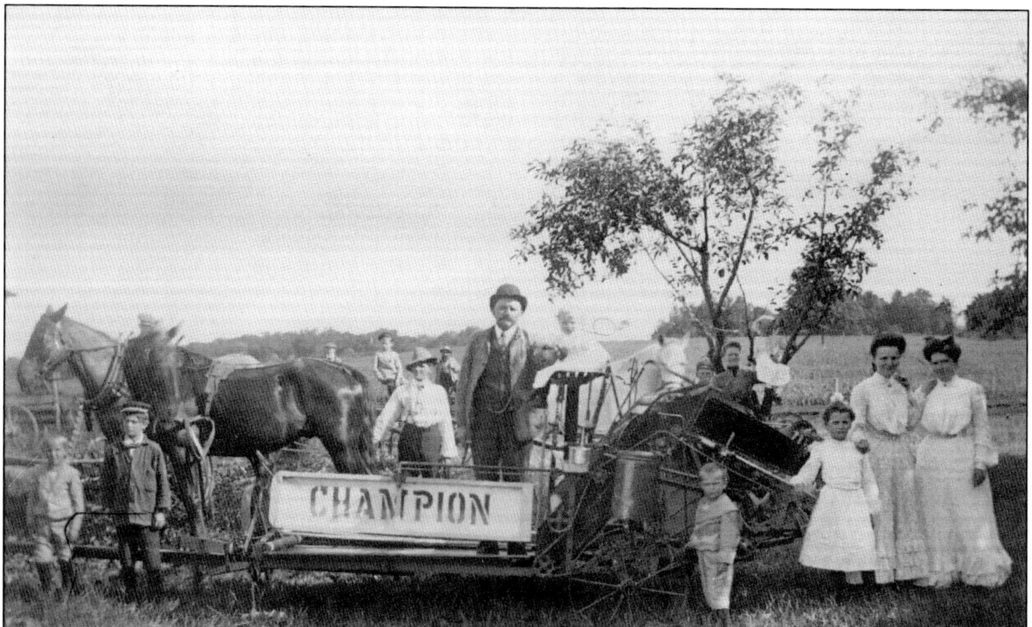


Here the Crowley family, who lived in the Brownsville neighborhood, pose with their Champion grain binder. The Champion brand was made by the Ellis Keystone Company for many decades. The model shown is a horse-drawn machine with traction wheels that power the mechanism. Mr. Crowley sold farm implements for many years.

In this 1956 photograph, Lewis F. Allen stands on one of the last logs harvested from the old millpond site, where they had been growing since 1916.

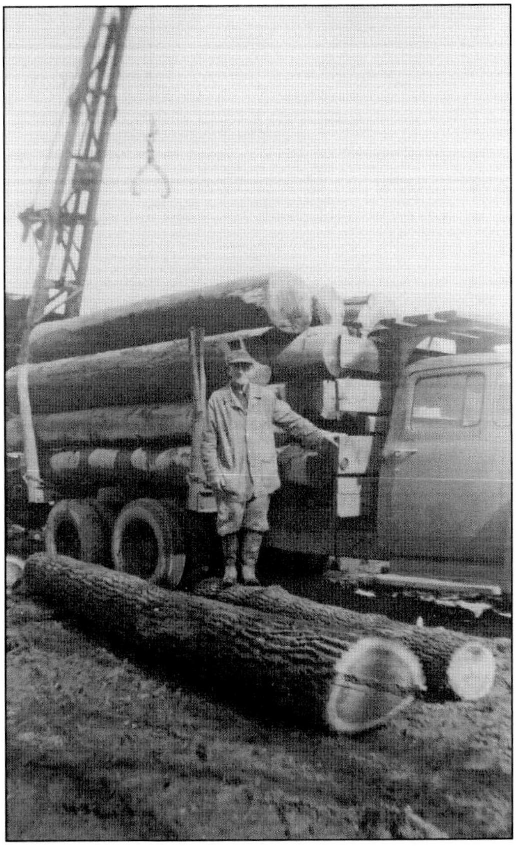

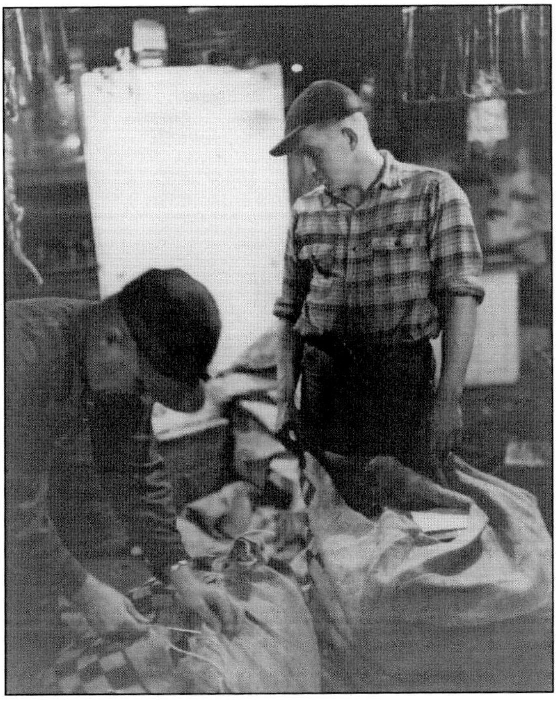

Arthur Herendeen and his son Allen are busy sorting furs in the winter of 1953. The Herendeens ran a successful fur business from the family farm on Allen-Padgham Road.

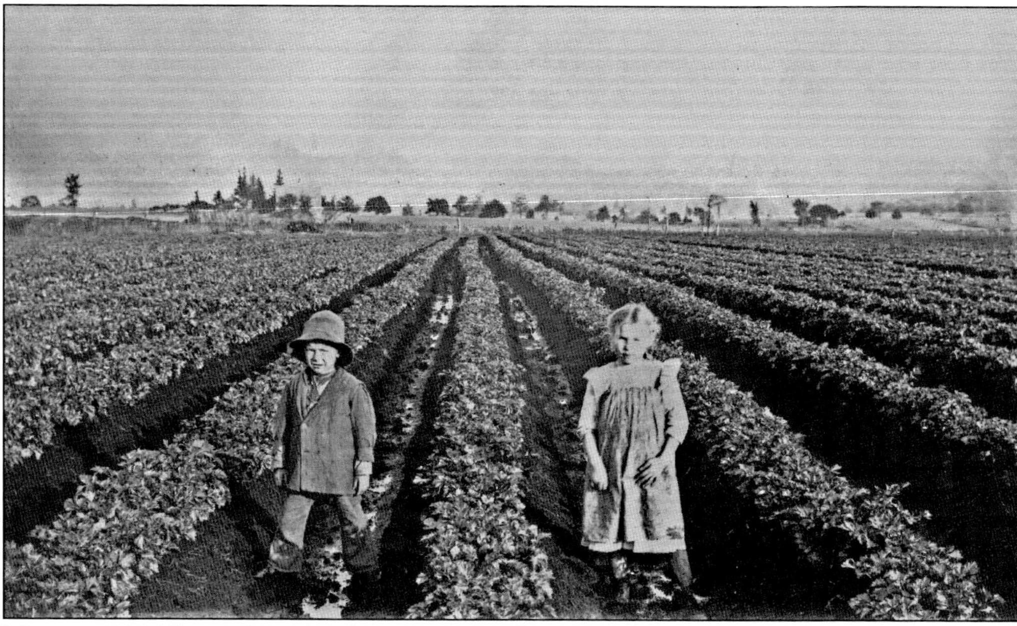

Margaret V. Miller and her brother are pictured in the early 1900s standing among the celery plants in the muck land of local farmer Verstraete. Farmington is home to several strips of rich organic muck land, which are perfect for growing root crops.

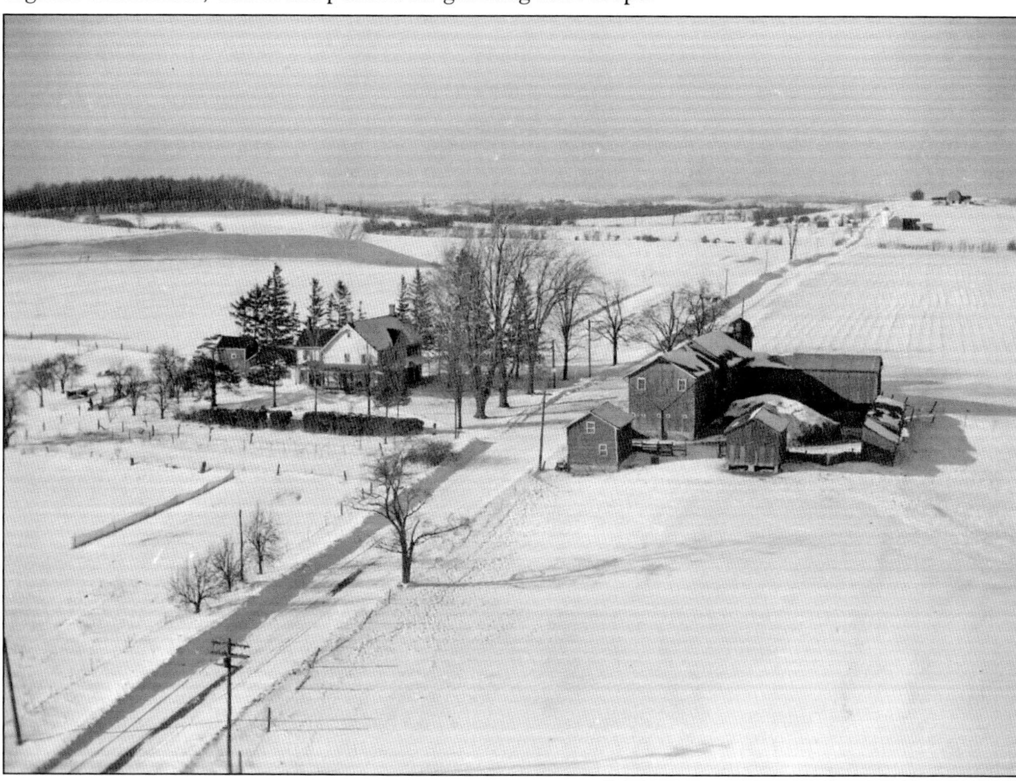

This aerial photograph of the farm on Allen-Padgham Road was taken in 1948, when it had been the homestead of the Allen family for 100 years.

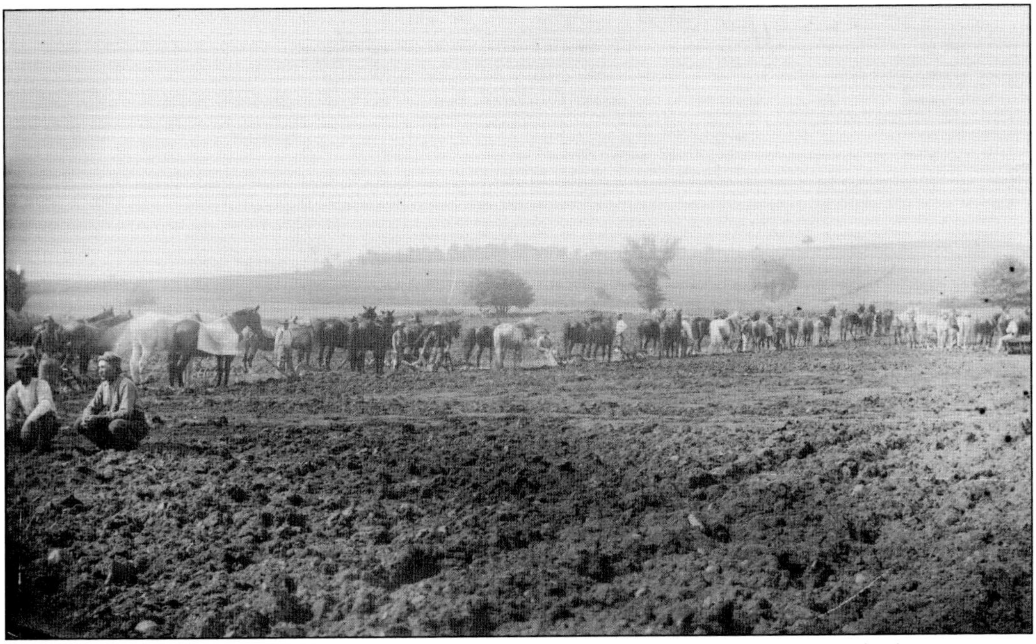

This is an undated photograph of Bert Stevenson's "plowing bee." A big crowd of Farmington men and horses has converged to plow a neighbor's field. These teams would move from field to field until all had been plowed. The Bert Stevenson farm was on the southeast corner of County Road 8 and Holtz Road. In the early 1900s it was known as Roselawn Farm.

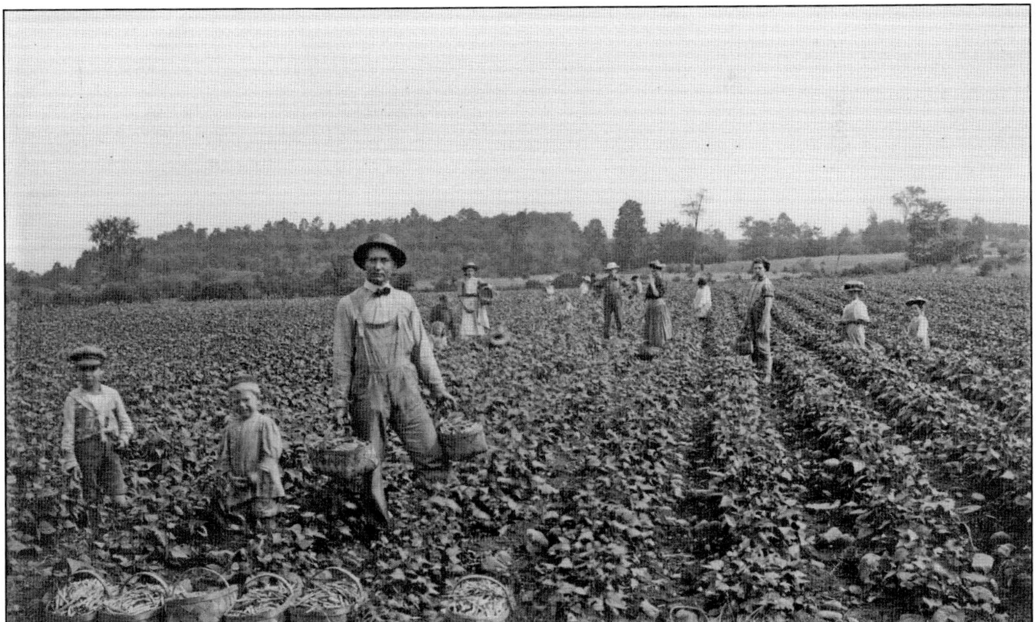

A. B. Katkamier is the man supervising the picking of string beans. In the early 1900s, it was customary to wear a hat, collar, and tie—even in the field. Harvesting was a family effort; men, women, and children all pitched in.

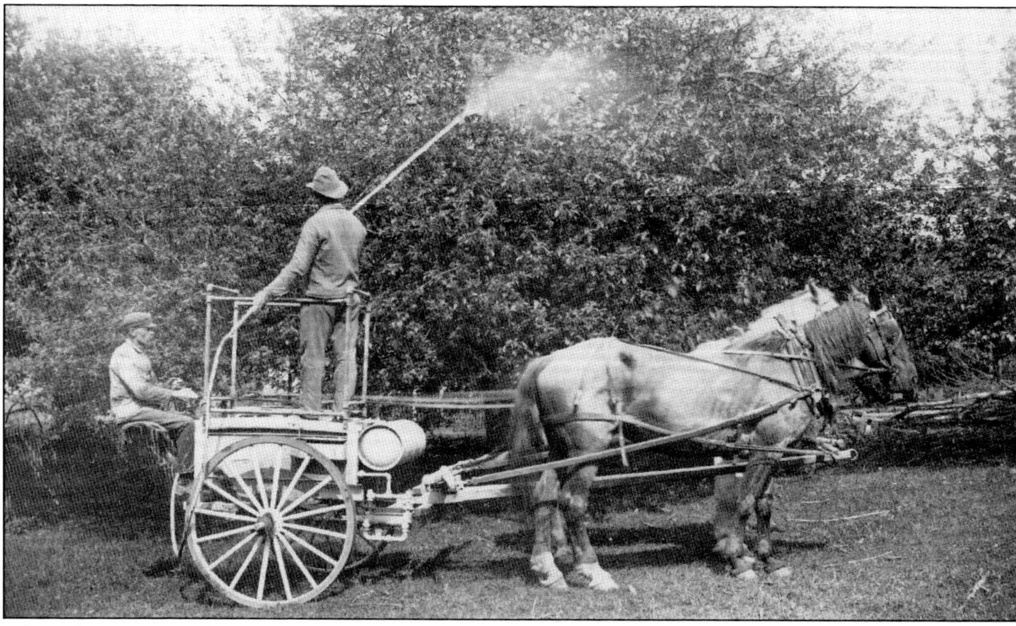

This photograph shows Richard S. "Vet" Buckley conducting the first orchard spraying in the Farmington area, with Fritz Schroth as the driver. Many of the chemicals once sprayed to protect orchards from agricultural pests are no longer used because of potential damage to the environment as well as people.

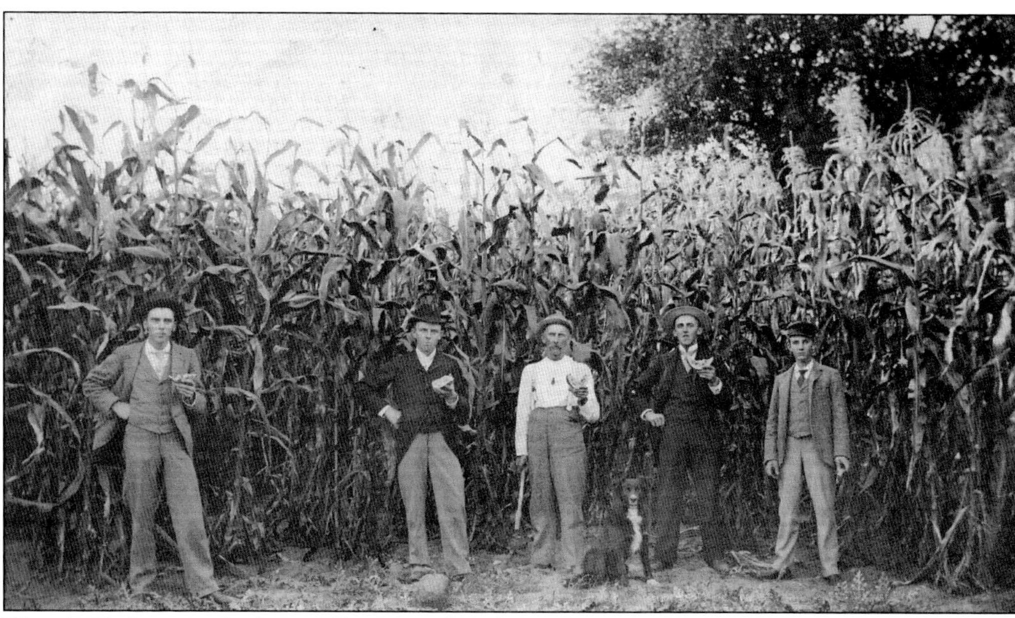

This 1895 photograph shows Ellery G. Allen (center) and his sons, (from left to right) George, Charles, Lewis, and Willard, eating watermelon beside the tall corn.

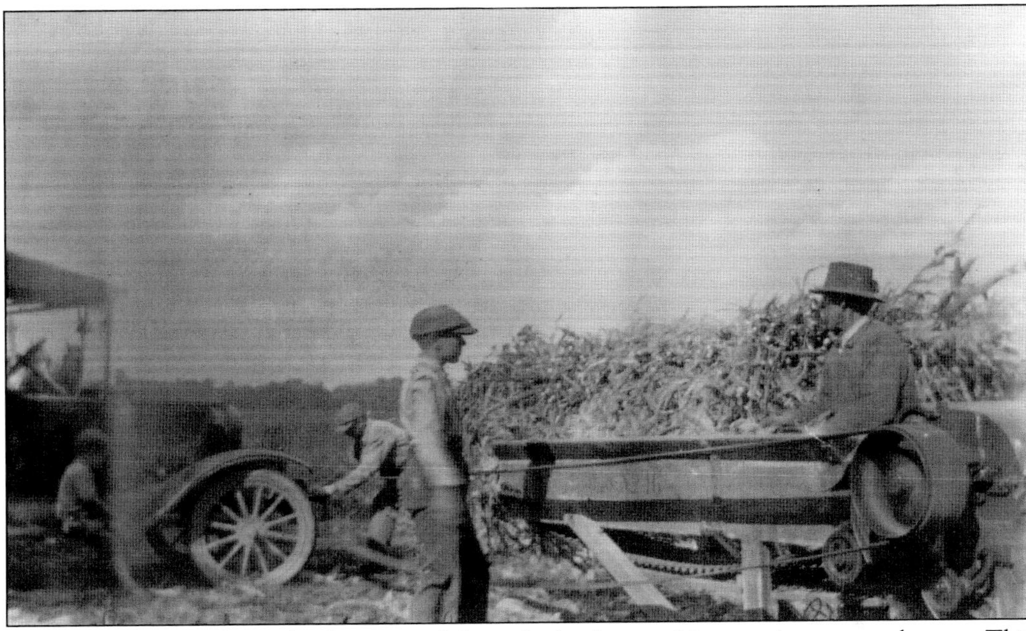

In 1938, a long belt driven by the automobile in the background is powering a corn chopper. This was a less expensive alternative to tractors or specialized machines for each job.

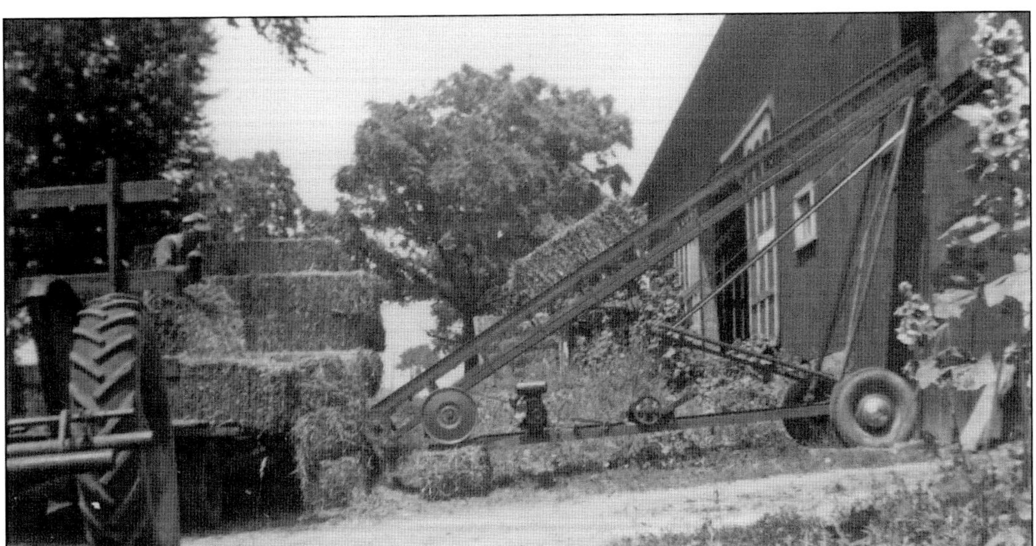

In 1948, loading hay bales into the barn is made easier with a gasoline-powered elevator.

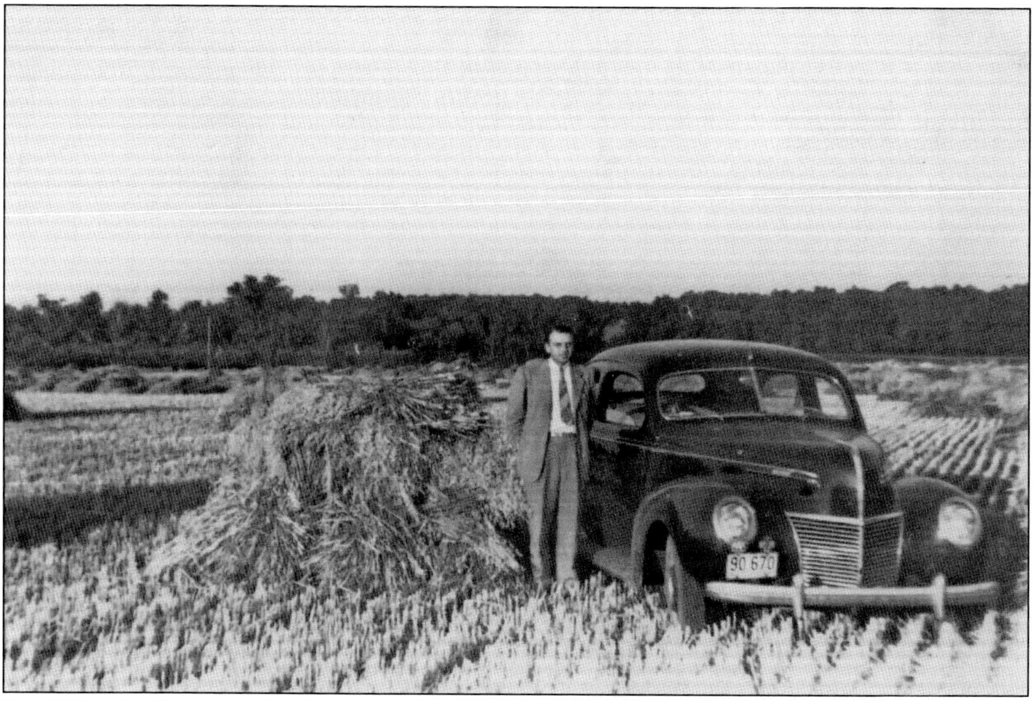

Dr. Willard Allen drove his brand-new car out into the field on the family farm to pose for this photograph in 1940.

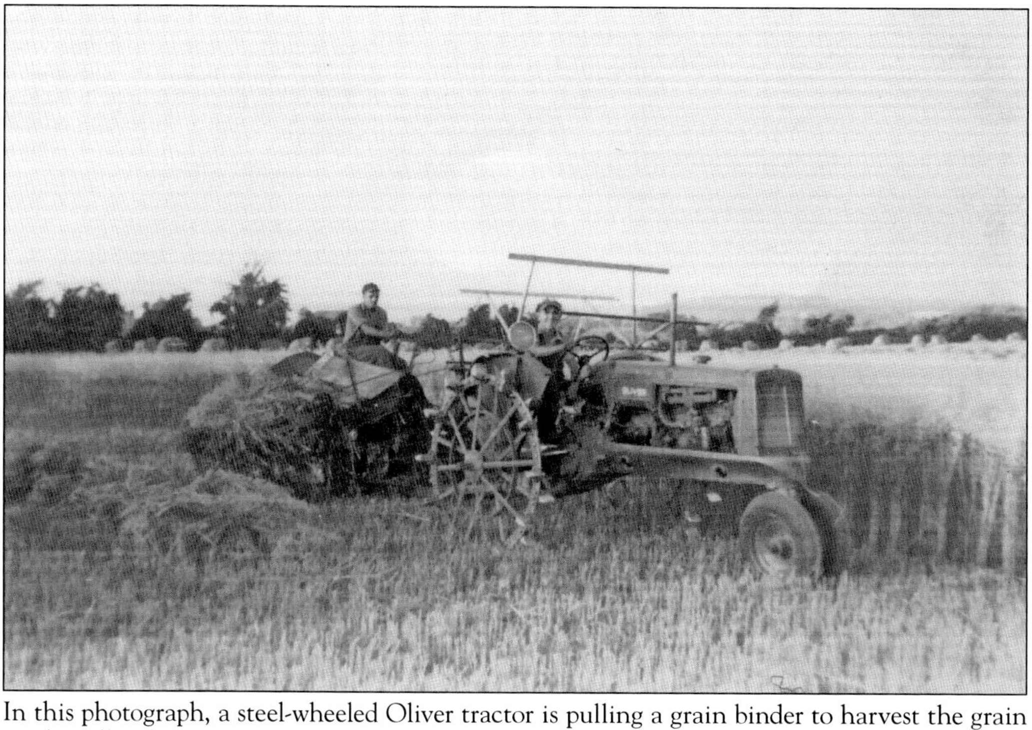

In this photograph, a steel-wheeled Oliver tractor is pulling a grain binder to harvest the grain on the Allen farm in 1940. Rubber tractor tires only became standard in the mid-1930s. By 1940, 95 percent of tractors had rubber tires.

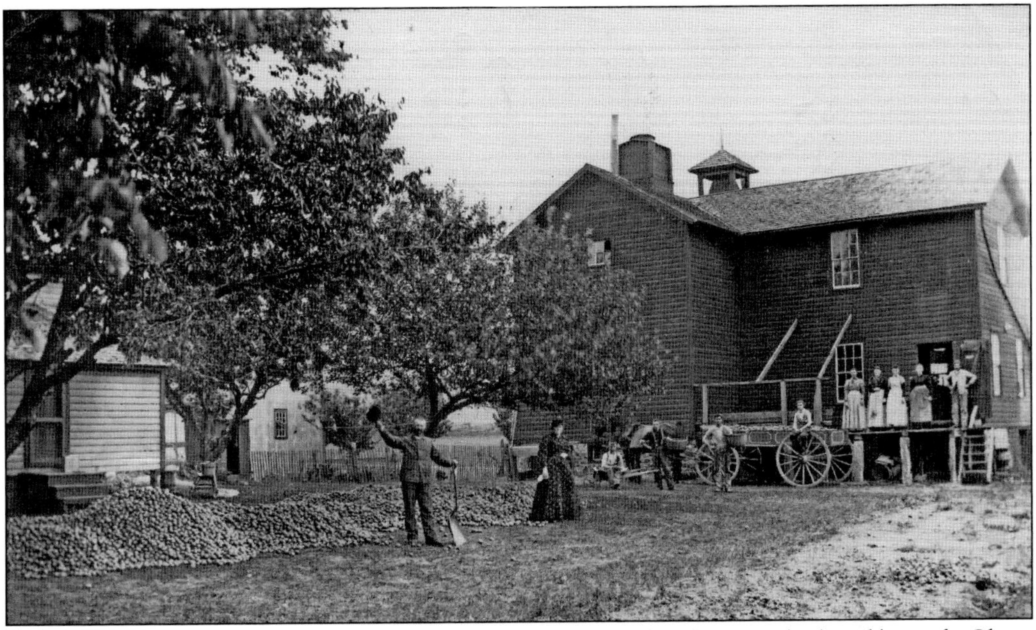

This 1910 photograph shows Charles H. Gardner (waving to the photographer) and his wife, Clara. Gardner's apple-drying house is in the background. Before commercial refrigeration was widely available, forced hot-air drying was an alternative way to preserve fruits. Some other individuals in this photograph are Ernest Crocker, Adelia Powers, and Ann Eliza Markham.

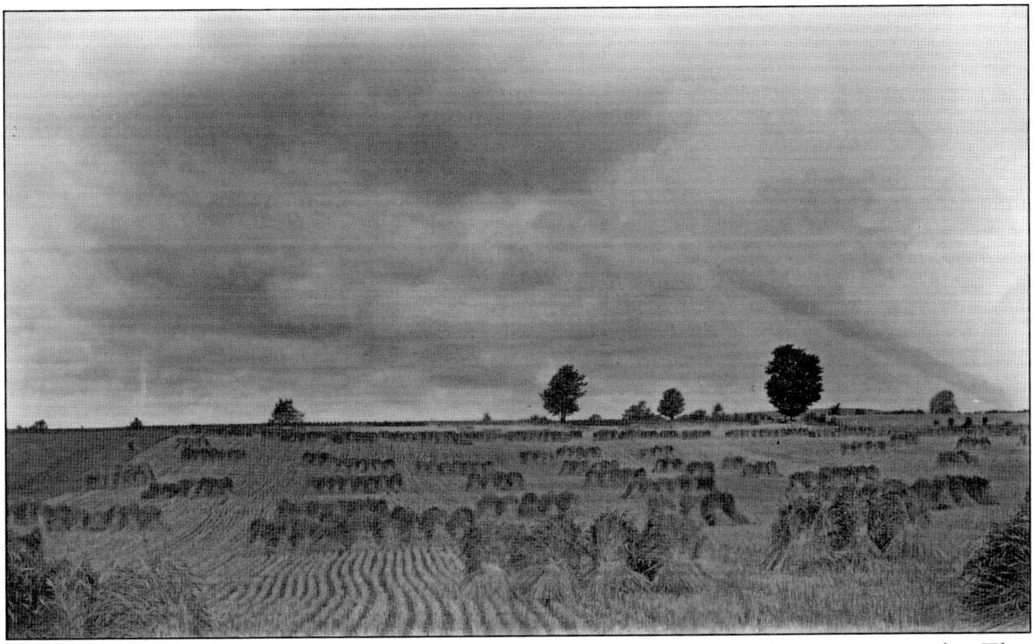

Seen here at harvest time, shocks of grain are stacked under a cloudy Farmington sky. This photograph of a bountiful harvest was taken in a field south of what was known as the "Gravel Pit House" at 320 County Road 8.

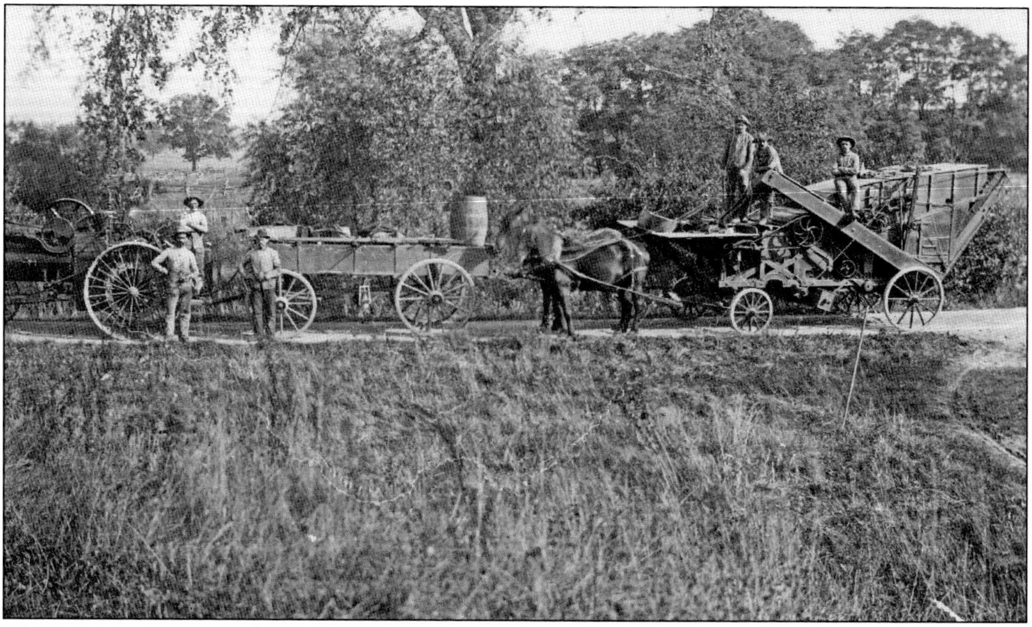

The inscription states that one of these men is James Neary, and this is a threshing outfit. The wagon between the two pieces of machinery probably carries the tools and spare parts along with water and fuel for the steam engine. Many farmers could not afford their own threshing machine, so they relied on equipment like this, which moved around the neighborhood. Each farmer's family would feed the crew when it visited their farm. Unlike most such rigs, this one has a built-in elevator.

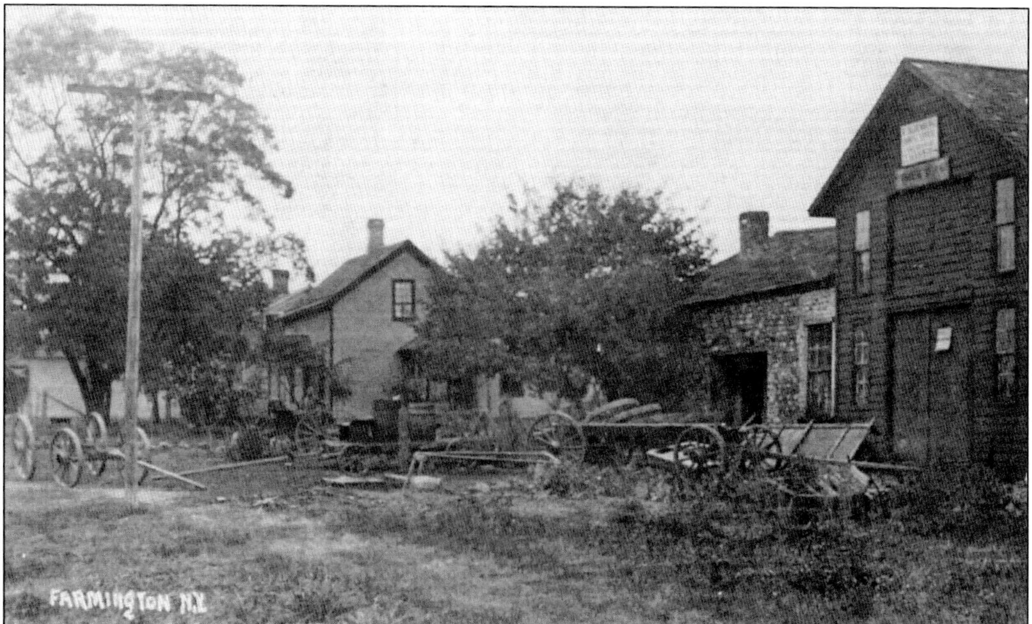


Wagon and carriage parts are piled outside a Farmington carriage shop on Allen-Padgham Road in this photo post card from the early 1900s. The building was near the former Betz store; it no longer exists.

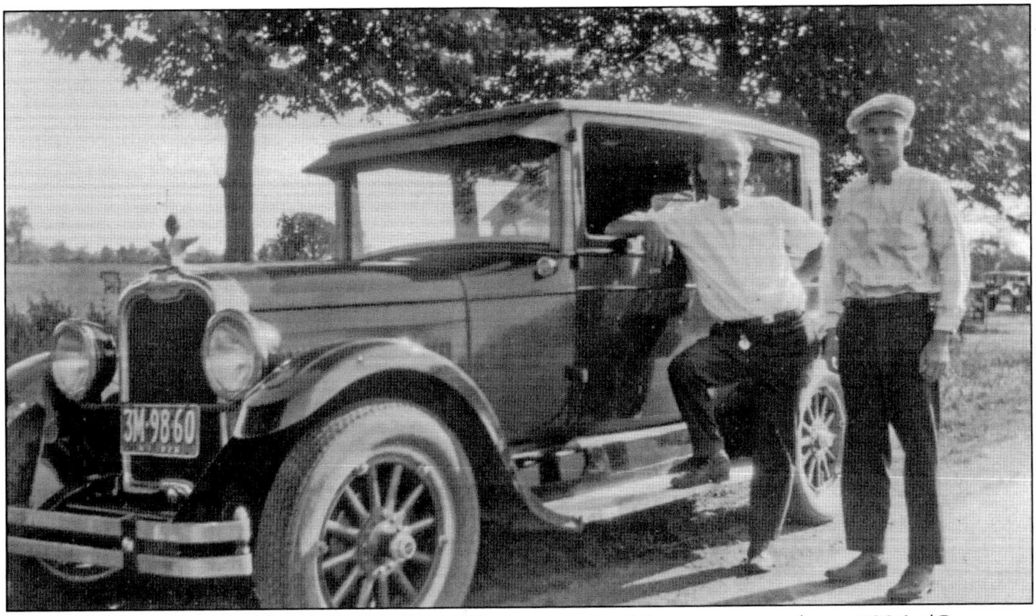


Farmingtonians Jim Schrader and Chet Mincer pose with a new car about 1926. (Courtesy Don Ford.)

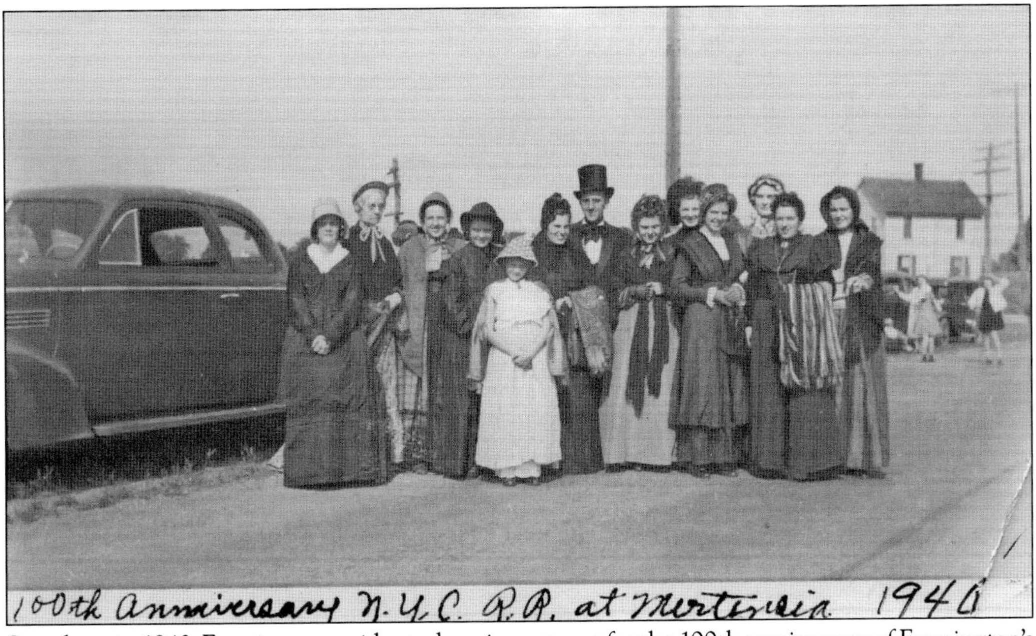


Seen here in 1940, Farmington residents dress in costume for the 100th anniversary of Farmington's railroad line at the Mertensia crossing. Among those pictured are Elma and Elsie Baker, Eleanor Purdy, Herbert Allen, and Virginia Hathaway.

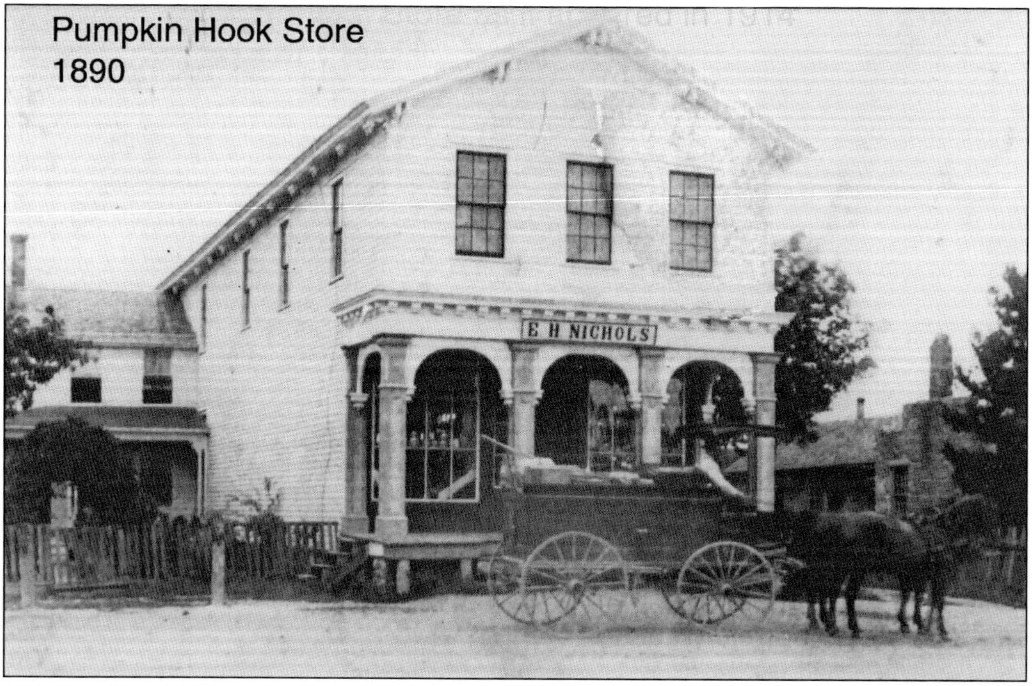


A merchant with a wagonload of goods has stopped in front of the Nichols store in Pumpkin Hook about 1890. There was a store in this building for generations. At one time, the second floor served as a community center and dance hall.

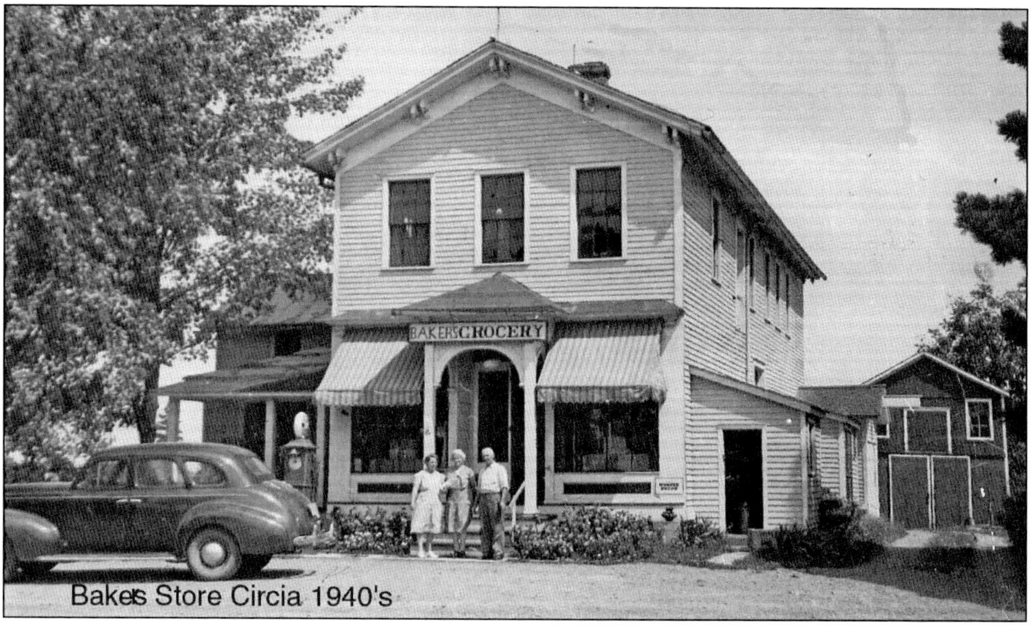


In 1940, the general store was operated by Adeline and Albert Baker. The building ceased to be a store sometime in the early 2000s.

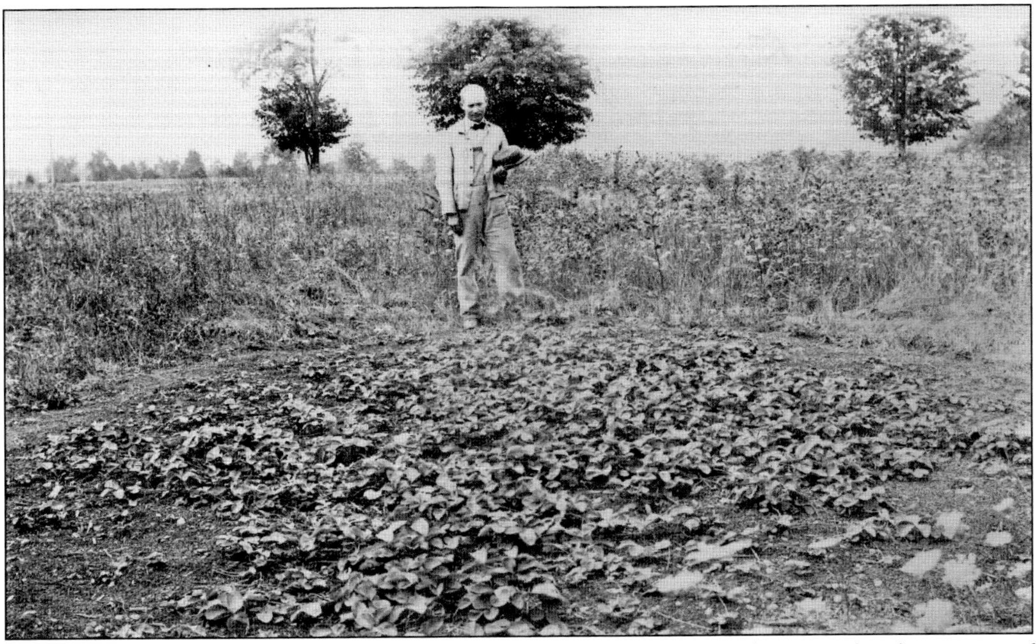

The caption on this photograph identifies this man as A. B. Katkamier, the discoverer of the "Granger" strawberry, standing in a patch of his strawberries. Mr. Katkamier was a noted horticulturist, plant hybridizer, and lecturer. He also operated the Iris Farm in Pumpkin Hook for many years.

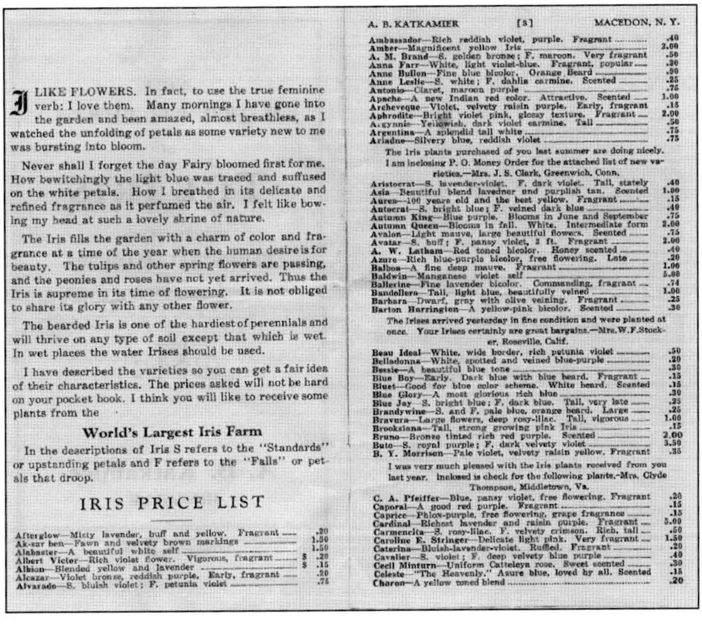

I LIKE FLOWERS. In fact, to use the true feminine verb: I love them. Many mornings I have gone into the garden and been amazed, almost breathless, as I watched the unfolding of petals as some variety new to me was bursting into bloom.

Never shall I forget the day Fairy bloomed first for me. How bewitchingly the light blue was traced and suffused on the white petals. How I breathed in its delicate and refined fragrance as it perfumed the air. I felt like bowing my head at such a lovely shrine of nature.

The Iris fills the garden with a charm of color and fragrance at a time of the year when the human desire is for beauty. The tulips and other spring flowers are passing, and the peonies and roses have not yet arrived. Thus the Iris is supreme in its time of flowering. It is not obliged to share its glory with any other flower.

The bearded Iris is one of the hardiest of perennials and will thrive on any type of soil except that which is wet. In wet places the water Irises should be used.

I have described the varieties so you can get a fair idea of their characteristics. The prices asked will not be hard on your pocket book. I think you will like to receive some plants from the

**World's Largest Iris Farm**

In the descriptions of Iris S refers to the "Standards" or upstanding petals and F refers to the "Falls" or petals that droop.

## IRIS PRICE LIST

| | | |
|---|---|---|
| **Afterglow**—Misty lavender, buff and yellow. Fragrant | | .20 |
| **Ak-sar ben**—Fawn and velvety brown markings | | 1.50 |
| **Alabaster**—A beautiful white self | | 1.50 |
| **Albert Victor**—Rich violet flower. Vigorous, fragrant | $ | .20 |
| **Albion**—Blended yellow and lavender | $ | .15 |
| **Alcazar**—Violet bronze, reddish purple. Early, fragrant | | .20 |
| **Alvarado**—S. bluish violet; F. petunia violet | | .75 |

A. B. KATKAMIER [3] MACEDON, N. Y.

| | |
|---|---|
| **Ambassador**—Rich reddish violet, purple. Fragrant | .40 |
| **Amber**—Magnificent yellow Iris | 2.00 |
| **A. M. Brand**—S. golden bronze; F. maroon. Very fragrant | .50 |
| **Anna Farr**—White, light violet-blue. Fragrant, popular | .30 |
| **Anne Bullen**—Fine blue bicolor. Orange Beard | .90 |
| **Anne Leslie**—S. white; F. dahlia carmine. Scented | .25 |
| **Antonio**—Claret, maroon purple | .75 |
| **Apache**—A new Indian red color. Attractive. Scented | 1.00 |
| **Archeveque**—Violet, velvety raisin purple. Early, fragrant | .15 |
| **Aphrodite**—Bright violet pink, glossy texture. Fragrant | 2.00 |
| **Argynnis**—Yellowish, dark violet carmine. Tall | .50 |
| **Argentina**—A splendid tall white | .75 |
| **Ariadne**—Silvery blue, reddish violet | .75 |

The Iris plants purchased of you last summer are doing nicely. I am inclosing P. O. Money Order for the attached list of new varieties.—Mrs. J. S. Clark, Greenwich, Conn.

| | |
|---|---|
| **Aristocrat**—S. lavender-violet. F. dark violet. Tall, stately | .40 |
| **Asia**—Beautiful blend lavedner and purplish tan. Scented | 1.00 |
| **Aurea**—100 years old and the best yellow. Fragrant | .15 |
| **Autocrat**—S. bright blue; F. veined dark blue | .40 |
| **Autumn King**—Blue purple. Blooms in June and September | .75 |
| **Autumn Queen**—Blooms in fall. White. Intermediate form | 2.00 |
| **Avalon**—Light mauve, large beautiful flowers. Scented | .75 |
| **Avatar**—S. buff; F. pansy violet, 3 ft. Fragrant | 2.00 |
| **A. W. Latham**—Red toned bicolor. Honey scented | .40 |
| **Azure**—Rich blue-purple bicolor, free flowering. Late | .20 |
| **Balboa**—A fine deep mauve. Fragrant | 1.00 |
| **Baldwin**—Manganese violet self | 5.00 |
| **Ballerine**—Fine lavender bicolor. Commanding, fragrant | .74 |
| **Bandollera**—Tall, light blue, beautifully veined | 1.00 |
| **Barbara**—Dwarf, gray with olive veining. Fragrant | .25 |
| **Barton Harrington**—A yellow-pink bicolor. Scented | .30 |

The Irises arrived yesterday in fine condition and were planted at once. Your Irises certainly are great bargains.—Mrs. W. F. Stocker, Roseville, Calif.

| | |
|---|---|
| **Beau Ideal**—White, wide border, rich petunia violet | .50 |
| **Belladonna**—White, spotted and veined blue-purple | .20 |
| **Bessie**—A beautiful blue tone | .30 |
| **Blue Boy**—Early. Dark blue with blue beard. Fragrant | .15 |
| **Bluet**—Good for blue color scheme. White beard. Scented | .15 |
| **Blue Glory**—A most glorious rich blue | .30 |
| **Blue Jay**—S. bright blue; F. dark blue. Tall, very late | .25 |
| **Brandywine**—S. and F. pale blue, orange beard. Large | .25 |
| **Bravura**—Large flowers, deep rosy-lilac. Tall, vigorous | 1.00 |
| **Brooksiana**—Tall, strong growing pink Iris | .15 |
| **Bruno**—Bronze tinted rich red purple. Scented | 2.00 |
| **Bute**—S. royal purple; F. dark velvety violet | 3.50 |
| **B. Y. Morrison**—Pale violet, velvety raisin yellow. Fragrant | .35 |

I was very much pleased with the Iris plants received from you last year. Inclosed is check for the following plants.—Mrs. Clyde Thompson, Middletown, Va.

| | |
|---|---|
| **C. A. Pfeiffer**—Blue, pansy violet, free flowering. Fragrant | .20 |
| **Caporal**—A good red purple. Fragrant | .15 |
| **Caprice**—Phlox-purple, free flowering, grape fragrance | .15 |
| **Cardinal**—Richest lavender and raisin purple. Fragrant | 5.00 |
| **Carmencita**—S. rosy-lilac. F. velvety crimson. Rich, tall | .50 |
| **Caroline E. Stringer**—Delicate light pink. Very fragrant | 1.50 |
| **Caterina**—Bluish-lavender-violet. Ruffled. Fragrant | .20 |
| **Cavalier**—S. violet; F. deep velvety blue purple | .40 |
| **Cecil Minturn**—Uniform Catteleya rose. Sweet scented | .30 |
| **Celeste**—"The Heavenly." Azure blue, loved by all. Scented | .15 |
| **Charon**—A yellow toned blend | .20 |

This is an inside page of the "World's Largest Iris Farm" 12 page catalog for 1930, with descriptions of some of the varieties sold. Although the catalog shows a Macedon mailing address for the firm, it was actually located in the Town of Farmington. Until Farmington received its own post office and zip code in the fall of 1986, residents' mailing addresses were in one of the five neighboring municipalities.

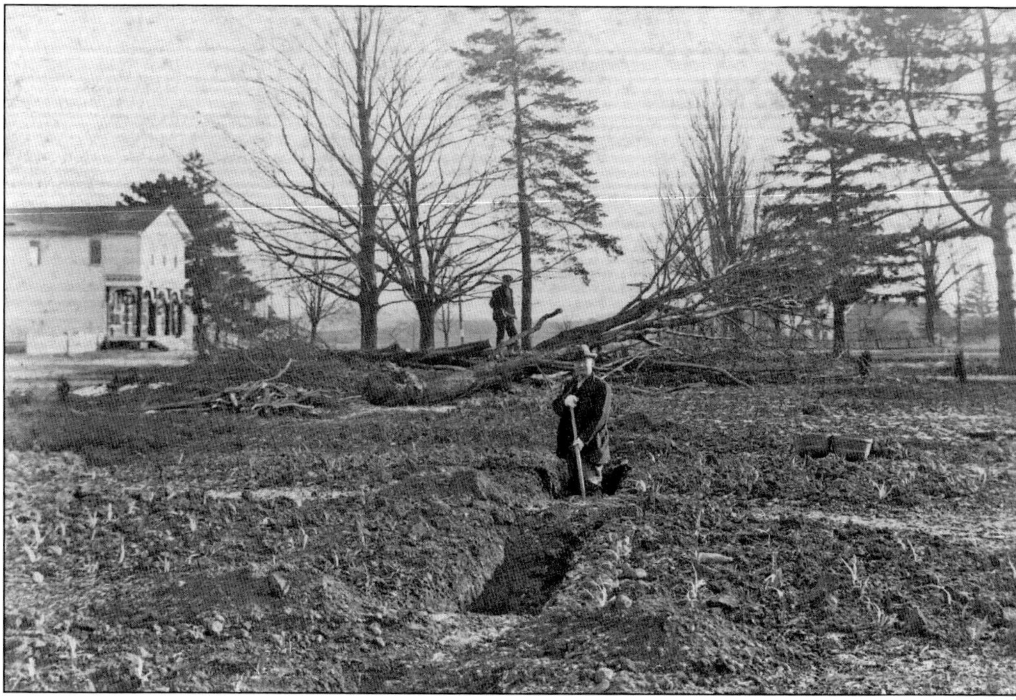

The caption on this undated photograph states, "Reopening gardens." A. B. Katkamier digs a trench near the northeast corner of Hook and Farmington Roads with the Nichols Store in the background. This was the site of the famous Iris Gardens. (Courtesy Diana and Rudy van der Velden.)

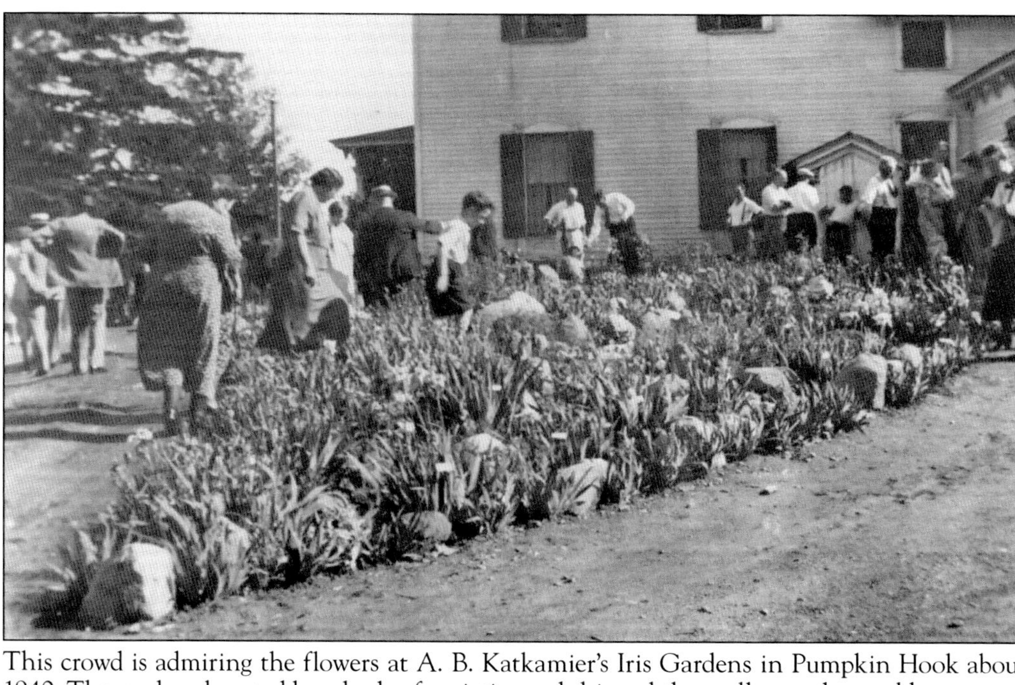

This crowd is admiring the flowers at A. B. Katkamier's Iris Gardens in Pumpkin Hook about 1940. The gardens boasted hundreds of varieties and shipped them all over the world.

Mr. Katkamier called his corner of the Hook "Irisville." Besides irises, he sold peonies, chrysanthemums, oriental poppies, and several other perennial varieties of flowers. (Courtesy Diana and Rudy van der Velden.)

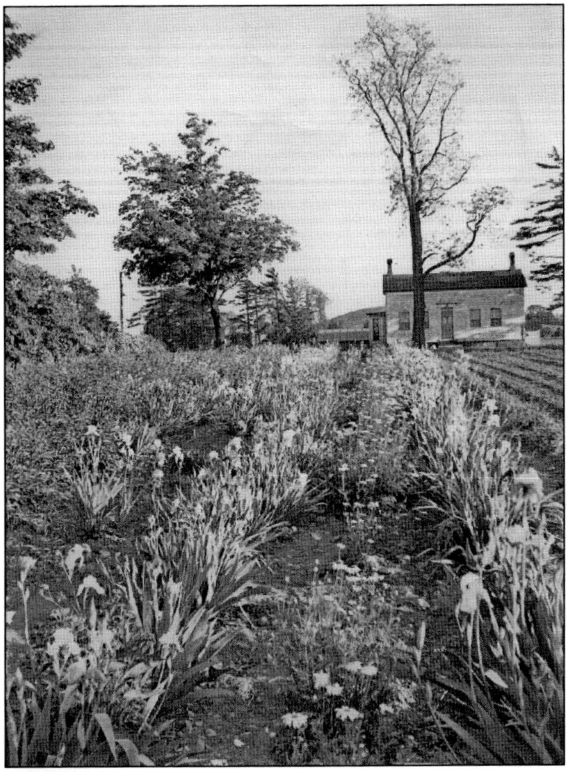

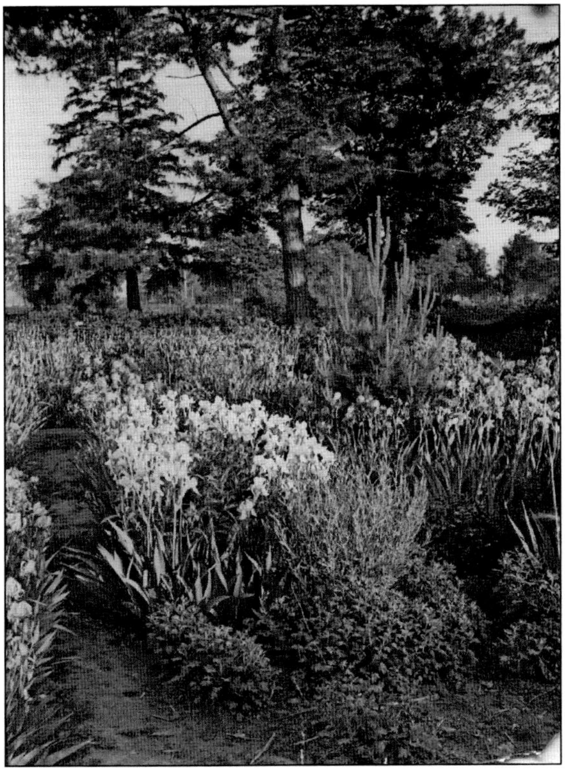

The gardens were across the road from a former hotel at the corner of Allen-Padgham and Hook Roads. Mr. Katkamier purchased that building in 1927. After the Iris Gardens went out of business, the house was opened as a bed-and-breakfast. In 2010, it is once again a private dwelling. (Courtesy Diana and Rudy van der Velden.)

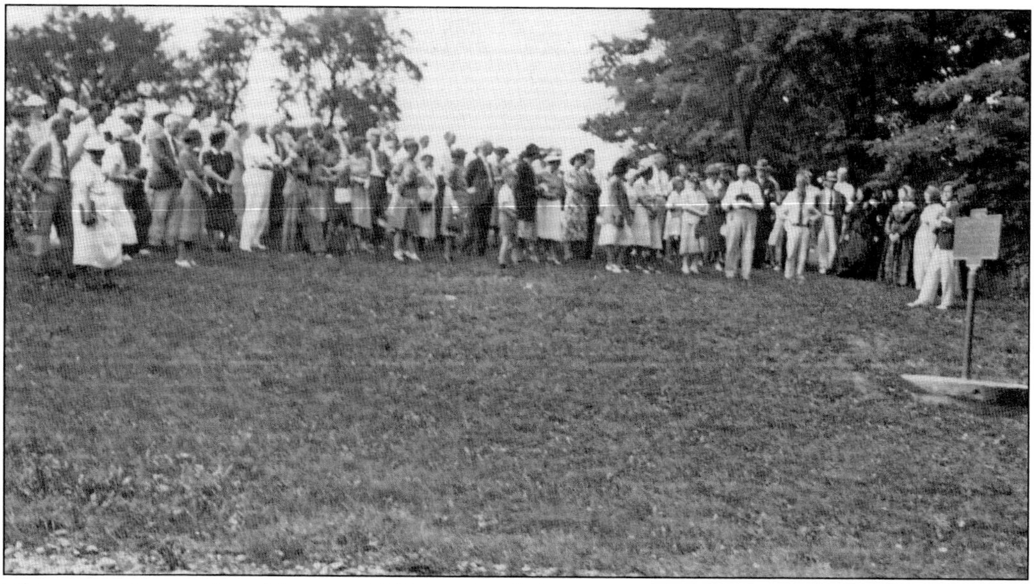

This crowd has gathered here in 1939 for the dedication of the historical marker to the right side of the photograph. It is located in the hamlet of Mertensia, near the northwest corner of Mertensia and Boughton Hill Roads. The marker recognizes one of the first mills in Farmington, which was built by pioneers Jacob and Joseph Smith. It was the site of both grist and saw mills, and both mills burned in the 1800s. Jacob Smith's home at 6272 County Road 41 was built in 1799 and still stands.

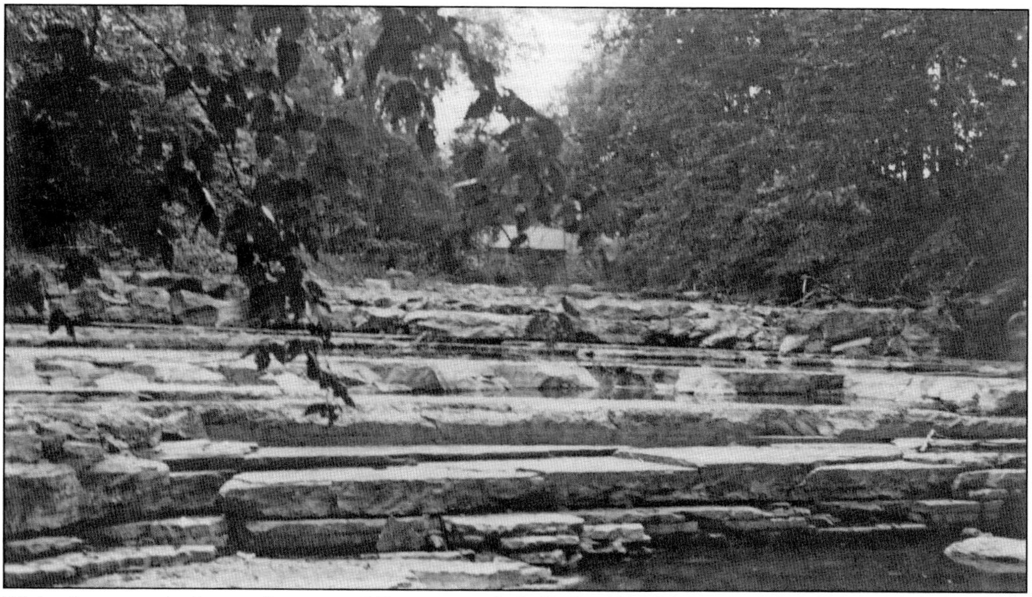

This photograph shows the area of Ganargua (Mud) Creek where it crosses Boughton Hill Road just west of Mertensia Road. This change in elevation provided waterpower for the Smith Mill. Pioneer Nathan Comstock drew logs several miles to this mill for lumber to build the first church and school in Farmington, which was constructed on the site of the present Farmington Friends Church on the corner of County Road 8 and Sheldon Road.

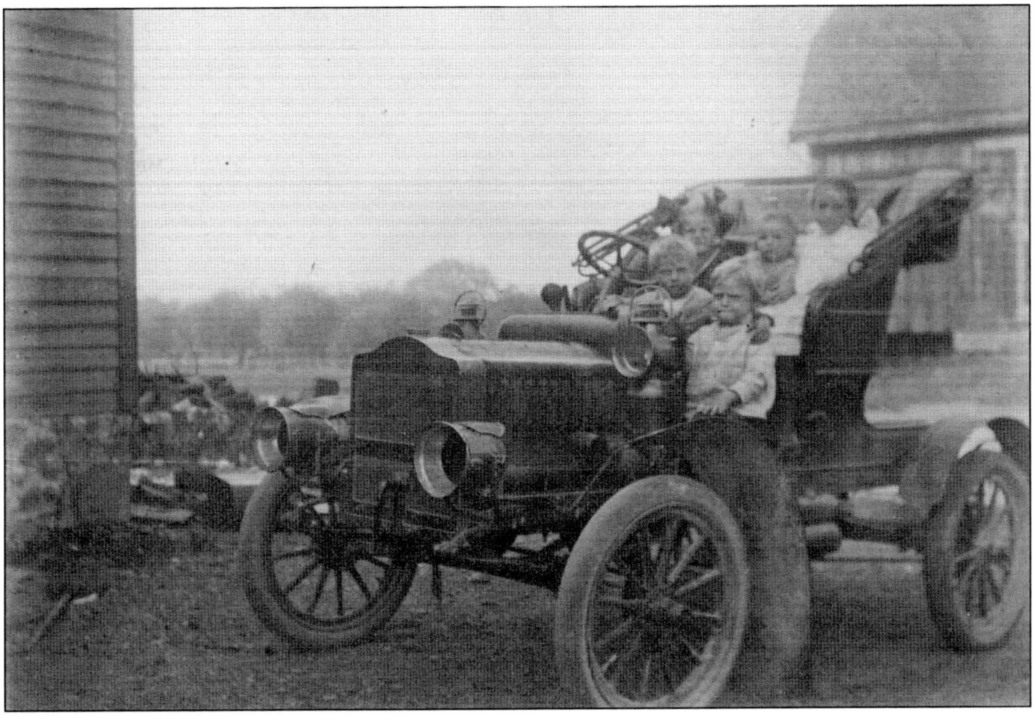

This photo postcard was sent to Lucille Gourlay by "The Bowerman Kids," who are posing in the family automobile in the early 1900s.

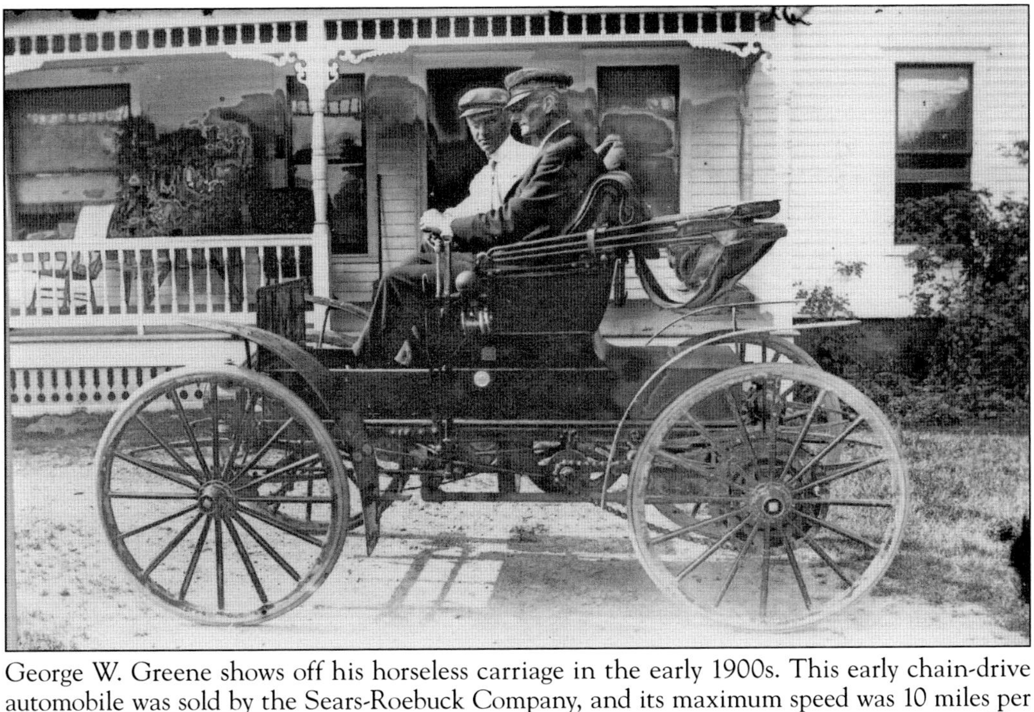

George W. Greene shows off his horseless carriage in the early 1900s. This early chain-drive automobile was sold by the Sears-Roebuck Company, and its maximum speed was 10 miles per hour; in 1910, that was the speed limit in most cities. This photograph was taken in front of the Gardner home on Hook Road. Lindley Gardner is Mr. Greene's passenger.

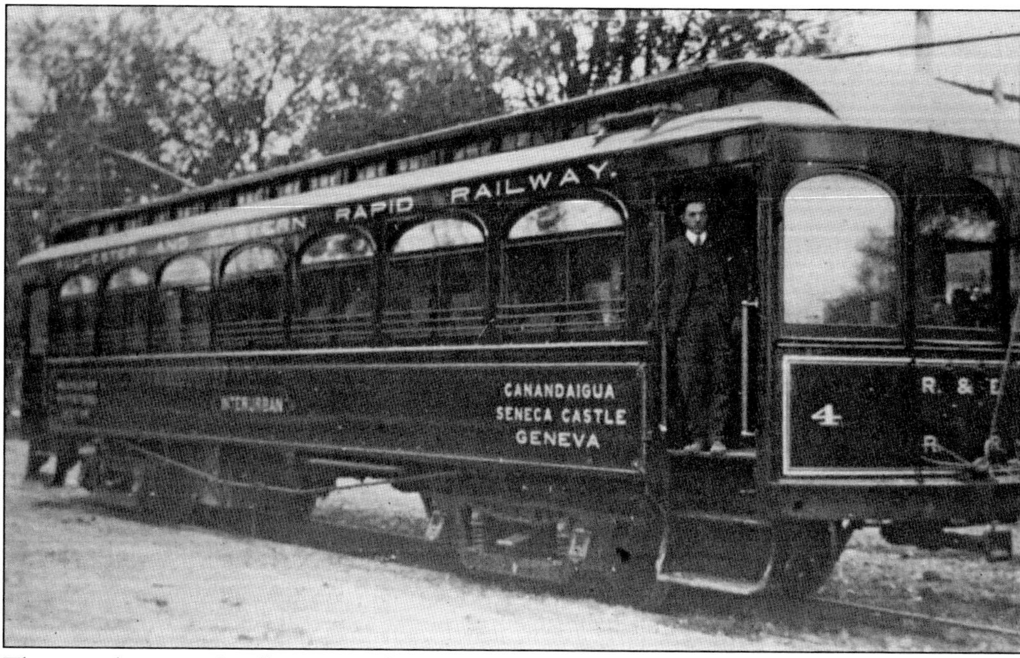


This was the type of trolley car used on the Rochester and Eastern Rapid Railway line through Farmington. The trolley line made several stops each day at Mertensia, Hathaway's Corners, and other locations in the southwest corner of the town. It ceased operation on August 1, 1930. (Courtesy Ray Henry, Canandaigua town historian.)

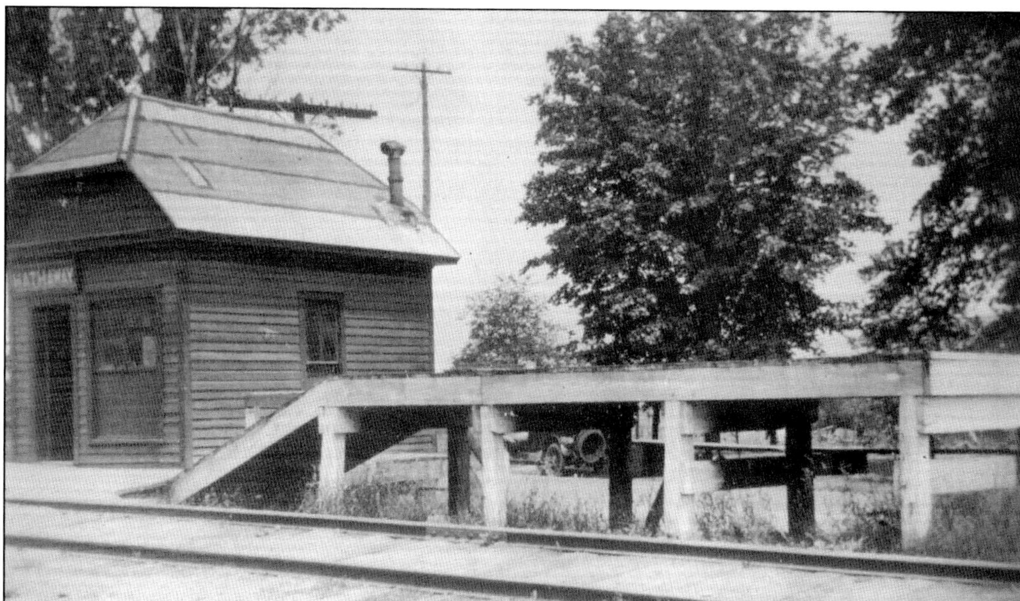


This is a view looking southwest of the trolley station at Hathaway's Corners in the 1920s, which was a stop on the Rochester and Eastern Rapid Railway. The trolley line paralleled the New York Central and Hudson River railroad line for part of its route through Farmington. The public had often speculated on which mode of travel was faster. In 1904, the competing lines staged a famous race; the electric trolley won. (Courtesy Ontario County Historical Society.)

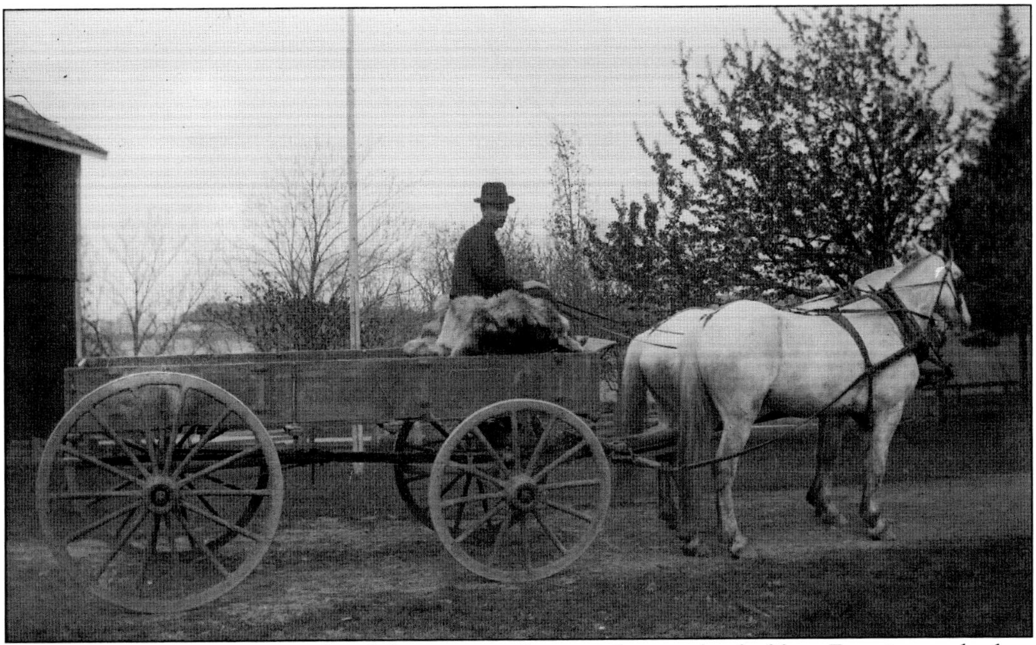

Richard Herendeen is pictured with his team and a partial wagonload of furs. Farmington had an active trapping and fur trading industry from the early 1900s up to the 1950s. (Courtesy Diana and Rudy van der Velden.)

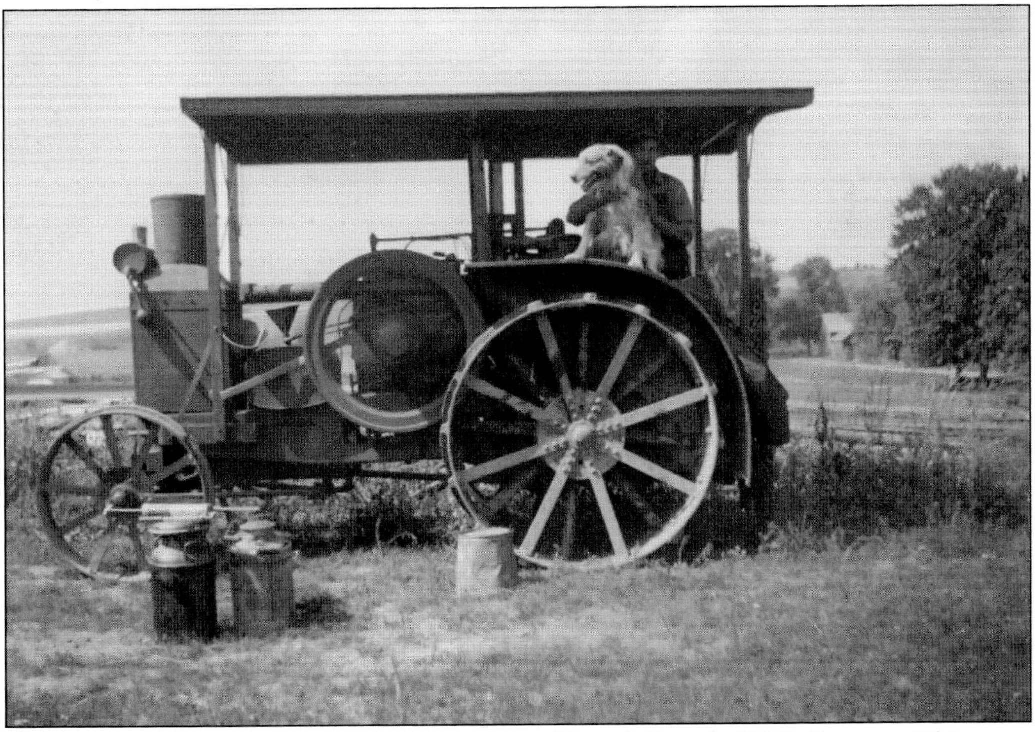

Henry Schrader and his dog are shown posing on Henry's Rumely Oil-Pull tractor. This was a famous kerosene-fueled tractor manufactured by the Rumely Company and was credited with opening the Great Plains to cultivation. (Courtesy Don Ford.)

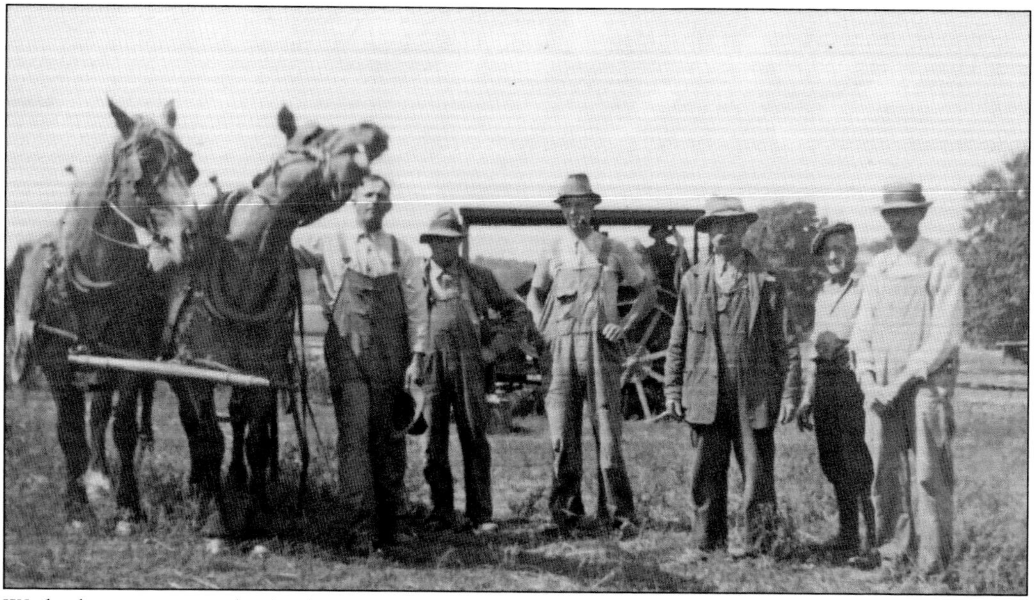

With the tractor in the background, workers pose for a photograph on the Schrader farm in Brownsville. From left to right the individuals are Willis Peglow, ? Devlin, Charles Schrader, John Peglow, Shorty Young, and Frank Yahn. (Courtesy Don Ford.)

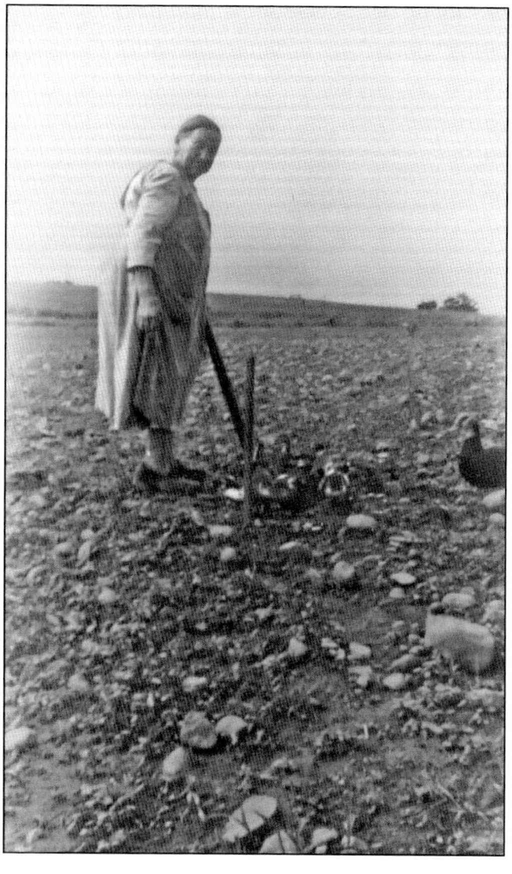

A curious duck family watches Jennie McFall working with a hand cultivator in a very rocky field about 1928. (Courtesy Don Ford.)

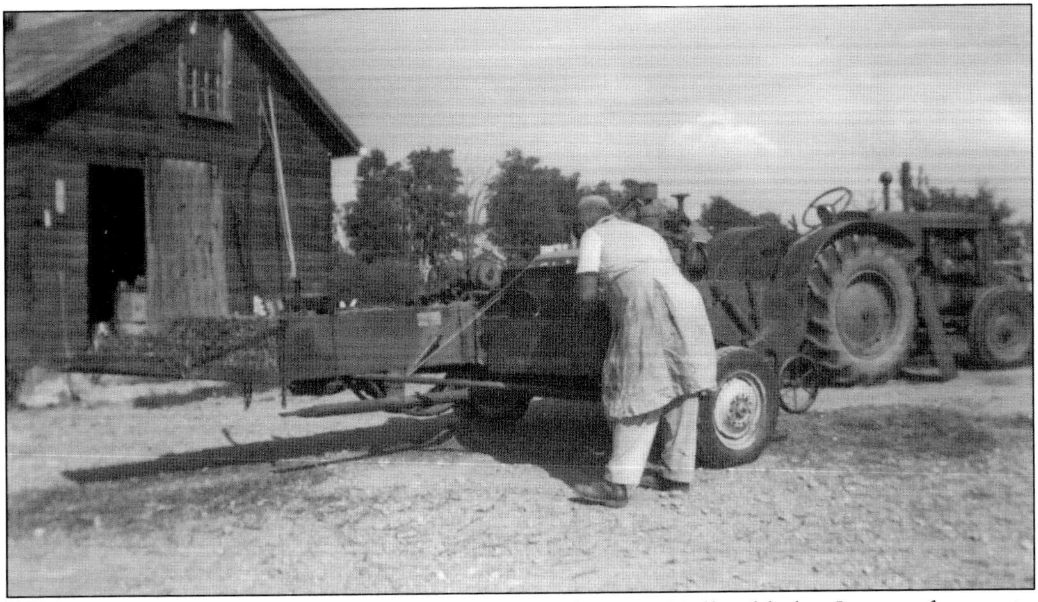

Here Joe Schrader is with an Oliver 80 tractor and a New Holland baler. Joe was famous in the Brownsville neighborhood for his talent at fixing machinery. When hay was being bailed, it was not unusual for a farmer to wear something over his clothing to protect himself from the abrasive stubble of the hay bails, which could wear through heavy denim in a few hours. (Courtesy Don Ford.)

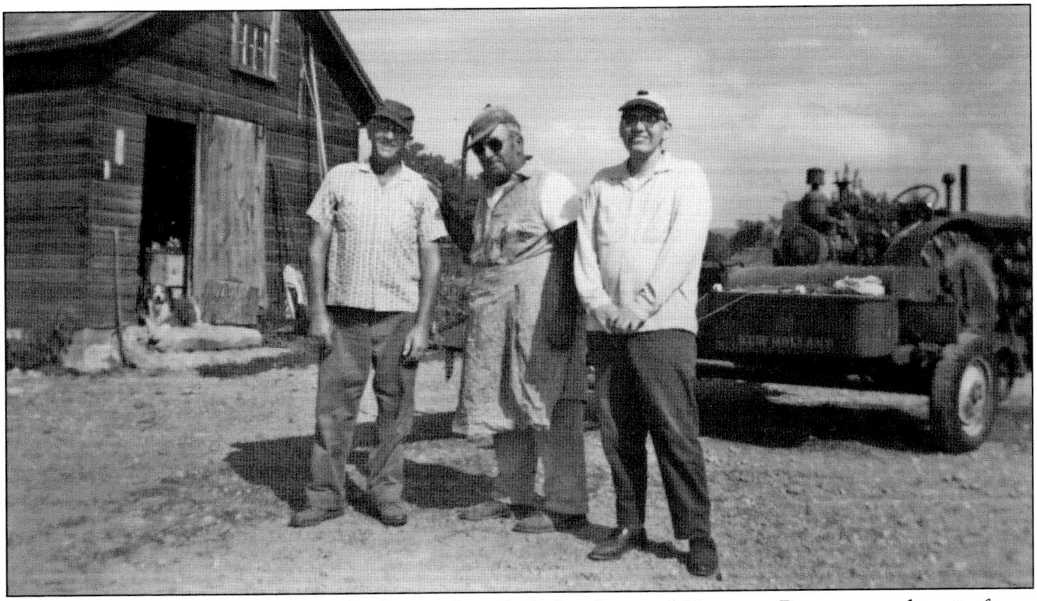

This snapshot shows Clement Thielman, Joseph Schrader, and Norman Brown standing in front of a tractor and New Holland farm implement. (Courtesy Don Ford.)

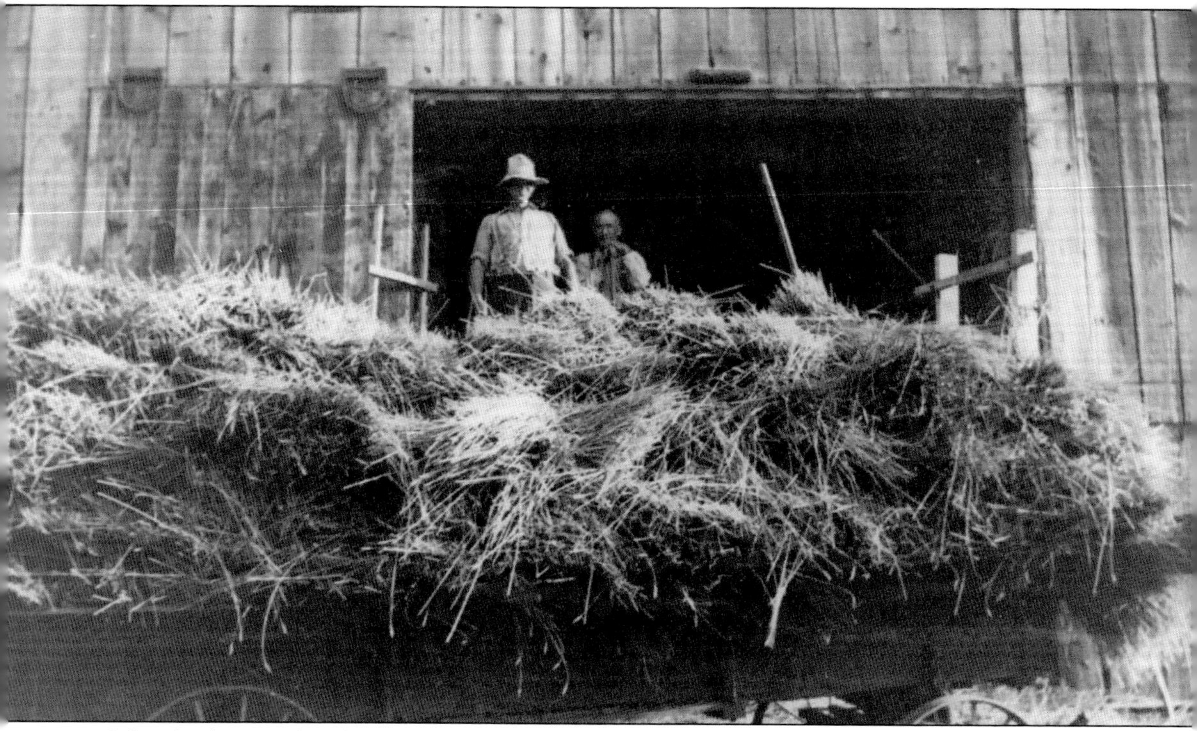

Schrader farmworkers have run this grain through the binder, and now it is ready to be forked into the hay barn. The Schrader farm was in the Brownsville area of Farmington. (Courtesy Don Ford.)

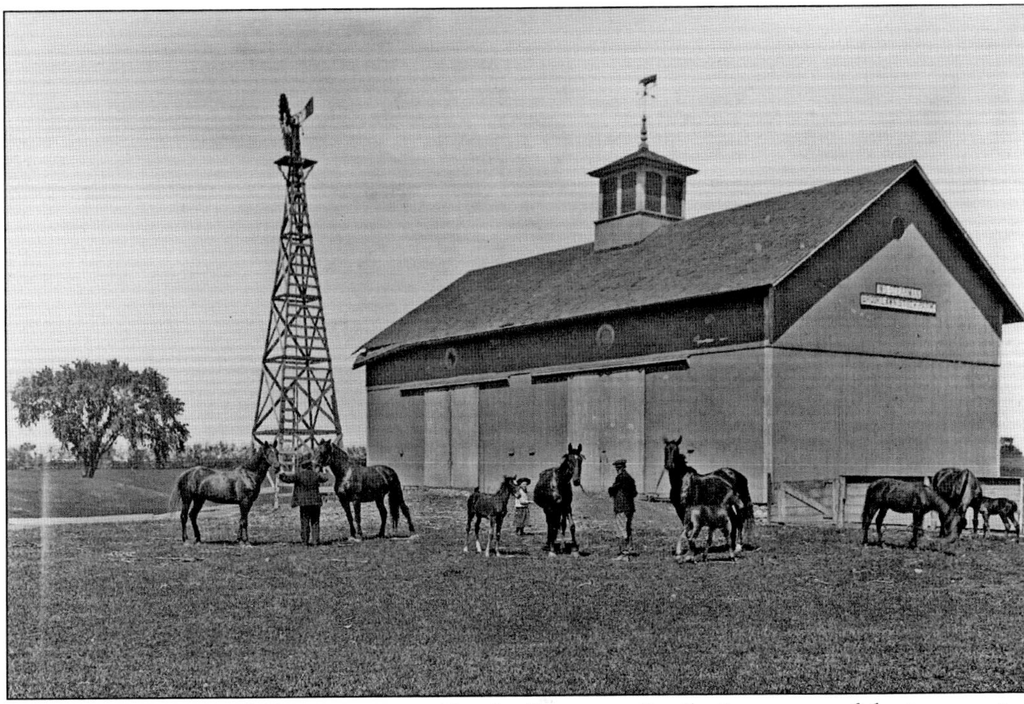

The Brook Lawn Stock Farm was owned by the Stearman family. It was east of the intersection of Shortsville Road and County Road 8. (Courtesy Diana and Rudy van der Velden.)

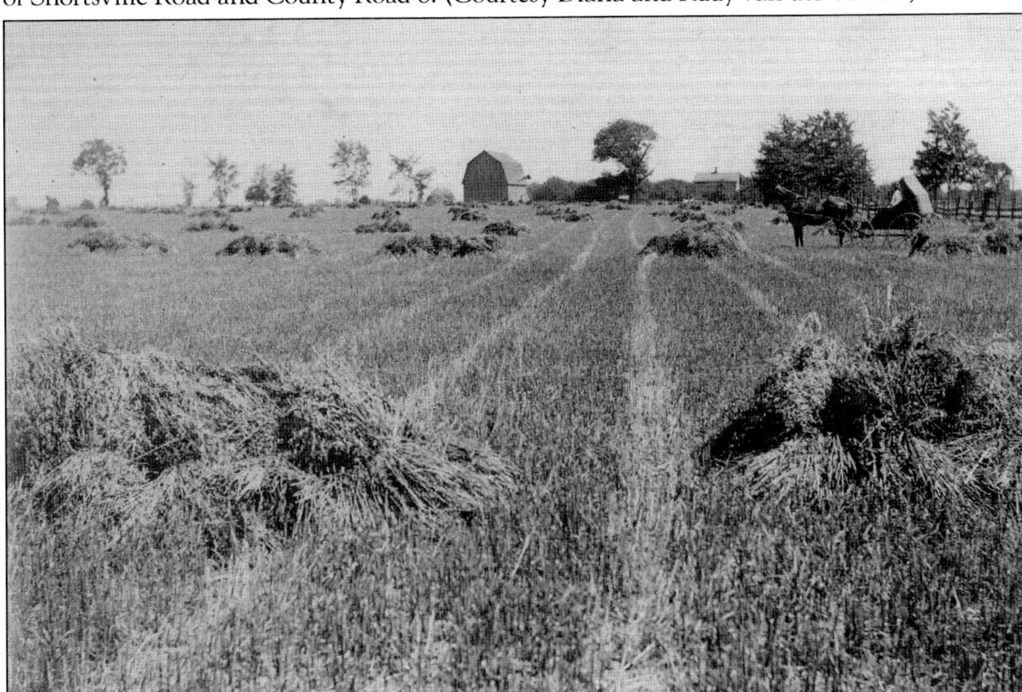

Here the photographer has documented a field of oats on the Stearman farm. The inscription identifies this as "Swedish Oats grown for S. G. Smith by A. Stearman, from seed supplied by Prof. Carlton of the US Department of Agriculture." (Courtesy Diana and Rudy van der Velden.)